Mastering Python

Master the art of writing beautiful and powerful Python by using all of the features that Python 3.5 offers

Rick van Hattem

BIRMINGHAM - MUMBAI

Mastering Python

First published: April 2016

Production reference: 1270416

Published by Packt Publishing Ltd.
Livery Place
35 Livery Street
Birmingham B3 2PB, UK.

ISBN 978-1-78528-972-9

www.packtpub.com

Credits

Author
Rick van Hattem

Reviewers
Randall Degges
Dave de Fijter
I. de Hoogt

Commissioning Editor
Sarah Crofton

Acquisition Editor
Reshma Raman

Content Development Editor
Arun Nadar

Technical Editors
Ryan Kochery
Tanmayee Patil

Copy Editor
Vikrant Phadke

Project Coordinator
Suzanne Coutinho

Proofreader
Safis Editing

Indexer
Mariammal Chettiyar

Production Coordinator
Nilesh Mohite

Cover Work
Nilesh Mohite

About the Author

Rick van Hattem is an experienced programmer, entrepreneur, and software/database architect with over 20 years of programming experience, including 15 with Python. Additionally, he has a lot of experience with high-performance architectures featuring large amounts of concurrent users and/or data.

Rick has founded several start-ups and has done consulting for many companies, including a few Y Combinator start-ups and several large companies. One of the startups he founded, Fashiolista.com, is one of the largest social networks for fashion in the world, featuring millions of users and the performance challenges to accompany those.

Rick was one of the reviewers on the book *PostgreSQL Server Programming, Packt Publishing*.

Thanks to my family, in particular Marloes, who supported me every step of the way; and my mother and sister, who have always been there for me.

About the Reviewers

Randall Degges is a happy programmer, speaker, author, and amateur bodybuilder living in California.

Growing up in Los Angeles, he was intensely interested in building command-line programs and writing quality software. His love of programming eventually propelled him into a successful career in software development.

Randall has been a life-long open source developer and has contributed to hundreds of popular projects in Python, Node.js, and Go. He's also the author of several popular libraries, which you can find on his public GitHub account at `https://github.com/rdegges`.

At 23, he cofounded an extremely popular API service in the telephony industry: OpenCNAM (`https://www.opencnam.com`). At 25, he joined Stormpath (`https://stormpath.com`) as the head of developer evangelism, whereby he writes open source security libraries full time and travels the world giving technical talks about building secure software.

In his free time, Randall writes and edits technical books, runs a security podcast called Stormcast (`https://www.stormca.st`), posts blogs on his personal website (`https://www.rdegges.com`), and tries to spend time with his high-school sweetheart, Samantha.

Dave de Fijter is a Python developer from the Netherlands. He always knew he would end up "doing something with computers." At a young age, he went to the library to read books about them even though he had no computer at that time. This obsession never really ended. In 2001, aged 14, he started his first part-time job, creating dynamic websites in PHP for a local web development company, and there he found his calling.

In 2007, he finished his bachelor's degree in ICT while already working full time as a PHP developer for over a year. In 2008, he switched from PHP to Python and Django for web development and loved this new technology stack so much that he never looked back.

After working as a Python developer for various start-ups and established companies, Dave used this experience to start his own business called Indentity (https://indentity.nl) in 2010, focusing on Python/Django development and advice. Up until now, he runs this company and mainly spends his time helping out start-ups with designing and building technologically advanced web applications from the ground up as an interim CTO/technical cofounder.

I. de Hoogt, with some basic experience wrought from university assignments in the field of modeling of multi-phase flows, got himself started in software development. His main experience in programming in Python stems from an internship at a company dealing in 3D printing software, where a package resulting in optimized object orientation and guaranteed mathematical mesh validity was created.

Other projects that he's been involved with have dealt with control systems such as self-parking cars, multi-legged robots, and quadcopters, but his current job is in the field of data analysis.

www.PacktPub.com

eBooks, discount offers, and more

Did you know that Packt offers eBook versions of every book published, with PDF and ePub files available? You can upgrade to the eBook version at `www.PacktPub.com` and as a print book customer, you are entitled to a discount on the eBook copy. Get in touch with us at `customercare@packtpub.com` for more details.

At `www.PacktPub.com`, you can also read a collection of free technical articles, sign up for a range of free newsletters and receive exclusive discounts and offers on Packt books and eBooks.

`https://www2.packtpub.com/books/subscription/packtlib`

Do you need instant solutions to your IT questions? PacktLib is Packt's online digital book library. Here, you can search, access, and read Packt's entire library of books.

Why subscribe?

- Fully searchable across every book published by Packt
- Copy and paste, print, and bookmark content
- On demand and accessible via a web browser

Table of Contents

Preface

Python is a language that is easy to learn and both powerful and convenient from the start. Mastering Python, however, is a completely different question.

Every programming problem you will encounter has at least several possible solutions and/or paradigms to apply within the vast possibilities of Python. This book will not only illustrate a range of different and new techniques but also explain where and when a method should be applied.

This book is not a beginner's guide to Python 3. It is a book that can teach you about the more advanced techniques possible within Python. Specifically targeting Python 3.5 and up, it also demonstrates several Python 3.5-only features such as async def and await statements.

As a Python programmer with many years of experience, I will attempt to rationalize the choices made in this book with relevant background information. These rationalizations are in no way strict guidelines, however. Several of these cases boil down to personal style in the end. Just know that they stem from experience and are, in many cases, the solutions recommended by the Python community.

Some of the references in this book might not be obvious to you if you are not a fan of Monty Python. This book extensively uses spam and eggs instead of foo and bar in code samples. To provide some background information, I recommend watching the "Spam" sketch by Monty Python. It is positively silly!

What this book covers

Chapter 1, *Getting Started – One Environment per Project*, introduces virtual Python environments using virtualenv or venv to isolate the packages in your Python projects.

Chapter 2, *Pythonic Syntax, Common Pitfalls, and Style Guide*, explains what Pythonic code is and how to write code that is Pythonic and adheres to the Python philosophy.

Chapter 3, Containers and Collections – Storing Data the Right Way, is where we use the many containers and collections bundled with Python to create code that is fast and readable.

Chapter 4, Functional Programming – Readability Versus Brevity, covers functional programming techniques such as list/dict/set comprehensions and lambda statements that are available in Python. Additionally, it illustrates their similarities with the mathematical principles involved.

Chapter 5, Decorators – Enabling Code Reuse by Decorating, explains not only how to create your own function/class decorators, but also how internal decorators such as property, staticmethod, and classmethod work.

Chapter 6, Generators and Coroutines – Infinity, One Step at a Time, shows how generators and coroutines can be used to lazily evaluate structures of infinite size.

Chapter 7, Async IO – Multithreading without Threads, demonstrates the usage of asynchronous functions using async def and await so that external resources no longer stall your Python processes.

Chapter 8, Metaclasses – Making Classes (Not Instances) Smarter, goes deeper into the creation of classes and how class behavior can be completely modified.

Chapter 9, Documentation – How to Use Sphinx and reStructuredText, shows how you can make Sphinx automatically document your code with very little effort. Additionally, it shows how the Napoleon syntax can be used to document function arguments in a way that is legible both in the code and the documentation.

Chapter 10, Testing and Logging – Preparing for Bugs, explains how code can be tested and how logging can be added to enable easy debugging in case bugs occur at a later time.

Chapter 11, Debugging – Solving the Bugs, demonstrates several methods of hunting down bugs with the use of tracing, logging, and interactive debugging.

Chapter 12, Performance – Tracking and Reducing Your Memory and CPU Usage, shows several methods of measuring and improving CPU and memory usage.

Chapter 13, Multiprocessing – When a Single CPU Core Is Not Enough, illustrates that the multiprocessing library can be used to execute your code, not just on multiple processors but even on multiple machines.

Chapter 14, Extensions in C/C++, System Calls, and C/C++ Libraries, covers the calling of C/C++ functions for both interoperability and performance using Ctypes, CFFI, and native C/C++.

Chapter 15, Packaging – Creating Your Own Libraries or Applications, demonstrates the usage of setuptools and setup.py to build and deploy packages on the Python Package Index (PyPI).

What you need for this book

The only hard requirement for this book is a Python interpreter. A Python 3.5 or newer interpreter is recommended, but many of the code examples will function in older Python versions, such as 2.7, with a simple from __future__ import print_statement added at the top of the file.

Additionally, *Chapter 14, Extensions in C/C++, System Calls, and C/C++ Libraries* requires a C/C++ compiler, such as GCC, Visual Studio, or XCode. A Linux machine is by far the easiest to execute the C/C++ examples, but these should function on Windows and OS X machines without too much effort as well.

Who this book is for

If you are beyond the absolute Python beginner level, then this book is for you. Even if you are already an expert Python programmer, I guarantee that you will find some useful techniques and insights in this book.

At the very least, it will allow Python 2 programmers to learn a lot more about the new features introduced in Python 3, and specifically Python 3.5.

Basic proficiency in Python is required as the installation of Python interpreters and the basic Python syntax are not covered.

Conventions

In this book, you will find a number of text styles that distinguish between different kinds of information. Here are some examples of these styles and an explanation of their meaning.

Code words in text, database table names, folder names, filenames, file extensions, pathnames, dummy URLs, user input, and Twitter handles are shown as follows: "It should be noted that the `type()` function has another use as well."

A block of code is set as follows:

```
import abc
import importlib


class Plugins(abc.ABCMeta):
    plugins = dict()

    def __new__(metaclass, name, bases, namespace):
        cls = abc.ABCMeta.__new__(
            metaclass, name, bases, namespace)
```

Any command-line input or output is written as follows where the >>> indicate the Python console and the # indicates a regular Linux/Unix shell:

```
>>> class Spam(object):
...     eggs = 'my eggs'

>>> Spam = type('Spam', (object,), dict(eggs='my eggs'))
```

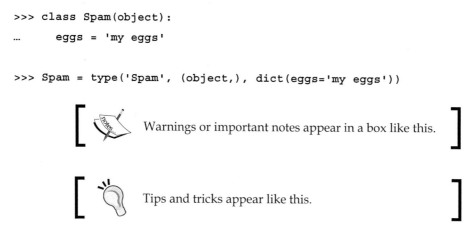

Warnings or important notes appear in a box like this.

Tips and tricks appear like this.

Reader feedback

Feedback from our readers is always welcome. Let us know what you think about this book—what you liked or disliked. Reader feedback is important for us as it helps us develop titles that you will really get the most out of.

To send us general feedback, simply e-mail feedback@packtpub.com, and mention the book's title in the subject of your message.

If there is a topic that you have expertise in and you are interested in either writing or contributing to a book, see our author guide at www.packtpub.com/authors.

Customer support

Now that you are the proud owner of a Packt book, we have a number of things to help you to get the most from your purchase.

Downloading the example code

You can download the example code files for this book from your account at `http://www.packtpub.com`. If you purchased this book elsewhere, you can visit `http://www.packtpub.com/support` and register to have the files e-mailed directly to you.

You can download the code files by following these steps:

1. Log in or register to our website using your e-mail address and password.
2. Hover the mouse pointer on the **SUPPORT** tab at the top.
3. Click on **Code Downloads & Errata**.
4. Enter the name of the book in the **Search** box.
5. Select the book for which you're looking to download the code files.
6. Choose from the drop-down menu where you purchased this book from.
7. Click on **Code Download**.

You can also download the code files by clicking on the **Code Files** button on the book's webpage at the Packt Publishing website. This page can be accessed by entering the book's name in the **Search** box. Please note that you need to be logged in to your Packt account.

Also, the code for the book is hosted on GitHub at `https://github.com/mastering-python/code`

Once the file is downloaded, please make sure that you unzip or extract the folder using the latest version of:

- WinRAR / 7-Zip for Windows
- Zipeg / iZip / UnRarX for Mac
- 7-Zip / PeaZip for Linux

Errata

Although we have taken every care to ensure the accuracy of our content, mistakes do happen. If you find a mistake in one of our books—maybe a mistake in the text or the code—we would be grateful if you could report this to us. By doing so, you can save other readers from frustration and help us improve subsequent versions of this book. If you find any errata, please report them by visiting http://www.packtpub.com/submit-errata, selecting your book, clicking on the **Errata Submission Form** link, and entering the details of your errata. Once your errata are verified, your submission will be accepted and the errata will be uploaded to our website or added to any list of existing errata under the Errata section of that title.

To view the previously submitted errata, go to https://www.packtpub.com/books/content/support and enter the name of the book in the search field. The required information will appear under the **Errata** section.

Piracy

Piracy of copyrighted material on the Internet is an ongoing problem across all media. At Packt, we take the protection of our copyright and licenses very seriously. If you come across any illegal copies of our works in any form on the Internet, please provide us with the location address or website name immediately so that we can pursue a remedy.

Please contact us at copyright@packtpub.com with a link to the suspected pirated material.

We appreciate your help in protecting our authors and our ability to bring you valuable content.

Questions

If you have a problem with any aspect of this book, you can contact us at questions@packtpub.com, and we will do our best to address the problem.

1
Getting Started – One Environment per Project

There is one aspect of the Python philosophy that always has been, and always will be, the most important in the entire language—readability, or Pythonic code. This book will help you master writing Python the way it was meant to be: readable, beautiful, explicit, and as simple as possible. In short, it will be Pythonic code. That is not to say that complicated subjects will not be covered. Naturally, they will, but whenever the philosophy of Python is at stake, you will be warned when and where the technique is justified.

Most of the code within this book will function on both Python 2 and Python 3, but the main target is Python 3. There are three reasons for doing this:

1. Python 3 was released in 2008, which is a very long time in the rapidly changing software world. It's not a new thing anymore, it's stable, it's usable, and, most importantly, it's the future.

2. Development for Python 2 effectively stopped in 2009. Certain features have been backported from Python 3 to Python 2, but any new development will be for Python 3 first.

3. Python 3 has become mature. While I have to admit that Python 3.2 and older versions still had a few small issues that made it hard to write code that functions on both Python 2 and 3, Python 3.3 did improve greatly in that aspect, and I consider it mature. This is evidenced by the marginally modified syntax in Python 3.4 and 3.5 and a lot of very useful features, which are covered in this book.

To summarize, Python 3 is an improvement over Python 2. I have been a skeptic for a very long time myself, but I do not see any reason not to use Python 3 for new projects, and even porting existing projects to Python 3 is generally possible with only minor changes. With cool new features such as `async with` in Python 3.5, you will want to upgrade just to try it.

This first chapter will show you how to properly set up an environment, create a new isolated environment, and make sure you get similar results when running the same code on different machines. Most Python programmers are already using `virtualenv` to create virtual Python environments, but the `venv` command, introduced in Python 3.3, is a very nice alternative. It is essentially a clone of the `virtualenv` package but is slightly simpler and bundled with Python. While its usage is mostly analogous to `virtualenv`, there are a few changes that are interesting to know.

Secondly, we will discuss the `pip` command. The `pip` command is automatically installed when using `venv` through the `ensurepip` package, a package introduced in Python 3.4. This package automatically bootstraps `pip` into an existing Python library while maintaining independent versions of Python and `pip`. Before Python 3.4, `venv` came without `pip` and had to be installed manually.

Finally, we will discuss how packages created with `distutils` can be installed. While pure Python packages are generally easy to install, it can get challenging when C modules are involved.

In this chapter, the following topics are covered:

- Creating a virtual Python environment using `venv`
- Bootstrapping pip using `ensurepip`
- Installing packages based on `distutils` (C/C++) with `pip`

Creating a virtual Python environment using venv

Most Python programmers are already be familiar with `venv` or `virtualenv`, but even if you're not, it's never too late to start using it. The `venv` module is designed to isolate your Python environments so that you can install packages specific to your current project without polluting your global namespace. For example, having a filename such as `sys.py` in your current directory can seriously break your code if you expect to have the standard Python `sys` library—your local sys libraries will be imported before the global one, effectively hiding the system library. In addition, because the packages are installed locally, you don't need system (root/administrator) access to install them.

The result is that you can make sure you have exactly the same version of a package on both your local development machine and production machines without interfering with other packages. For example, there are many Django packages around that require specific versions of the Django project. Using venv, you can easily install Django 1.4 for project A and Django 1.8 for project B without them ever knowing that there are different versions installed in other environments. By default, the environments are even configured in such a way that the global packages are not visible. The benefit of this is that to get an exact list of all installed packages within the environment, simply a `pip freeze` will suffice. The downside is that some of the heavier packages (for example, `numpy`) will have to be installed in every separate environment. Needless to say, which choice is the best for your project depends on the project. For most projects, I would keep the default setting of not having the global packages, but when messing around with projects that have lots of C/C++ extensions, it would be convenient to simply enable the global site packages. The reason is simple; if you do not have a compiler available, installing the package locally can be difficult, while the global install has an executable for Windows or an installable package for Linux/Unix available.

The venv module (`https://docs.python.org/3/library/venv.html`) can be seen as a slightly simplified version of the `virtualenv` tool (`https://virtualenv.pypa.io/`), which has been bundled with Python since version 3.3 (refer to PEP 0405 -- Python Virtual Environments: `https://www.python.org/dev/peps/pep-0405/`).

The `virtualenv` package can generally be used as a drop-in replacement for venv, which is especially relevant for older Python versions (below 3.3) that do not come bundled with venv.

Creating your first venv

Creating an environment is quite easy. The basic command comes down to pyvenv PATH_TO_THE_NEW_VIRTUAL_ENVIRONMENT, so let's give it a try. Note that this command works on Linux, Unix, and Mac; the Windows command will follow shortly:

```
# pyvenv test_venv
# . ./test_venv/bin/activate
(test_venv) #
```

Some Ubuntu releases (notably 14.04 LTS) maim the Python installation by not including the full `pyvenv` package with `ensurepip`. The standard workaround is to call `pyvenv --without-pip test_env`, which requires a manual `pip` installation through the `get_pip.py` file available on the `pip` home page.

This creates an environment called `test_venv`, and the second line activates the environment.

On Windows, everything is slightly different but similar overall. By default, the `pyvenv` command won't be in your PATH, so running the command is slightly different. The three options are as follows:

- Add the `Python\Tools\Scripts\` directory to your PATH
- Run the module:

  ```
  python -m venv test_venv
  ```

- Run the script directly:

  ```
  python Python\Tools\Scripts\pyvenv.py test_venv
  ```

For convenience, I would recommend that you add the `Scripts` directory to your PATH anyhow, since many other applications/scripts (such as `pip`) will be installed there as well.

Here is the full example for Windows:

```
C:\envs>python -m venv test_venv
C:\envs>test_venv\Scripts\activate.bat
(test_venv) C:\envs>
```

 When using Windows PowerShell, the environment can be activated by using `test_venv\Scripts\Activate.ps1` instead. Note that you really do need backslashes here.

venv arguments

So far, we have just created a plain and regular `venv`, but there are a few, really useful flags for customizing your `venv` specifically to your needs.

First, let's look at the `venv` help:

Parameter	Description
`--system-site-packages`	It gives the virtual environment access to the `system-site-packages` directory
`--symlinks`	Try to use `symlinks` rather than copies when symlinks are not the default for the platform
`--copies`	Try to use copies rather than symlinks even when symlinks are the default for the platform
`--clear`	Delete the contents of the environment directory, if it exists, before environment creation
`--upgrade`	Upgrade the environment directory to use this version of Python, assuming that Python has been upgraded in-place
`--without-pip`	This skips installing or upgrading pip in the virtual environment (pip is bootstrapped by default)

The most important argument to note is `--system-site-packages`, which enables the global site packages within the environment. This means that if you have a package installed in your global Python version, it will be available within your environment as well. However, if you try to update it to a different version, it will be installed locally. Whenever possible, I would recommend disabling the `--system-site-packages` flag because it gives you a simple environment without too many variables. A simple update of the system packages could break your virtual environment otherwise, but worse, there is no way to know which packages are needed locally and which ones are just installed for other purposes.

To enable this for an existing environment, you can simply run the environment creation command again, but this time adding the `--system-site-packages` flag to enable the global site packages.

To disable it again, you can simply run the environment creation command without the flag. This will keep the locally (within the environment) installed packages available but will remove the global packages from your Python scope.

 When using `virtualenvwrapper`, this can also be done with the `toggleglobalsitepackages` command from within the activated environment.

The --symlinks and --copies arguments can generally be ignored, but it is important to know the difference. These arguments decide whether the files will be copied from the base python directory or whether they will be symlinked.

> Symlinks are a Linux/Unix/Mac thing; instead of copying a file it creates a symbolic link that tells the system where to find the actual file.

By default, venv will try to symlink the files, and if that fails, it will fall back to copying. Since Windows Vista and Python 3.2, this is also supported on Windows, so unless you're using a very old system, you will most likely be using symlinks in your environment. The benefit of symlinks is that it saves disk space and stays in sync with your Python installation. The downside is that if your system's Python version undergoes an upgrade, it can break the packages installed within your environment, but that can easily be fixed by reinstalling the packages using pip.

Finally, the --upgrade argument is useful if your system Python version has been upgraded in-place. The most common use case for this argument is for repairing broken environments after upgrading the system Python with a copied (as opposed to symlinked) environment.

Differences between virtualenv and venv

Since the venv module is essentially a simpler version of virtualenv, they are mostly the same, but some things are different. Also, since virtualenv is a package that is distributed separately from Python, it does have some advantages.

The following are the advantages of venv over virtualenv:

- venv is distributed with Python 3.3 and above, so no separate install is needed
- venv is simple and straightforward with no features besides the bare necessities

Advantages of virtualenv over venv:

- virtualenv is distributed outside of Python, so it can be updated separately.
- virtualenv works on old Python versions, but Python 2.6 or a higher version is recommended. However, Python 2.5 support is possible with older versions (1.9.x or lower).
- It supports convenient wrappers, such as virtualenvwrapper (http://virtualenvwrapper.readthedocs.org/)

In short, if venv is enough for you, use it. If you are using an old Python version or want some extra convenience, such as virtualenvwrapper, use virtualenv instead. Both projects essentially do the same thing, and efforts have been made to easily switch between them. The biggest and most significant difference between the two is the wide variety of Python versions that virtualenv supports.

Bootstrapping pip using ensurepip

Slowly, the pip package manager has been replacing easy_install since its introduction in 2008. Since Python 3.4, it has even become the default and is bundled with Python. Since Python 3.4 onward, it is installed by default within both the regular Python environment and that of pyvenv; before that, a manual install is required. To automatically install pip in Python 3.4 and above, the ensurepip library is used. This is a library that handles automatic installation and/or upgrades of pip, so it is at least as recent as the one bundled with ensurepip.

ensurepip usage

The usage of ensurepip is fairly straightforward. Just run python -m ensurepip to guarantee a pip version or python -m ensurepip --upgrade to make sure that pip will be at least the version that is bundled with ensurepip.

In addition to installing the regular pip shortcut, this will also install the pipX and pipX.Y links, which allow you to select a specific Python version. When using Python 2 and Python 3 simultaneously, this allows you to install packages within Python 2 and Python 3 with pip2 and pip3, respectively. This means that if you use python -m ensurepip on Python 3.5 you will get pip, pip3, and pip3.5 commands installed in your environment.

Manual pip install

The ensurepip package is great if you are using Python 3.4 or above. Below that, however, you need to install pip manually. Actually, this is surprisingly easy. It involves just two steps:

1. Download the get-pip.py file: https://bootstrap.pypa.io/get-pip.py.

2. Execute the get-pip.py file: python get-pip.py.

 If the ensurepip command fails due to permission errors, it can be useful to supply the --user argument. This allows you to install pip inside the user specific site packages directory, so root/admin access is not required.

Installing C/C++ packages

Most Python packages are purely Python and blissfully easy to install, just as a simple `pip install packagename` does the trick. However, there are cases where compilation is involved and installation goes from a simple pip install to searching for hours to see which dependencies are needed to install a certain package.

The specific error message will differ as per the project and environment, but there is a common pattern in these errors, and understanding what you are looking at can help a lot when searching for a solution.

For example, when installing `pillow` on a standard Ubuntu machine, you'll get a few pages full of errors, warnings, and other messages that end like this:

```
    x86_64-linux-gnu-gcc: error: build/temp.linux-x86_64-3.4/libImaging/
Jpeg2KDecode.o: No such file or directory
    x86_64-linux-gnu-gcc: error: build/temp.linux-x86_64-3.4/libImaging/
Jpeg2KEncode.o: No such file or directory
    x86_64-linux-gnu-gcc: error: build/temp.linux-x86_64-3.4/libImaging/
BoxBlur.o: No such file or directory
    error: command 'x86_64-linux-gnu-gcc' failed with exit status 1


    ----------------------------------------
Command "python3 -c "import setuptools, tokenize;__file__='/tmp/pip-
build-_f0ryusw/pillow/setup.py';exec(compile(getattr(tokenize, 'open',
open)(__file__).read().replace('\r\n', '\n'), __file__, 'exec'))" install
--record /tmp/pip-kmmobum2-record/install-record.txt --single-version-
externally-managed --compile --install-headers include/site/python3.4/
pillow" failed with error code 1 in /tmp/pip-build-_f0ryusw/pillow
```

Upon seeing messages like these, you might be tempted to search for one of the lines such as `x86_64-linux-gnu-gcc: error: build/temp.linux-x86_64-3.4/libImaging/Jpeg2KDecode.o: No such file or directory`. While this might give you some relevant results, most likely it will not. The trick with installations like these is to scroll up until you see messages about missing headers. Here is an example:

```
  In file included from libImaging/Imaging.h:14:0,
                   from libImaging/Resample.c:16:
  libImaging/ImPlatform.h:10:20: fatal error: Python.h: No such file or
directory
    #include "Python.h"
                  ^
  compilation terminated.
```

The key message here is that `Python.h` is missing. These are part of the Python headers and are needed for the compilation of most C/C++ packages within Python. Depending on the operating system, the solutions will vary—unfortunately. So, I recommend that you skip all parts of this paragraph that are not relevant for your case.

Debian and Ubuntu

In Debian and Ubuntu, the package to be installed is `python3-dev` or `python2-dev` if you're still using Python 2. The command to execute is as follows:

```
# sudo apt-get install python3-dev
```

However, this installs the development headers only. If you want the compiler and other headers bundled with the install, then the `build-dep` command is also very useful. Here is an example:

```
# sudo apt-get build-dep python3
```

Red Hat, CentOS, and Fedora

Red Hat, CentOS, and Fedora are rpm-based distros that use the `yum` package manager to install the requirements. Most development headers are available through `<package-name>-devel` and are easily installable as such. To install the Python 3 development headers, use this line:

```
# sudo apt-get install python3-devel
```

To make sure you have all the requirements such as development headers and compilers to build packages such as Python, the `yum-builddep` command is available:

```
# yum-builddep python3
```

OS X

The install procedure on OS X consists of three steps before the actual package can be installed.

First, you have to install Xcode. This can be done through the OS X App Store at `https://itunes.apple.com/en/app/xcode/id497799835?mt=12`.

Then you have to install the Xcode command-line tools:

```
# xcode-select --install
```

Finally, you need to install the **Homebrew** package manager. The steps are available at http://brew.sh/, but the install command is as follows:

```
# /usr/bin/ruby -e "$(curl -fsSL https://raw.githubusercontent.com/
Homebrew/install/master/install)"
```

 Other package managers, such as Macports, are also possible, but Homebrew is currently the OS X package manager with the most active development and community.

Once all of these steps have been completed, you should have a working Homebrew installation. The working of Homebrew can be verified using the brew doctor command. If there are no major errors in the output, then you should be ready to install your first packages through brew. Now we simply need to install Python and we're done:

```
# brew install python3
```

Windows

On Windows, manual compilation of C Python packages is generally a non-trivial task to say the least. Most packages have been written with Linux/Unix systems in mind (OS X falls under the Unix category), and Windows is a nice-to-have for developers. The result is that packages are difficult to compile on Windows because there are few people testing them and many of the libraries require manual installation, making it a very tedious task. So, unless you really have to, try and stay away from manually compiling Python packages on Windows. Most packages are available as installable binary downloads with a bit of searching, and there are alternatives such as Anaconda that include binary packages for most important C Python packages.

If you still feel inclined to manually compile C Python packages, then there is another option, and it is generally an easier alternative. The Cygwin project (http://cygwin.com/) attempts to make Linux applications run natively on Windows. This is generally an easier solution than making packages work with Visual Studio.

If you do wish to take the Visual Studio path, I would like to point you towards *Chapter 14, Extensions in C/C++, System Calls, and C/C++ Libraries*, which covers manual writing of C/C++ extensions and some information on which Visual Studio versions you need for your Python version.

Summary

With the inclusion of packages such as `pip` and `venv`, I feel that Python 3 has become a complete package that should suit most people. Beyond legacy applications, there is no real reason not to choose Python 3 anymore. The initial Python 3 release in 2008 was definitely a bit raw compared to the well-rounded Python 2.6 version released the same year, but a lot has changed in that aspect. The last major Python 2 release was Python 2.7, which was released in 2010; within the software world, that is a very, very long time. While Python 2.7 still receives maintenance, it will not receive any of the amazing new features that Python 3 is getting—features such as Unicode strings by default, `dict` generators (Chapter 6, *Generators and Coroutines – Infinity, One Step at a Time*), and `async` methods (Chapter 7, *Async IO – Multithreading without Threads*).

After finishing this chapter, you should be able to create a clean and recreatable virtual environment and know where to look if an installation of C/C++ packages fails.

Here are the most important notes for this chapter:

- For a clean and simple environment, use `venv`. If compatibility with Python 2 is needed, use `virtualenv`.
- If C/C++ packages fail to install, look for the error about missing includes.

The next chapter covers the Python style guide, which rules are important, and why they matter. Readability is one of the most important aspects of the Python philosophy, and you will learn methods and styles for writing cleaner and more readable Python code.

2
Pythonic Syntax, Common Pitfalls, and Style Guide

The design and development of the Python programming language have always been in the hands of its original author, Guido van Rossum, in many cases lovingly referred to as the **Benevolent Dictator For Life** (**BDFL**). Even though van Rossum is thought to have a time machine (he has repeatedly answered feature requests with "I just implemented that last night": `http://www.catb.org/jargon/html/G/Guido.html`), he is still just a human and needs help with the maintenance and development of Python. To facilitate that, the **Python Enhancement Proposal** (**PEP**) process has been developed. This process allows anyone to submit a PEP with a technical specification of the feature and a rationale to defend its usefulness. After a discussion on the Python mailing lists and possibly some improvements, the BDFL will make a decision to accept or reject the proposal.

The Python style guide (`PEP 8`: `https://www.python.org/dev/peps/pep-0008/`) was once submitted as one of those PEPs, and it is has been accepted and improved regularly since. It has a lot of great and widely accepted conventions as well as a few disputed ones. Especially, the maximum line length of 79 characters is a topic of many discussions. Limiting a line to 79 characters does have some merits, however. In addition to this, while just the style guide itself does not make code Pythonic, as "The Zen of Python" (`PEP 20`: `https://www.python.org/dev/peps/pep-0020/`) elegantly says: "Beautiful is better than ugly." `PEP 8` defines how code should be formatted in an exact way, and `PEP 20` is more of a philosophy and mindset.

The common pitfalls are a list of common mistakes made, varying from beginner mistakes to advanced ones. They range from passing a list or dictionary (which are mutable) as arguments to late-binding problems in closures. An even more important issue is how to work around circular imports in a clean way.

Some of the techniques used in the examples in this chapter might be a bit too advanced for such an early chapter, but please don't worry. This chapter is about style and common pitfalls. The inner workings of the techniques used will be covered in later chapters.

We will cover the following topics in this chapter:

- Code style (PEP 8, pyflakes, flake8, and more)
- Common pitfalls (lists as function arguments, pass by value versus pass by reference, and inheritance behavior)

 The definition of Pythonic code is highly subjective and mainly reflects the opinion of this author. When working on a project, it is more important to stay consistent with the coding styles of that project than with the coding guidelines given by Python or this book.

Code style – or what is Pythonic code?

Pythonic code — when you first hear of it, you might think it is a programming paradigm, similar to object-oriented or functional programming. While some of it could be considered as such, it is actually more of a design philosophy. Python leaves you free to choose to program in an object-oriented, procedural, functional, aspect-oriented or even logic-oriented way. These freedoms make Python a great language to write in, but as always, freedom has the drawback of requiring a lot of discipline to keep the code clean and readable. The PEP8 standard tells us how to format code, but there is more to Pythonic code than syntax alone. That is what the Pythonic philosophy (PEP20) is all about, code that is:

- Clean
- Simple
- Beautiful
- Explicit
- Readable

Most of these sound like common sense, and I think they should be. There are cases however, where there is not a single obvious way to do it (unless you're Dutch, of course, as you'll read later in this chapter). That is the goal of this chapter — to learn what code is beautiful and why certain decisions have been made in the Python style guide.

Some programmers once asked Guido van Rossum whether Python would ever support braces. Since that day, braces have been available through a `__future__` import:

```
>>> from __future__ import braces
  File "<stdin>", line 1
SyntaxError: not a chance
```

Formatting strings – printf-style or str.format?

Python has supported both `printf-style` (%) and `str.format` for a long time, so you are most likely familiar with both already.

Within this book, `printf-style` formatting will be used for a few reasons:

- The most important reason is that it comes naturally to me. I have been using `printf` in many different programming languages for about 20 years now.

- The `printf` syntax is supported in most programming languages, which makes it familiar for a lot of people.

- While only relevant for the purposes of the examples in this book, it takes up slightly less space, requiring less formatting changes. As opposed to monitors, books have not gotten wider over the years.

In general most people recommend `str.format` these days, but it mainly comes down to preference. The `printf-style` is simpler, while the `str.format` method is more powerful.

If you wish to learn more about how `printf-style` formatting can be replaced with `str.format` (or the other way around, of course), then I recommend the PyFormat site at `https://pyformat.info/`.

PEP20, the Zen of Python

Most of the Pythonic philosophy can be explained through PEP20. Python has a nice little Easter egg to always remind you of PEP20. Simply type `import this` in a Python console and you will get the PEP20 lines. To quote PEP20:

> *"Long time Pythoneer Tim Peters succinctly channels the BDFL's guiding principles for Python's design into 20 aphorisms, only 19 of which have been written down."*

The next few paragraphs will explain the intentions of these 19 lines.

 The examples within the PEP20 section are not necessarily all identical in working, but they do serve the same purpose. Many of the examples here are fictional and serve no purpose other than explaining the rationale of the paragraph.

For clarity, let's see the output of `import this` before we begin:

```
>>> import this
The Zen of Python, by Tim Peters


Beautiful is better than ugly.
Explicit is better than implicit.
Simple is better than complex.
Complex is better than complicated.
Flat is better than nested.
Sparse is better than dense.
Readability counts.
Special cases aren't special enough to break the rules.
Although practicality beats purity.
Errors should never pass silently.
Unless explicitly silenced.
In the face of ambiguity, refuse the temptation to guess.
There should be one-- and preferably only one --obvious way to do it.
Although that way may not be obvious at first unless you're Dutch.
Now is better than never.
Although never is often better than *right* now.
If the implementation is hard to explain, it's a bad idea.
If the implementation is easy to explain, it may be a good idea.
Namespaces are one honking great idea -- let's do more of those!
```

Beautiful is better than ugly

While beauty is quite subjective, there are some Python style rules to adhere to: limiting line lengths, keeping statements on separate lines, splitting imports on separate lines, and so on.

In short, instead of a somewhat complex function such as this:

```
def filter_modulo(items, modulo):
    output_items = []
    for i in range(len(items)):
        if items[i] % modulo:
            output_items.append(items[i])
    return output_items
```

Or this:

```
filter_modulo = lambda i, m: [i[j] for i in range(len(i))
                                    if i[j] % m]
```

Just do the following:

```
def filter_modulo(items, modulo):
    for item in items:
        if item % modulo:
            yield item
```

Simpler, easier to read, and a bit more beautiful!

 These examples are not identical in results. The first two return lists whereas the last returns a generator. Generators will be discussed more thoroughly in *Chapter 6, Generators and Coroutines – Infinity, One Step at a Time.*

Explicit is better than implicit

Imports, arguments, and variable names are just some of the many cases where explicit code is far easier to read at the cost of a little bit more effort and/or verbosity when writing the code.

Here is an example:

```
from spam import *
from eggs import *

some_function()
```

While this saves you some typing, it becomes quite difficult to see where `some_function` is defined. Is it defined in `foo`? In `bar`? Perhaps in both modules? There are editors with advanced introspection that can help you here, but why not keep it explicit so that everyone (even when simply viewing the code online) can see what it's doing?

```
import spam
import eggs


spam.some_function()
eggs.some_function()
```

The added benefit is that we can explicitly call the function from either `spam` or `eggs` here, and everyone will have a better idea what the code does.

The same goes for functions with `*args` and `**kwargs`. They can be very useful at times, but they do have the downside of making it less obvious which arguments are valid for a function:

```
def spam(egg, *args, **kwargs):
    processed_egg = process_egg(egg, *args, **kwargs)
    return Spam(processed_egg)
```

Documentation can obviously help for cases like these and I don't disagree with the usage of `*args` and `**kwargs` in general, but it is definitely a good idea to keep at least the most common arguments explicit. Even when it requires you to repeat the arguments for a parent class, it just makes the code that much clearer. When refactoring the parent class in future, you'll know whether there are subclasses that still use some parameters.

Simple is better than complex

"Simple is better than complex. Complex is better than complicated."

The most important question to ask yourself when starting a new project is: how complex does it need to be?

For example, let's assume that we've written a small program and now we need to store a bit of data. What options do we have here?

- A full database server, such as PostgreSQL or MySQL
- A simple file system database, such as SQLite or AnyDBM
- Flat file storage, such as CSV and TSV

- Structured storage, such as JSON, YAML, or XML
- Serialized Python, such as Pickle or Marshal

All of these options have their own use cases as well as advantages and disadvantages depending on the use case:

- Are you storing a lot of data? Then full database servers and flat file storage are generally the most convenient options.

- Should it be easily portable to different systems without any package installation? That makes anything besides full database servers convenient options.

- Do we need to search the data? This is much easier using one of the database systems, both filesystem and full servers.

- Are there other applications that need to be able to edit the data? That makes universal formats such as flat file storage and the structured storage convenient options, but excludes serialized Python.

Many questions! But the most important one is: how complex does it need to be? Storing data in a `pickle` file is something you can do in three lines, while connecting to a database (even with SQLite) will be more complicated and, in many cases, not needed:

```
import pickle  # Or json/yaml
With open('data.pickle', 'wb') as fh:
    pickle.dump(data, fh, pickle.HIGHEST_PROTOCOL)
```

Versus:

```
import sqlite3
connection = sqlite3.connect('database.sqlite')
cursor = connection.cursor()
cursor.execute('CREATE TABLE data (key text, value text)')
cursor.execute('''INSERT INTO data VALUES ('key', 'value')''')
connection.commit()
connection.close()
```

These examples are far from identical, of course, as one stores a complete data object whereas the other simply stores some key/value pairs within a SQLite database. That is not the point, however. The point is that the code is far more complex while it is actually less versatile in many cases. With proper libraries, this can be simplified, but the basic premise stays the same. Simple is better than complex and if the complexity is not needed, it's better to avoid it.

Flat is better than nested

Nested code quickly becomes unreadable and hard to understand. There are no strict rules here, but generally when you have three levels of nested loops, it is time to refactor.

Just take a look the following example, which prints a list of two-dimensional matrices. While nothing is specifically wrong here, splitting it into a few more functions might make it easier to understand the purpose and easier to test:

```python
def print_matrices():
    for matrix in matrices:
        print('Matrix:')
        for row in matrix:
            for col in row:
                print(col, end='')
            print()
        print()
```

The somewhat flatter version is as follows:

```python
def print_row(row):
    for col in row:
        print(col, end='')

def print_matrix(matrix):
    for row in matrix:
        print_row(row)
        print()

def print_matrices(matrices):
    for matrix in matrices:
        print('Matrix:')
        print_matrix(matrix)
        print()
```

This example might be a bit convoluted, but the idea is sound. Having deeply nested code can easily become very unreadable.

Sparse is better than dense

Whitespace is generally a good thing. Yes, it will make your files longer and your code will take more space, but it can help a lot with readability if you split your code logically:

```python
>>> def make_eggs(a,b):'while',['technically'];print('correct');\
...     {'this':'is','highly':'unreadable'};print(1-a+b**4/2**2)
```

```
...
>>> make_eggs(1,2)
correct
4.0
```

While technically correct, this is not all that readable. I'm certain that it would take me some effort to find out what the code actually does and what number it would print without trying it:

```
>>> def make_eggs(a, b):
...     'while', ['technically']
...     print('correct')
...     {'this': 'is', 'highly': 'unreadable'}
...     print(1 - a + ((b ** 4) / (2 ** 2)))
...
>>> make_eggs(1, 2)
correct
4.0
```

Still, this is not the best code, but at least it's a bit more obvious what is happening in the code.

Readability counts

Shorter does not always mean easier to read:

```
fib=lambda n:reduce(lambda x,y:(x[0]+x[1],x[0]),[(1,1)]*(n-2))[0]
```

Although the short version has a certain beauty in conciseness, I personally find the following far more beautiful:

```
def fib(n):
    a, b = 0, 1
    while True:
        yield a
        a, b = b, a + b
```

Practicality beats purity

> *"Special cases aren't special enough to break the rules. Although practicality beats purity."*

Breaking the rules can be tempting at times, but it tends to be a slippery slope. Naturally, this applies to all rules. If your quick fix is going to break the rules, you should really try to refactor it immediately. Chances are that you won't have the time to fix it later and will regret it.

No need to go overboard though. If the solution is good enough and refactoring would be much more work, then choosing the working method might be better. Even though all of these examples pertain to imports, this guideline applies to nearly all cases.

To prevent long lines, imports can be made shorter by using a few methods, adding a backslash, adding parentheses, or just shortening the imports:

```
from spam.eggs.foo.bar import spam, eggs, extra_spam, extra_eggs,
extra_stuff  from spam.eggs.foo.bar import spam, eggs, extra_spam,
extra_eggs
```

This case can easily be avoided by just following PEP8 (one import per line):

```
from spam.eggs.foo.bar import spam from spam.eggs.foo.bar import eggs
from spam.eggs.foo.bar import extra_spam from spam.eggs.foo.bar import
extra_eggs from spam.eggs.foo.bar import extra_stuff  from spam.eggs.
foo.bar import spam
from spam.eggs.foo.bar import eggs
from spam.eggs.foo.bar import extra_spam
from spam.eggs.foo.bar import extra_eggs
```

But what about really long imports?

```
from spam_eggs_and_some_extra_spam_stuff import
my_spam_and_eggs_stuff_which_is_too_long_for_a_line
```

Yes... even though adding a backslash for imports is generally not recommended, there are some cases where it's still the best option:

```
from spam_eggs_and_some_extra_spam_stuff \
    import my_spam_and_eggs_stuff_which_is_too_long_for_a_line
```

Errors should never pass silently

"Errors should never pass silently. Unless explicitly silenced."

To paraphrase Jamie Zawinsky: Some people, when confronted with an error, think "I know, I'll use a `try/except/pass` block." Now they have two problems.

Bare or too broad exception catching is already a bad idea. Not passing them along will make you (or some other person working on the code) wonder for ages what is happening:

```
try:
    value = int(user_input)
except:
    pass
```

If you really need to catch all errors, be very explicit about it:

```
try:
    value = int(user_input)
except Exception as e:
    logging.warn('Uncaught exception %r', e)
```

Or even better, catch it specifically and add a sane default:

```
try:
    value = int(user_input)
except ValueError:
    value = 0
```

The problem is actually even more complicated. What about blocks of code that depend on whatever is happening within the exception? For example, consider the following code block:

```
try:
    value = int(user_input)
    value = do_some_processing(value)
    value = do_some_other_processing(value)
except ValueError:
    value = 0
```

If `ValueError` is raised, which line is causing it? Is it `int(user_input)`, `do_some_processing(value)`, or `do_some_other_processing(value)`? With silent catching of the error, there is no way to know when regularly executing the code, and this can be quite dangerous. If for some reason the processing of the other functions changes, it becomes a problem to handle exceptions in this way. So, unless it was actually intended to behave like that, use this instead:

```
try:
    value = int(user_input)
except ValueError:
    value = 0
else:
    value = do_some_processing(value)
    value = do_some_other_processing(value)
```

In the face of ambiguity, refuse the temptation to guess

While guesses will work in many cases, they can bite you if you're not careful. As already demonstrated in the "explicit is better than implicit" paragraph, when having a few `from ... import *`, you cannot always be certain which module is providing you the variable you were expecting.

Ambiguity should generally be avoided, so guessing can be avoided. Clear and unambiguous code generates fewer bugs. A useful case where ambiguity is likely is function calling. Take, for example, the following two function calls:

```
spam(1, 2, 3, 4, 5)
spam(spam=1, eggs=2, a=3, b=4, c=5)
```

They could be the same, but they might also not be. It's impossible to say without seeing the function. If the function were implemented in the following way, the results would be vastly different between the two:

```
def spam(a=0, b=0, c=0, d=0, e=0, spam=1, eggs=2):
    pass
```

I'm not saying you should use keyword arguments in all cases, but if there are many arguments involved and/or hard-to-identify parameters (such as numbers), it would be a good idea. Instead of using keyword arguments, you can choose logical variable names to pass the arguments as well, as long as the meaning is clearly conveyed from the code.

For example, the following is a similar call that uses custom variable names to convey the intent:

```
a = 3
b = 4
c = 5
spam(a, b, c)
```

One obvious way to do it

"There should be one — and preferably only one — obvious way to do it. Although that way may not be obvious at first unless you're Dutch."

In general, after thinking about a difficult problem for a while, you will find that there is one solution that is clearly preferable over the alternatives. There are cases where this is not the case, however, and in that case, it can be useful if you're Dutch. The joke here is that Guido van Rossum, the BDFL and original author of Python, is Dutch (as is yours truly).

Now is better than never

"Now is better than never. Although never is often better than *right* now."

It's better to fix a problem right now than push it into the future. There are cases, however, where fixing it right away is not an option. In those cases, a good alternative can be to mark a function as deprecated instead so that there is no chance of accidentally forgetting the problem:

```
import warnings
warnings.warn('Something deprecated', DeprecationWarning)
```

Hard to explain, easy to explain

"If the implementation is hard to explain, it's a bad idea. If the implementation is easy to explain, it may be a good idea."

As always, keep things as simple as you can. While complicated code can be nice to test with, it is more prone to bugs. The simpler you can keep things, the better.

Namespaces are one honking great idea

"Namespaces are one honking great idea — let's do more of those!"

Namespaces can make code a lot clearer to use. Naming them properly makes it even better. For example, what does the following line of code do?

```
load(fh)
```

Not too clear, right?

How about the version with the namespace?

```
pickle.load(fh)
```

And now we do understand.

To give an example of a namespace, the full length of which renders it impractical to use, we will take a look at the User class in Django. Within the Django framework, the User class is stored in django.contrib.auth.models.User. Many projects use the object in the following way:

```
from django.contrib.auth.models import User
# Use it as: User
```

While this is fairly clear, it might make someone think that the User class is local to the current class. Doing the following instead lets people know that it is in a different module:

```
from django.contrib.auth import models
# Use it as: models.User
```

This quickly clashes with other models' imports though, so personally I would recommend the following instead:

```
from django.contrib.auth import models as auth_models
# Use it as auth_models.User
```

Here is another alternative:

```
import django.contrib.auth as auth_models
# Use it as auth_models.User
```

Conclusion

Now we should have some idea of what the Pythonic ideology is about. Creating code that is:

- Beautiful
- Readable
- Unambiguous
- Explicit enough
- Not completely void of whitespace

So let's move on to some more examples of how to create beautiful, readable, and simple code using the Python style guide.

Explaining PEP8

The previous paragraphs have already shown a lot of examples using PEP20 as a reference, but there are a few other important guidelines to note as well. The PEP8 style guide specifies the standard Python coding conventions. Simply following the PEP8 standard doesn't make your code Pythonic though, but it is most certainly a good start. Which style you use is really not that much of a concern as long as you are consistent. The only thing worse than not using a proper style guide is being inconsistent with it.

Duck typing

Duck typing is a method of handling variables by behavior. To quote Alex Martelli (one of my Python heroes, also nicknamed the MartelliBot by many):

> *"Don't check whether it IS-a duck: check whether it QUACKS-like-a duck, WALKS-like-a duck, etc, etc, depending on exactly what subset of duck-like behaviour you need to play your language-games with. If the argument fails this specific-ducklyhood-subset-test, then you can shrug, ask "why a duck?"*

In many cases, when people make a comparison such as `if spam != '':`, they are actually just looking for anything that is considered a true value. While you can compare the value to the string value `''`, you generally don't have to make it so specific. In many cases, simply doing `if spam:` is more than enough and actually functions better.

For example, the following lines of code use the value of `timestamp` to generate a filename:

```
filename = '%s.csv' % timestamp
```

Because it is named `timestamp`, one might be tempted to check whether it is actually a `date` or `datetime` object, like this:

```
import datetime
if isinstance(timestamp, (datetime.date, datetime.datetime)):
    filename = '%s.csv' % timestamp
else:
    raise TypeError(
        'Timestamp %r should be date(time) object, got %s'
        % (timestamp, type(timestamp)))
```

While this is not inherently wrong, comparing types is considered a bad practice in Python, as there is oftentimes no need for it. In Python, duck typing is preferred instead. Just try converting it to a string and don't care what it actually is. To illustrate how little difference this can make for the end result, see the following code:

```python
import datetime
timestamp = datetime.date(2000, 10, 5)
filename = '%s.csv' % timestamp
print('Filename from date: %s' % filename)

timestamp = '2000-10-05'
filename = '%s.csv' % timestamp
print('Filename from str: %s' % filename)
```

As you might expect, the result is identical:

```
Filename from date: 2000-10-05.csv
Filename from str: 2000-10-05.csv
```

The same goes for converting a number to a float or an integer; instead of enforcing a certain type, just require certain features. Need something that can pass as a number? Just try to convert to `int` or `float`. Need a `file` object? Why not just check whether there is a `read` method with `hasattr`?

So, don't do this:

```python
if isinstance(value, int):
```

Instead, just use the following:

```python
value = int(value)
```

And instead of this:

```python
import io

if isinstance(fh, io.IOBase):
```

Simply use the following line:

```python
if hasattr(fh, 'read'):
```

Differences between value and identity comparisons

There are several methods of comparing objects in Python, the standard greater than and less than, equal and unequal. But there are actually a few more, and one of them is a bit special. That's the identity comparison operator: instead of using if spam == eggs, you use if spam is eggs. The big difference is that one compares the value and the other compares the identity. This sounds a little vague, but it's actually fairly simple. At least within the CPython implementation, the memory address is being compared, which means that it is one of the lightest lookups you can get. Whereas a value needs to make sure that the types are comparable and perhaps check the sub-values, the identity check just checks whether the unique identifier is the same.

 If you've ever written Java, you should be familiar with this principle. In Java, a regular string comparison (spam == eggs) will use the identity instead of the value. To compare the value, you need to use spam.equals(eggs) to get the correct results.

Look at this example:

```
a = 200 + 56
b = 256
c = 200 + 57
d = 257

print('%r == %r: %r' % (a, b, a == b))
print('%r is %r: %r' % (a, b, a is b))
print('%r == %r: %r' % (c, d, c == d))
print('%r is %r: %r' % (c, d, c is d))
```

While the values are the same, the identities are different. The actual result from this code is as follows:

```
256 == 256: True
256 is 256: True
257 == 257: True
257 is 257: False
```

The catch is that Python keeps an internal array of integer objects for all integers between -5 and 256; that's why it works for 256 but not for 257.

You might wonder why anyone would ever want to use is instead of ==. There are multiple valid answers; depending on the case, one is correct and the other isn't. But performance can also be a very important consideration. The basic guideline is that when comparing Python singletons such as True, False, and None, always compare using is.

As for the performance consideration, think of the following example:

```
spam = range(1000000)
eggs = range(1000000)
```

When doing `spam == eggs`, this will compare every item in both lists to each other, so effectively it is doing 1,000,000 comparisons internally. Compare this with only one simple identity check when using `spam is eggs`.

To look at what Python is actually doing internally with the `is` operator, you can use the `id` function. When executing `if spam is eggs`, Python will actually execute `if id(spam) == id(eggs)` internally.

Loops

Coming from other languages, one might be tempted to use `for` loops or even `while` loops to process the items of a `list`, `tuple`, `str`, and so on. While valid, it is more complex than needed. For example, consider this code:

```
i = 0
while i < len(my_list):
    item = my_list[i]
    i += 1
    do_something(i, item)
```

Instead you can do the following:

```
for i, item in enumerate(my_list):
    do_something(i, item)
```

While this can be written even shorter, it's generally not recommended, as it does not improve readability:

```
[do_something(i, item) for i, item in enumerate(my_list)]
```

The last option might be clear to some but not all. Personally, I prefer to limit the usage of list comprehensions, dict comprehensions, and map and filter statements for when the result is actually being stored.

For example:

```
spam_items = [x for x in items if x.startswith('spam_')]
```

But still, only if it doesn't hurt the readability of the code.

Consider this bit of code:

```
eggs = [is_egg(item) or create_egg(item) for item in list_of_items if
egg and hasattr(egg, 'egg_property') and isinstance(egg, Egg)]  eggs =
[is_egg(item) or create_egg(item) for item in list_of_items
        if egg and hasattr(egg, 'egg_property')
        and isinstance(egg, Egg)]
```

Instead of putting everything in the list comprehension, why not split it into a few functions?

```
def to_egg(item):
    return is_egg(item) or create_egg(item)


def can_be_egg(item):
    has_egg_property = hasattr(egg, 'egg_property')
    is_egg_instance = isinstance(egg, Egg)
    return egg and has_egg_property and is_egg_instance


eggs = [to_egg(item) for item in list_of_items if can_be_egg(item)]
eggs = [to_egg(item) for item in list_of_items if
        can_be_egg(item)]
```

While this code is a bit longer, I would personally argue that it's more readable this way.

Maximum line length

Many Python programmers think 79 characters is too constricting and just keep the lines longer. While I am not going to argue for 79 characters specifically, setting a low and fixed limit such as 79 or 99 is a good idea. While monitors get wider and wider, limiting your lines can still help a lot with readability and it allows you to put multiple files next to each other. It's a regular occurrence for me to have four Python files opened next to each other. If the line width were more than 79 characters, that simply wouldn't fit.

The PEP8 guide tells us to use backslashes in cases where lines get too long. While I agree that backslashes are preferable over long lines, I still think they should be avoided if possible. Here's an example from PEP8:

```
with open('/path/to/some/file/you/want/to/read') as file_1, \
        open('/path/to/some/file/being/written', 'w') as file_2:
    file_2.write(file_1.read())
```

Instead of using backslashes, I would reformat it like this:

```
filename_1 = '/path/to/some/file/you/want/to/read'
filename_2 = '/path/to/some/file/being/written'
```

```
with open(filename_1) as file_1, open(filename_2, 'w') as file_2:
    file_2.write(file_1.read())
```

Or perhaps the following:

```
filename_1 = '/path/to/some/file/you/want/to/read'
filename_2 = '/path/to/some/file/being/written'
with open(filename_1) as file_1:
    with open(filename_2, 'w') as file_2:
        file_2.write(file_1.read())
```

Not always an option, of course, but it's a good consideration to keep the code short and readable. It actually gives a bonus of adding more information to the code. If, instead of `filename_1`, you use a name that conveys the goal of the filename, it immediately becomes clearer what you are trying to do.

Verifying code quality, pep8, pyflakes, and more

There are many tools for checking code quality in Python. The simplest ones, such as `pep8`, just validate a few simple PEP8 errors. The more advanced ones, such as `pylint`, do advanced introspections to detect potential bugs in otherwise working code. A large portion of what `pylint` offers is a bit over the top for many projects, but still interesting to look at.

flake8

The `flake8` tool combines pep8, pyflakes, and McCabe to set up a quality standard for code. The `flake8` tool is one of the most important packages for maintaining code quality in my packages. All the packages that I maintain have a 100% `flake8` compliance requirement. It does not promise readable code, but at least it requires a certain level of consistency, which is very important when writing on a project with multiple programmers.

Pep8

One of the simplest tools used to check the quality of Python code is the `pep8` package. It doesn't check everything that is in the PEP8 standard, but it goes a long way and is still updated regularly to add new checks. Some of the most important things checked by `pep8` are as follows:

- Indentation, while Python will not check how many spaces you use to indent, it does not help with the readability of your code
- Missing whitespace, such as `spam=123`

- Too much whitespace, such as `def eggs(spam = 123):`
- Too many or too few blank lines
- Too long lines
- Syntax and indentation errors
- Incorrect and/or superfluous comparisons (`not in`, `is not`, `if spam is True`, and type comparisons without `isinstance`)

The conclusion is that the `pep8` tool helps a lot with testing whitespace and some of the more common styling issues, but it is still fairly limited.

pyflakes

This is where pyflakes comes in. pyflakes is a bit more intelligent than `pep8` and warns you about style issues such as:

- Unused imports
- Wildcard imports (`from module import *`)
- Incorrect `__future__` imports (after other imports)

But more importantly, it warns about potential bugs, such as the following:

- Redefinitions of names that were imported
- Usage of undefined variables
- Referencing variables before assignment
- Duplicate argument names
- Unused local variables

The last bit of PEP8 is covered by the pep8-naming package. It makes sure that your naming is close to the standard dictated by PEP8:

- Class names as *CapWord*
- Function, variable, and argument names all in lowercase
- Constants as full uppercase and being treated as constants
- The first argument of instance methods and class methods as *self* and *cls*, respectively

McCabe

Lastly, there is the McCabe complexity. It checks the complexity of code by looking at the **Abstract Syntax Tree** (**AST**). It finds out how many lines, levels, and statements are there and warns you if your code has more complexity than a preconfigured threshold. Generally, you will use McCabe through `flake8`, but a manual call is possible as well. Using the following code:

```
def spam():
    pass


def eggs(matrix):
    for x in matrix:
        for y in x:
            for z in y:
                print(z, end='')
            print()
        print()
```

McCabe will give us the following output:

```
# pip install mccabe
...
# python -m mccabe cabe_test.py 1:1: 'spam' 1
5:1: 'eggs' 4
```

Your maximum threshold is configurable, of course, but the default is 10. The McCabe test returns a number that is influenced by parameters such as the size of a function, the nested depths, and a few others. If your function reaches 10, it might be time to refactor the code.

flake8

All of this combined is `flake8`, a tool that combines these tools and outputs a single report. Some of the warnings generated by `flake8` might not fit your taste, so each and every one of the checks can be disabled, both per file and for the entire project if needed. For example, I personally disable `W391` for all my projects, which warns about blank lines at the end of a file. This is something I find useful while working on code so that I can easily jump to the end of the file and start writing code instead of having to append a few lines first.

In general, before committing your code and/or putting it online, just run `flake8` from your source directory to check everything recursively.

Here is a demonstration with some poorly formatted code:

```
def spam(a,b,c):
    print(a,b+c)

def eggs():
    pass
```

It results in the following:

```
# pip install flake8
...
# flake8 flake8_test.py
flake8_test.py:1:11: E231 missing whitespace after ','
flake8_test.py:1:13: E231 missing whitespace after ','
flake8_test.py:2:12: E231 missing whitespace after ','
flake8_test.py:2:14: E226 missing whitespace around arithmetic operator
flake8_test.py:4:1: E302 expected 2 blank lines, found 1
```

Pylint

`pylint` is a far more advanced—and in some cases better—code quality checker. The power of `pylint` does come with a few drawbacks, however. Whereas `flake8` is a really fast, light, and safe quality check, `pylint` has far more advanced introspection and is much slower for this reason. In addition, `pylint` will most likely give you a large number of warnings, which are irrelevant or even wrong. This could be seen as a flaw in `pylint`, but it's actually more of a restriction of passive code analysis. Tools such as `pychecker` actually load and execute your code. In many cases, this is safe, but there are cases where it is not. Just think of what could happen when executing a command that deletes files.

While I have nothing against `pylint`, in general I find that most important problems are handled by `flake8`, and others can easily be avoided with some proper coding standards. It can be a very useful tool if configured correctly, but without configuration, it is very verbose.

Common pitfalls

Python is a language meant to be clear and readable without any ambiguities and unexpected behaviors. Unfortunately, these goals are not achievable in all cases, and that is why Python does have a few corner cases where it might do something different than what you were expecting.

This section will show you some issues that you might encounter when writing Python code.

Scope matters!

There are a few cases in Python where you might not be using the scope that you are actually expecting. Some examples are when declaring a class and with function arguments.

Function arguments

The following example shows a case that breaks due to a careless choice in default parameters:

```
def spam(key, value, list_=[], dict_={}):
    list_.append(value)
    dict_[key] = value

    print('List: %r' % list_)
    print('Dict: %r' % dict_)

spam('key 1', 'value 1')
spam('key 2', 'value 2')
```

You would probably expect the following output:

```
List: ['value 1']
Dict: {'key 1': 'value 1'}
List: ['value 2']
Dict: {'key 2': 'value 2'}
```

But it's actually this:

```
List: ['value 1']
Dict: {'key 1': 'value 1'}
List: ['value 1', 'value 2']
Dict: {'key 1': 'value 1', 'key 2': 'value 2'}
```

The reason is that list_ and dict_ are actually shared between multiple calls. The only time this is actually useful is if you are doing something hacky, so please avoid using mutable objects as default parameters in a function.

The safe alternative of the same example is as follows:

```
def spam(key, value, list_=None, dict_=None):
    if list_ is None:
```

```
        list_ = []

    if dict_ is None:
        dict_ {}

    list_.append(value)
    dict_[key] = value
```

Class properties

The problem also occurs when defining classes. It is very easy to mix class attributes and instance attributes. Especially when coming from other languages such as C#, this can be confusing. Let's illustrate it:

```
class Spam(object):
    list_ = []
    dict_ = {}

    def __init__(self, key, value):
        self.list_.append(value)
        self.dict_[key] = value

        print('List: %r' % self.list_)
        print('Dict: %r' % self.dict_)


Spam('key 1', 'value 1')
Spam('key 2', 'value 2')
```

As with the function arguments, the list and dictionaries are shared. So, the output is as follows:

```
List: ['value 1']
Dict: {'key 1': 'value 1'}
List: ['value 1', 'value 2']
Dict: {'key 1': 'value 1', 'key 2': 'value 2'}
```

A better alternative is to initialize the mutable objects within the __init__ method of the class. This way, they are not shared between instances:

```
class Spam(object):
    def __init__(self, key, value):
        self.list_ = [key]
        self.dict_ = {key: value}

        print('List: %r' % self.list_)
        print('Dict: %r' % self.dict_)
```

Another important thing to note when dealing with classes is that a class property will be inherited, and that's where things might prove to be confusing. When inheriting, the original properties will stay (unless overwritten), even in subclasses:

```
>>> class A(object):
...     spam = 1



>>> class B(A):
...     pass



Regular inheritance, the spam attribute of both A and B are 1 as
you would expect.
>>> A.spam
1
>>> B.spam
1


Assigning 2 to A.spam now modifies B.spam as well
>>> A.spam = 2

>>> A.spam
2
>>> B.spam
2
```

While this is to be expected due to inheritance, someone else using the class might not suspect the variable to change in the meantime. After all, we modified A.spam, not B.spam.

There are two easy ways to prevent this. It is obviously possible to simply set spam for every class separately. But the better solution is never to modify class properties. It's easy to forget that the property will change in multiple locations, and if it has to be modifiable anyway, it's usually better to put it in an instance variable instead.

Modifying variables in the global scope

A common problem when accessing variables from the global scope is that setting a variable makes it local, even when accessing the global variable.

This works:

```
>>> def eggs():
...     print('Spam: %r' % spam)


>>> eggs()
Spam: 1
```

But the following does not:

```
>>> spam = 1



>>> def eggs():
...     spam += 1
...     print('Spam: %r' % spam)


>>> eggs()
Traceback (most recent call last):
    ...
UnboundLocalError: local variable 'spam' referenced before assignment
```

The problem is that spam += 1 actually translates to spam = spam + 1, and anything containing spam = makes the variable local to your scope. Since the local variable is being assigned at that point, it has no value yet and you are trying to use it. For these cases, there is the global statement, although I would really recommend that you avoid globals altogether.

Overwriting and/or creating extra built-ins

While it can be useful in some cases, generally you will want to avoid overwriting global functions. The PEP8 convention for naming your functions—similar to built-in statements, functions, and variables—is to use a trailing underscore.

So, do not use this:

```
    list = [1, 2, 3]
```

Instead, use the following:

```
    list_ = [1, 2, 3]
```

For lists and such, this is just a good convention. For statements such as `from`, `import`, and `with`, it's a requirement. Forgetting about this can lead to very confusing errors:

```
>>> list = list((1, 2, 3))
>>> list
[1, 2, 3]


>>> list((4, 5, 6))
Traceback (most recent call last):
    ...
TypeError: 'list' object is not callable


>>> import = 'Some import'
Traceback (most recent call last):
    ...
SyntaxError: invalid syntax
```

If you actually want to define a built-in that is available everywhere, it's possible. For debugging purposes, I've been known to add this code to a project while developing:

```
import builtins
import inspect
import pprint
import re


def pp(*args, **kwargs):
    '''PrettyPrint function that prints the variable name when
    available and pprints the data'''
    name = None
    # Fetch the current frame from the stack
    frame = inspect.currentframe().f_back
    # Prepare the frame info
    frame_info = inspect.getframeinfo(frame)

    # Walk through the lines of the function
    for line in frame_info[3]:
        # Search for the pp() function call with a fancy regexp
        m = re.search(r'\bpp\s*\(\s*([^)]*)\s*\)', line)
        if m:
            print('# %s:' % m.group(1), end=' ')
```

```
        break

    pprint.pprint(*args, **kwargs)

builtins.pf = pprint.pformat
builtins.pp = pp
```

Much too hacky for production code, but it is still useful when working on a large project where you need print statements to debug. Alternative (and better) debugging solutions can be found in Chapter 11, *Debugging – Solving the Bugs*.

The usage is quite simple:

```
x = 10
pp(x)
```

Here is the output:

```
# x: 10
```

Modifying while iterating

At one point or another, you will run into this problem: while iterating through mutable objects such as lists, dicts, or sets, you cannot modify them. All of these result in a RuntimeError telling you that you cannot modify the object during iteration:

```
dict_ = {'spam': 'eggs'}
list_ = ['spam']
set_ = {'spam', 'eggs'}

for key in dict_:
    del dict_[key]

for item in list_:
    list_.remove(item)

for item in set_:
    set_.remove(item)
```

This can be avoided by copying the object. The most convenient option is by using the list function:

```
dict_ = {'spam': 'eggs'}
list_ = ['spam']
set_ = {'spam', 'eggs'}

for key in list(dict_):
```

```
del dict_[key]

for item in list(list_):
    list_.remove(item)

for item in list(set_):
    set_.remove(item)
```

Catching exceptions – differences between Python 2 and 3

With Python 3, catching an exception and storing it has been made more obvious with the `as` statement. The problem is that many people are still used to the `except Exception, variable` syntax, which doesn't work anymore. Luckily, the Python 3 syntax has been backported to Python 2, so now you can use the following syntax everywhere:

```
try:
    ... # do something here
except (ValueError, TypeError) as e:
    print('Exception: %r' % e)
```

Another important difference is that Python 3 makes this variable local to the exception scope. The result is that you need to declare the exception variable before the `try`/`except` block if you want to use it later:

```
def spam(value):
    try:
        value = int(value)
    except ValueError as exception:
        print('We caught an exception: %r' % exception)

    return exception


spam('a')
```

You might expect that since we get an exception here, this works; but actually, it doesn't, because `exception` does not exist at the point of the `return` statement.

The actual output is as follows:

```
We caught an exception: ValueError("invalid literal for int() with
base 10: 'a'",)
Traceback (most recent call last):
  File "test.py", line 14, in <module>
```

```
    spam('a')
  File "test.py", line 11, in spam
    return exception
UnboundLocalError: local variable 'exception' referenced before
assignment
```

Personally I would argue that the preceding code is broken in any case: what if there isn't an exception somehow? It would have raised the same error. Luckily, the fix is simple; just write the value to a variable outside of the scope. One important thing to note here is that you explicitly need to save the variable to the parent scope. This code does not work either:

```
def spam(value):
    exception = None
    try:
        value = int(value)
    except ValueError as exception:
        print('We caught an exception: %r' % exception)


    return exception
```

We really need to save it explicitly because Python 3 automatically deletes anything saved with `as variable` at the end of the `except` statements. The reason for this is that exceptions in Python 3 contain a `__traceback__` attribute. Having this attribute makes it much more difficult for the garbage collector to handle as it introduces a recursive self-referencing cycle (*exception -> traceback -> exception -> traceback... ad nauseum*). To solve this, Python essentially does the following:

```
exception = None
try:
    value = int(value)
except ValueError as exception:
    try:
        print('We caught an exception: %r' % exception)
    finally:
        del exception
```

The solution is simple enough—luckily—but you should keep in mind that this can introduce memory leaks into your program. The Python garbage collector is smart enough to understand that the variables are not visible anymore and will delete it eventually, but it can take a lot more time. How the garbage collection actually works is covered in *Chapter 12, Performance – Tracking and Reducing Your Memory and CPU Usage*. Here is the working version of the code:

```
def spam(value):
    exception = None
```

```
try:
    value = int(value)
except ValueError as e:
    exception = e
    print('We caught an exception: %r' % exception)

return exception
```

Late binding – be careful with closures

Closures are a method of implementing local scopes in code. They make it possible to locally define variables without overriding variables in the parent (or global) scope and hide the variables from the outside scope later. The problem with closures in Python is that Python tries to bind its variables as late as possible for performance reasons. While generally useful, it does have some unexpected side effects:

```
eggs = [lambda a: i * a for i in range(3)]

for egg in eggs:
    print(egg(5))
```

The expected result? Should be something along the lines of this, right?

```
0
5
10
```

No, unfortunately not. This is similar to how class inheritance works with properties. Due to late binding, the variable i gets called from the surrounding scope at call time, and not when it's actually defined.

The actual result is as follows:

```
10
10
10
```

So what to do instead? As with the cases mentioned earlier, the variable needs to be made local. One alternative is to force immediate binding by currying the function with partial:

```
import functools


eggs = [functools.partial(lambda i, a: i * a, i) for i in
range(3)]
```

```
for egg in eggs:
    print(egg(5))
```

A better solution would be to avoid binding problems altogether by not introducing extra scopes (the `lambda`), that use external variables. If both `i` and `a` were specified as arguments to `lambda`, this will not be a problem.

Circular imports

Even though Python is fairly tolerant towards circular imports, there are some cases where you will get errors.

Let's assume we have two files.

`eggs.py`:

```
from spam import spam


def eggs():
    print('This is eggs')
    spam()
```

`spam.py`:

```
from eggs import eggs


def spam():
    print('This is spam')


if __name__ == '__main__':
    eggs()
```

Running `spam.py` will result in a circular `import` error:

```
Traceback (most recent call last):
  File "spam.py", line 1, in <module>
    from eggs import eggs
  File "eggs.py", line 1, in <module>
    from spam import spam
  File "spam.py", line 1, in <module>
    from eggs import eggs
ImportError: cannot import name 'eggs'
```

There are a few ways to work around this. Restructuring the code is usually the best to go around, but the best solution depends on the problem. In the preceding case, it can be solved easily. Just use module imports instead of function imports (which I recommend regardless of circular imports).

`eggs.py`:

```
import spam


def eggs():
    print('This is eggs')
    spam.spam()
```

`spam.py`:

```
import eggs


def spam():
    print('This is spam')


if __name__ == '__main__':
    eggs.eggs()
```

An alternative solution is to move the imports within the functions so that they occur at runtime. This is not the prettiest solution but it does the trick in many cases.

`eggs.py`:

```
def eggs():
    from spam import spam
    print('This is eggs')
    spam()
```

`spam.py`:

```
def spam():
    from eggs import eggs
    print('This is spam')


if __name__ == '__main__':
    eggs()
```

Lastly there is the solution of moving the imports below the code that actually uses them. This is generally not recommended because it can make it non-obvious where the imports are, but I still find it preferable to having the `import` within the function calls.

`eggs.py`:

```python
def eggs():
    print('This is eggs')
    spam()


from spam import spam
```

`spam.py`:

```python
def spam():
    print('This is spam')


from eggs import eggs


if __name__ == '__main__':
    eggs()
```

And yes, there are still other solutions such as dynamic imports. One example of this is how the Django `ForeignKey` fields support strings instead of actual classes. But those are generally a really bad idea to use since they will be checked only at runtime. Because of this, bugs will introduce themselves only when executing any code that uses it instead of when modifying the code. So please try to avoid these whenever possible, or make sure you add proper automated tests to prevent unexpected bugs. Especially when they cause circular imports internally, they become an enormous pain to debug.

Import collisions

One problem that can be extremely confusing is having colliding imports—multiple packages/modules with the same name. I have had more than a few bug reports on my packages where, for example, people tried to use my `numpy-stl` project, which resides in a package named `stl` from a test file named `stl.py`. The result: it was importing itself instead of the `stl` package. While this case is difficult to avoid, at least within packages, a relative import is generally a better option. This is because it also tells other programmers that the import comes from the local scope instead of another package. So, instead of writing `import spam`, write `from . import spam`. This way, the code will always load from the current package instead of any global package that happens to have the same name.

In addition to this there is also the problem of packages being incompatible with each other. Common names might be used by several packages, so be careful when installing those packages. When in doubt, just create a new virtual environment and try again. Doing this can save you a lot of debugging.

Summary

This chapter showed us what the Pythonic philosophy is all about and explained to us what the Zen of Python is all about. While code style is highly personal, Python has a few, very helpful guidelines that at least keep people mostly on the same page and style. In the end, we are all consenting adults; everyone has the right to write code as he/she sees fit. But I do request you. Please read through the style guides and try to adhere to them unless you have a really good reason not to.

With all that power comes great responsibility, and so do a few pitfalls, though there aren't too many. Some are tricky enough to fool me regularly and I've been writing Python for a long time! Python improves all the time though. Many pitfalls have been taken care of since Python 2, but some will always remain. For example, recursive imports and definitions can easily bite you in most languages that support them, but that doesn't mean we'll stop trying to improve Python.

A good example of the improvements in Python over the years is the collections module. It contains many useful collections that have been added by users because there was a need. Most of them are actually implemented in pure Python, and because of that, they are easy enough to be read by anyone. Understanding might take a bit more effort, but I truly believe that if you make it to the end of this book, you will have no problem understanding what the collections do. Fully understanding how the internals work is something I cannot promise though; some parts of that go more towards generic computer science than Python mastery.

The next chapter will show you some of the collections available in Python and how they are constructed internally. Even though you are undoubtedly familiar with collections such as lists and dictionaries, you might not be aware of the performance characteristics involved with some of the operations. If some of the examples in this chapter were less than clear, you don't have to worry. The next chapter will at least revisit some of them, and more will come in later chapters.

3
Containers and Collections – Storing Data the Right Way

Python comes bundled with several very useful collections, a few of which are basic Python collection data types. The rest are advanced combinations of these types. In this chapter, we will explain some of these collections, how to use them, and the pros and cons of each of them.

Before we can properly discuss data structures and the related performance, a basic understanding of time complexity (and specifically the big O notation) is required. No need to worry! The concept is really simple, but without it, we cannot easily explain the performance characteristics of operations.

Once the big O notation is clear, we will discuss the basic data structures:

- `list`
- `dict`
- `set`
- `tuple`

Building on the basic data structures, we will continue with more advanced collections, such as the following:

- Dictionary-like types:
    - `ChainMap`
    - `Counter`
    - `Defaultdict`
    - `OrderedDict`

- List types:
  - Deque
  - Heapq

- Tuple types:
  - NamedTuple

- Other types:
  - Enum

Time complexity – the big O notation

Before we can begin with this chapter, there is a simple notation that you need to understand. This chapter heavily uses the big O notation to indicate the time complexity for an operation. Feel free to skip this paragraph if you are already familiar with this notation. While this notation sounds really complicated, the concept is actually quite simple.

When we say that a function takes `O(1)` time, it means that it generally only takes 1 step to execute. Similarly, a function with `O(n)` would take n steps to execute, where n is generally the size of the object. This time complexity is just a basic indication of what to expect when executing the code, as it is generally what matters most.

The purpose of this system is to indicate the approximate performance of an operation; this is separate from code speed but it is still relevant. A piece of code that executes a single step `1000` times faster but needs `O(2**n)` steps to execute will still be slower than another version of it that takes only `O(n)` steps for a value of n equal to `10` or more. This is because `2**n` for n=10 is `2**10=1024`, that is, 1,024 steps to execute the same code. This makes choosing the right algorithm very important. Even though `C` code is generally faster than Python, if it uses the wrong algorithm, it won't help at all.

For example, suppose you have a list of `1000` items and you walk through them. This will take `O(n)` time because there are n=1000 items. Checking whether or not an item exists in the list takes `O(n)`, so that's 1,000 steps. Doing this 100 times will take you `100*O(n) = 100 * 1000 = 100,000` steps. When you compare this to a `dict`, where checking whether the item exists or not takes only `O(1)` time the difference is huge. With a `dict`, it would be `100*O(1) = 100 * 1 = 100` steps. So, using a `dict` instead of a `list` will be roughly 1,000 times faster for an object with 1,000 items:

```
n = 1000
a = list(range(n))
b = dict.fromkeys(range(n))
```

```
for i in range(100):
    i in a  # takes n=1000 steps
    i in b  # takes 1 step
```

To illustrate O(1), O(n), and O(n**2) functions:

```
def o_one(items):
    return 1  # 1 operation so O(1)


def o_n(items):
    total = 0
    # Walks through all items once so O(n)
    for item in items:
        total += item
    return total


def o_n_squared(items):
    total = 0
    # Walks through all items n*n times so O(n**2)
    for a in items:
        for b in items:
            total += a * b
    return total


n = 10
items = range(n)
o_one(items)  # 1 operation
o_n(items)  # n = 10 operations
o_n_squared(items)  # n*n = 10*10 = 100 operations
```

It should be noted that the big O in this chapter is about the average case and not the worst case. In some cases, they can be much worse, but those are rare enough to be ignored for the general case.

Core collections

Before we can look at the more advanced combined collections later in this chapter, you need to understand the workings of the core Python collections. This is not just about the usage, however; it is also about the time complexities involved, which can strongly affect how your application will behave as it grows. If you are well versed with the time complexities of these objects and know the possibilities of Python 3's tuple packing and unpacking by heart, then feel free to jump to the *Advanced collections* section.

list – a mutable list of items

The `list` is most likely the container structure that you've used most in Python. It is simple in its usage, and for most cases, it exhibits great performance.

While you may already be well versed with the usage of list, you might not be aware of the time complexities of the `list` object. Luckily, many of the time complexities of `list` are very low; append, get, set, and len all take `O(1)` time — the best possible. However, you might not be aware of the fact that remove and insert have `O(n)` time complexity. So, to delete a single item out of 1,000 items, Python will have to walk-through 1,000 items. Internally, the remove and insert operations execute something along these lines:

```python
>>> def remove(items, value):
...     new_items = []
...     found = False
...     for item in items:
...         # Skip the first item which is equal to value
...         if not found and item == value:
...             found = True
...             continue
...         new_items.append(item)
...
...     if not found:
...         raise ValueError('list.remove(x): x not in list')
...
...     return new_items


>>> def insert(items, index, value):
...     new_items = []
...     for i, item in enumerate(items):
...         if i == index:
...             new_items.append(value)
...         new_items.append(item)
...     return new_items

>>> items = list(range(10))
>>> items
```

```
[0, 1, 2, 3, 4, 5, 6, 7, 8, 9]

>>> items = remove(items, 5)
>>> items
[0, 1, 2, 3, 4, 6, 7, 8, 9]

>>> items = insert(items, 2, 5)
>>> items
[0, 1, 5, 2, 3, 4, 6, 7, 8, 9]
```

To remove or insert a single item from/into the list, Python needs to copy the entire list, which is especially heavy with larger lists. When executing this only once, it is of course not all that bad. But when executing a large number of deletions, a `filter` or `list` comprehension is a much faster solution because, if properly structured, it needs to copy the list only once. For example, suppose we wish to remove a specific set of numbers from the list. We have quite a few options for this. The first is a solution using `remove`, followed by a list comprehension, and then comes a `filter` statement. *Chapter 4, Functional Programming – Readability Versus Brevity*, will explain `list` comprehensions and the `filter` statement in more detail. But first, let's check out the example:

```
>>> primes = set((1, 2, 3, 5, 7))

# Classic solution
>>> items = list(range(10))
>>> for prime in primes:
...     items.remove(prime)
>>> items
[0, 4, 6, 8, 9]

# List comprehension
>>> items = list(range(10))
>>> [item for item in items if item not in primes]
[0, 4, 6, 8, 9]

# Filter
>>> items = list(range(10))
>>> list(filter(lambda item: item not in primes, items))
[0, 4, 6, 8, 9]
```

The latter two are much faster for large lists of items. This is because the operations are much faster. To compare using n=len(items) and m=len(primes), the first takes O(m*n)=5*10=50 operations, whereas the latter two take O(n*1)=10*1=10 operations.

> The first method is actually slightly better than that since n decreases during the loop. So, it's effectively 10+9+8+7+6=40, but this is an effect that is negligible enough to ignore. In the case of n=1000, that would be the difference between 1000+999+998+997+996=4990 and 5*1000=5000, which is negligible in most cases.

Of course, min, max, and in all take O(n) as well, but that is expected for a structure that is not optimized for these types of lookups.

They can be implemented like this:

```
>>> def in_(items, value):
...         for item in items:
...             if item == value:
...                 return True
...         return False


>>> def min_(items):
...         current_min = items[0]
...         for item in items[1:]:
...             if current_min > item:
...                 current_min = item
...         return current_min


>>> def max_(items):
...         current_max = items[0]
...         for item in items[1:]:
...             if current_max < item:
...                 current_max = item
...         return current_max


>>> items = range(5)
>>> in_(items, 3)
True
```

```
>>> min_(items)
0
>>> max_(items)
4
```

With these examples, it's obvious as well that the in operator could work O(1) if you're lucky, but we count it as O(n) because it might not exist, in which case all values need to be checked.

dict – unsorted but a fast map of items

The dict has to be at least among the top three container structures you use in Python. It's fast, simple to use, and very effective. The average time complexity is exactly as you would expect—O(1) for get, set, and del—but there are cases where this is not true. The way a dict works is by converting the key to a hash using the hash function (calls the __hash__ function of an object) and storing it in a hash table. There are two problems with hash tables, however. The first and the most obvious is that the items will be sorted by hash, which appears at random in most cases. The second problem with hash tables is that they can have hash collisions, and the result of a hash collision is that in the worst case, all the former operations can take O(n) instead. Hash collisions are not all that likely to occur, but they can occur, and if a large dict performs subpar, that's the place to look.

Let's see how this actually works in practice. For the sake of this example, I will use the simplest hashing algorithm I can think of, which is the most significant digit of a number. So, for the case of 12345, it will return 1, and for 56789, it will return 5:

```
>>> def most_significant(value):
...     while value >= 10:
...         value //= 10
...     return value

>>> most_significant(12345)
1
>>> most_significant(99)
9
>>> most_significant(0)
0
```

Now we will emulate a `dict` using a `list` of lists with this hashing method. We know that our hashing method can only return numbers from 0 to 9, so we need only 10 buckets in our list. Now we will add a few values and show how the spam in eggs might work:

```
>>> def add(collection, key, value):
...     index = most_significant(key)
...     collection[index].append((key, value))

>>> def contains(collection, key):
...     index = most_significant(key)
...     for k, v in collection[index]:
...         if k == key:
...             return True
...     return False

# Create the collection of 10 lists
>>> collection = [[], [], [], [], [], [], [], [], [], []]

# Add some items, using key/value pairs
>>> add(collection, 123, 'a')
>>> add(collection, 456, 'b')
>>> add(collection, 789, 'c')
>>> add(collection, 101, 'c')

# Look at the collection
>>> collection
[[], [(123, 'a'), (101, 'c')], [], [],
 [(456, 'b')], [], [], [(789, 'c')], [], []]

# Check if the contains works correctly
>>> contains(collection, 123)
True
>>> contains(collection, 1)
False
```

This code is obviously not identical to the `dict` implementation, but it is actually quite similar internally. Because we can just get item 1 for a value of 123 by simple indexing, we have only O(1) lookup costs in the general case. However, since both keys, 123 and 101, are within the 1 bucket, the runtime can actually increase to O(n) in the worst case where all keys have the same hash. That is what we call a hash collision.

 To debug hash collisions, you can use the `hash()` function paired with the counter collection, discussed in the *counter – keeping track of the most occurring elements* section.

In addition to the hash collision performance problem, there is another behavior that might surprise you. When deleting items from a dictionary, it won't actually resize the dictionary in memory yet. The result is that both copying and iterating the entire dictionary take O(m) time (where m is the maximum size of the dictionary); n, the current number of items is not used. So, if you add 1,000 items to a `dict` and remove 999, iterating and copying will still take 1,000 steps. The only way to work around this issue is by recreating the dictionary, which is something that both the `copy` and `insert` operations will perform internally. Note that recreation during an `insert` operation is not guaranteed and depends on the number of free slots available internally.

set – like a dict without values

A `set` is a structure that uses the hash method to get a unique collection of values. Internally, it is very similar to a `dict`, with the same hash collision problem, but there are a few handy features of set that need to be shown:

```
# All output in the table below is generated using this function
>>> def print_set(expression, set_):
...     'Print set as a string sorted by letters'
...     print(expression, ''.join(sorted(set_)))

>>> spam = set('spam')
>>> print_set('spam:', spam)
spam: amps

>>> eggs = set('eggs')
>>> print_set('eggs:', spam)
eggs: amps
```

The first few are pretty much as expected. At the operators, it gets interesting.

Expression	Output	Explanation
spam	amps	All unique items. A `set` doesn't allow for duplicates.
eggs	egs	
spam & eggs	s	Every item in both.
spam | eggs	aegmps	Every item in either or both.
spam ^ eggs	aegmp	Every item in either but not in both.
spam - eggs	amp	Every item in the first but not the latter.
eggs - spam	eg	
spam > eggs	False	True if every item in the latter is in the first.
eggs > spam	False	
spam > sp	True	
spam < sp	False	True if every item in the first is contained in the latter.

One useful example for `set` operations is calculating the differences between two objects. For example, let's assume we have two lists:

- `current_users`: The current users in a group
- `new_users`: The new list of users in a group

In permission systems, this is a very common scenario—mass adding and/or removing users from a group. Within many permission databases, it's not easily possible to set the entire list at once, so you need a list to insert and a list to delete. This is where `set` comes in really handy:

The set function takes a sequence as argument so the double (is required.

```
>>> current_users = set((
...      'a',
...      'b',
...      'd',
... ))

>>> new_users = set((
...      'b',
...      'c',
...      'd',
...      'e',
```

```
... ))

>>> to_insert = new_users - current_users
>>> sorted(to_insert)
['c', 'e']
>>> to_delete = current_users - new_users
>>> sorted(to_delete)
['a']
>>> unchanged = new_users & current_users
>>> sorted(unchanged)
['b', 'd']
```

Now we have lists of all users who were added, removed, and unchanged. Note that `sorted` is only needed for consistent output, since a `set`, similar to a `dict`, has no predefined sort order.

tuple – the immutable list

A `tuple` is an object that you use very often without even noticing it. When you look at it initially, it seems like a useless data structure. It's like a list that you can't modify, so why not just use a `list`? There are a few cases where a `tuple` offers some really useful functionalities that a `list` does not.

Firstly, they are hashaable. This means that you can use a `tuple` as a key in a `dict`, which is something a `list` can't do:

```
>>> spam = 1, 2, 3
>>> eggs = 4, 5, 6

>>> data = dict()
>>> data[spam] = 'spam'
>>> data[eggs] = 'eggs'

>>> import pprint  # Using pprint for consistent and sorted output
>>> pprint.pprint(data)
{(1, 2, 3): 'spam', (4, 5, 6): 'eggs'}
```

However, it can actually be more than simple numbers. As long as all elements of a `tuple` are hashable, it will work. This means that you can use nested tuples, strings, numbers, and anything else for which the `hash()` function returns a consistent result:

```
>>> spam = 1, 'abc', (2, 3, (4, 5)), 'def'
>>> eggs = 4, (spam, 5), 6

>>> data = dict()
>>> data[spam] = 'spam'
>>> data[eggs] = 'eggs'
>>> import pprint  # Using pprint for consistent and sorted output
>>> pprint.pprint(data)
{(1, 'abc', (2, 3, (4, 5)), 'def'): 'spam',
 (4, ((1, 'abc', (2, 3, (4, 5)), 'def'), 5), 6): 'eggs'}
```

You can make these as complex as you need. As long as all the parts are hashable, it will function as expected.

Perhaps, even more useful is the fact that tuples also support tuple packing and unpacking:

```
# Assign using tuples on both sides
>>> a, b, c = 1, 2, 3
>>> a
1

# Assign a tuple to a single variable
>>> spam = a, (b, c)
>>> spam
(1, (2, 3))

# Unpack a tuple to two variables
>>> a, b = spam
>>> a
1
>>> b
(2, 3)
```

In addition to regular packing and unpacking, from Python 3 onwards, we can actually pack and unpack objects with a variable number of items:

```
# Unpack with variable length objects which actually assigns as a
list, not a tuple
>>> spam, *eggs = 1, 2, 3, 4
>>> spam
1
>>> eggs
[2, 3, 4]


# Which can be unpacked as well of course
>>> a, b, c = eggs
>>> c
4


# This works for ranges as well
>>> spam, *eggs = range(10)
>>> spam
0
>>> eggs
[1, 2, 3, 4, 5, 6, 7, 8, 9]


# Which works both ways
>>> a
2
>>> a, b, *c = a, *eggs
>>> a, b
(2, 1)
>>> c
[2, 3, 4, 5, 6, 7, 8, 9]
```

This very method can be applied in many cases, even for function arguments:

```
>>> def eggs(*args):
...     print('args:', args)


>>> eggs(1, 2, 3)
args: (1, 2, 3)
```

And its equally useful to return multiple arguments from a function:

```
>>> def spam_eggs():
...     return 'spam', 'eggs'


>>> spam, eggs = spam_eggs()
>>> print('spam: %s, eggs: %s' % (spam, eggs))
spam: spam, eggs: eggs
```

Advanced collections

The following collections are mostly just extensions of base collections, some of them fairly simple and others a bit more advanced. For all of them though, it is important to know the characteristics of the underlying structures. Without understanding them, it will be difficult to comprehend the characteristics of these collections.

There are a few collections that are implemented in native C code for performance reasons, but all of them can easily be implemented in pure Python as well.

ChainMap – the list of dictionaries

Introduced in Python 3.3, `ChainMap` allows you to combine multiple mappings (dictionaries for example) into one. This is especially useful when combining multiple contexts. For example, when looking for a variable in your current scope, by default, Python will search in `locals()`, `globals()`, and lastly `builtins`.

Normally, you would do something like this:

```
import builtins

builtin_vars = vars(builtins)
if key in locals():
    value = locals()[key]
elif key in globals():
    value = globals()[key]
elif key in builtin_vars:
    value = builtin_vars[key]
else:
    raise NameError('name %r is not defined' % key)
```

This works, but it's ugly to say the least. We can make it prettier, of course:

```python
import builtins

mappings = globals(), locals(), vars(builtins)
for mapping in mappings:
    if key in mapping:
        value = mapping[key]
        break
else:
    raise NameError('name %r is not defined' % key)
```

A lot better! Moreover, this can actually be considered a nice solution. But since Python 3.3, it's even easier. Now we can simply use the following code:

```python
import builtins
import collections

mappings = collections.ChainMap(globals(), locals(), vars(builtins))
value = mappings[key]
```

The `ChainMap` collection is very useful for command-line applications. The most important configuration happens through command-line arguments, followed by directory local config files, followed by global config files, followed by defaults:

```python
import argparse
import collections

defaults = {
    'spam': 'default spam value',
    'eggs': 'default eggs value',
}

parser = argparse.ArgumentParser()
parser.add_argument('--spam')
parser.add_argument('--eggs')

args = vars(parser.parse_args())
# We need to check for empty/default values so we can't simply use
vars(args)
filtered_args = {k: v for k, v in args.items() if v}

combined = collections.ChainMap(filtered_args, defaults)

print(combined ['spam'])
```

Note that accessing specific mappings is still possible:

```
print(combined.maps[1]['spam'])

for map_ in combined.maps:
    print(map_.get('spam'))
```

counter – keeping track of the most occurring elements

The `counter` is a class for keeping track of the number of occurrences of an element. Its basic usage is as you would expect:

```
>>> import collections

>>> counter = collections.Counter('eggs')
>>> for k in 'eggs':
...     print('Count for %s: %d' % (k, counter[k]))
Count for e: 1
Count for g: 2
Count for g: 2
Count for s: 1
```

However, `counter` can do more than simply return the count. It also has a few very useful and fast (it uses `heapq`) methods for getting the most common elements. Even with a million elements added to the counter, it still executes within a second:

```
>>> import math
>>> import collections

>>> counter = collections.Counter()
>>> for i in range(0, 100000):
...     counter[math.sqrt(i) // 25] += 1

>>> for key, count in counter.most_common(5):
...     print('%s: %d' % (key, count))
11.0: 14375
10.0: 13125
9.0: 11875
8.0: 10625
12.0: 10000
```

But wait, there's more! In addition to getting the most frequent elements, it's also possible to add, subtract, intersect, and "union" counters very similarly to the `set` operations that we saw earlier. So what is the difference between adding two counters and making a union of them? As you would expect, they are similar, but there is a small difference. Let's look at its workings:

```
>>> import collections


>>> def print_counter(expression, counter):
...     sorted_characters = sorted(counter.elements())
...     print(expression, ''.join(sorted_characters))


>>> eggs = collections.Counter('eggs')
>>> spam = collections.Counter('spam')
>>> print_counter('eggs:', eggs)
eggs: eggs
>>> print_counter('spam:', spam)
spam: amps
>>> print_counter('eggs & spam:', eggs & spam)
eggs & spam: s
>>> print_counter('spam & eggs:', spam & eggs)
spam & eggs: s
>>> print_counter('eggs - spam:', eggs - spam)
eggs - spam: egg
>>> print_counter('spam - eggs:', spam - eggs)
spam - eggs: amp
>>> print_counter('eggs + spam:', eggs + spam)
eggs + spam: aeggmpss
>>> print_counter('spam + eggs:', spam + eggs)
spam + eggs: aeggmpss
>>> print_counter('eggs | spam:', eggs | spam)
eggs | spam: aeggmps
>>> print_counter('spam | eggs:', spam | eggs)
spam | eggs: aeggmps
```

The first two are obvious. The `eggs` string is just a sequence of characters with two "g"s, one "s", and one "e", and spam is almost the same but with different letters.

The result of spam & eggs (and the reverse) is also quite predictable. The only letter that's shared between spam and eggs is s, so that's the result. When it comes to counts, it simply does a min(element_a, element_b) per shared element from both and gets the lowest.

When subtracting the letters s, p, a, and m from eggs, you are left with e and g. Similarly, when removing e, g, and s from spam, you are left with p, a, and m.

Now, adding is as you would expect—just an element-by-element addition of both counters.

So how is the union (OR) any different? It gets the max(element_a, element_b) per element in either of the counters instead of adding them; regardless as is the case with the addition.

Lastly, as is demonstrated in the preceding code, the elements method returns an expanded list of all elements repeated by the count.

 The Counter object will automatically remove elements that are zero or less during the execution of mathematical operations.

deque – the double ended queue

The deque (short for Double Ended Queue) object is one of the oldest collections. It was introduced in Python 2.4, so it has been available for over 10 years by now. Generally, this object will be too low-level for most purposes these days, as many operations that would otherwise use it have well-supported libraries available, but that doesn't make it less useful.

Internally, deque is created as a doubly linked list, which means that every item points to the next and the previous item. Since deque is double-ended, the list itself points to both the first and the last element. This makes both adding and removing items from either the beginning or the end a very light O(1) operation, since only the pointer to the beginning/end of the list needs to change and a pointer needs to be added to the first/last item, depending on whether an item is added at the beginning or the end.

For simple stack/queue purposes, it seems wasteful to use a double-ended queue, but the performance is good enough for us not to care about the overhead incurred. The deque class is fully implemented in C (with CPython).

Its usage as a queue is very straightforward:

```
>>> import collections

>>> queue = collections.deque()
>>> queue.append(1)
>>> queue.append(2)
>>> queue
deque([1, 2])
>>> queue.popleft()
1
>>> queue.popleft()
2
>>> queue.popleft()
Traceback (most recent call last):
    ...
IndexError: pop from an empty deque
```

As expected, the items are followed by an `IndexError` since there are only two items and we are trying to get three.

The usage as a stack is almost identical, but we have to use `pop` instead of `popleft` (or `appendleft` instead of `append`):

```
>>> import collections

>>> queue = collections.deque()
>>> queue.append(1)
>>> queue.append(2)
>>> queue
deque([1, 2])
>>> queue.pop()
2
>>> queue.pop()
1
>>> queue.pop()
Traceback (most recent call last):
    ...
IndexError: pop from an empty deque
```

Another very useful feature is that `deque` can be used as a circular queue with the `maxlen` parameter. By using this, it can be used to keep the last n status messages or something similar:

```
>>> import collections


>>> circular = collections.deque(maxlen=2)
>>> for i in range(5):
...     circular.append(i)
...     circular
deque([0], maxlen=2)
deque([0, 1], maxlen=2)
deque([1, 2], maxlen=2)
deque([2, 3], maxlen=2)
deque([3, 4], maxlen=2)
>>> circular
deque([3, 4], maxlen=2)
```

Whenever you require a queue or stack class within a single-threaded application, `deque` is a very convenient option. If you require the object to be synchronized for multithreading operations, then the `queue.Queue` class would be better suited. Internally, it wraps `deque`, but it's a thread-safe alternative. In the same category, there is also an `asyncio.Queue` for asynchronous operations and `multiprocessing.Queue` for multiprocessing operations. Examples of `asyncio` and `multiprocessing` can be found in *Chapter 7, Async IO – Multithreading without Threads* and *Chapter 13, Multiprocessing – When a Single CPU Core Is Not Enough* respectively.

defaultdict – dictionary with a default value

The `defaultdict` is by far my favorite object in the collections package. I still remember writing my own versions of it before it was added to the core. While it's a fairly simple object, it is extremely useful for all sorts of design patterns. Instead of having to check for the existence of a key and adding a value every time, you can just declare the default from the beginning, and there is no need to worry about the rest.

For example, let's say we are building a very basic graph structure from a list of connected nodes.

This is our list of connected nodes (one way):

```
nodes = [
    ('a', 'b'),
```

```
        ('a', 'c'),
        ('b', 'a'),
        ('b', 'd'),
        ('c', 'a'),
        ('d', 'a'),
        ('d', 'b'),
        ('d', 'c'),
    ]
```

Now let's put this graph into a normal dictionary:

```
>>> graph = dict()
>>> for from_, to in nodes:
...     if from_ not in graph:
...         graph[from_] = []
...     graph[from_].append(to)

>>> import pprint
>>> pprint.pprint(graph)
{'a': ['b', 'c'],
 'b': ['a', 'd'],
 'c': ['a'],
 'd': ['a', 'b', 'c']}
```

Some variations are possible, of course, using `setdefault` for example. But they remain more complex than they need to be.

The truly Pythonic version uses `defaultdict` instead:

```
>>> import collections

>>> graph = collections.defaultdict(list)
>>> for from_, to in nodes:
...     graph[from_].append(to)

>>> import pprint
>>> pprint.pprint(graph)
defaultdict(<class 'list'>,
            {'a': ['b', 'c'],
             'b': ['a', 'd'],
             'c': ['a'],
             'd': ['a', 'b', 'c']})
```

Isn't that a beautiful bit of code? The `defaultdict` can actually be seen as the precursor of the `counter` object. It's not as fancy and doesn't have all the bells and whistles that `counter` has, but it does the job in many cases:

```
>>> counter = collections.defaultdict(int)
>>> counter['spam'] += 5
>>> counter
defaultdict(<class 'int'>, {'spam': 5})
```

The default value for `defaultdict` needs to be a callable object. In the previous cases, these were `int` and `list`, but you can easily define your own functions to use as a default value. That's what the following example uses, although I won't recommend production usage since it lacks a bit of readability. I do believe, however, that it is a beautiful example of the power of Python.

This is how we create a `tree` in a single line of Python:

```
import collections
def tree(): return collections.defaultdict(tree)
```

Brilliant, isn't it? Here's how we can actually use it:

```
>>> import json
>>> import collections



>>> def tree():
...     return collections.defaultdict(tree)


>>> colours = tree()
>>> colours['other']['black'] = 0x000000
>>> colours['other']['white'] = 0xFFFFFF
>>> colours['primary']['red'] = 0xFF0000
>>> colours['primary']['green'] = 0x00FF00
>>> colours['primary']['blue'] = 0x0000FF
>>> colours['secondary']['yellow'] = 0xFFFF00
>>> colours['secondary']['aqua'] = 0x00FFFF
>>> colours['secondary']['fuchsia'] = 0xFF00FF


>>> print(json.dumps(colours, sort_keys=True, indent=4))
{
```

```
    "other": {
        "black": 0,
        "white": 16777215
    },
    "primary": {
        "blue": 255,
        "green": 65280,
        "red": 16711680
    },
    "secondary": {
        "aqua": 65535,
        "fuchsia": 16711935,
        "yellow": 16776960
    }
}
```

The nice thing is that you can make it go as deep as you'd like. Because of the defaultdict base, it generates itself recursively.

namedtuple – tuples with field names

The namedtuple object is exactly what the name implies—a tuple with a name. It has a few useful use cases, though I must admit that I haven't found too many in the wild, except for some Python modules such as inspect and urllib.parse. Points in 2D or 3D space are a nice example of where it is definitely useful:

```
>>> import collections

>>> Point = collections.namedtuple('Point', ['x', 'y', 'z'])
>>> point_a = Point(1, 2, 3)
>>> point_a
Point(x=1, y=2, z=3)

>>> point_b = Point(x=4, z=5, y=6)
>>> point_b
Point(x=4, y=6, z=5)
```

Not too much can be said about `namedtuple`; it does what you would expect, and the greatest advantage is that the properties can be executed both by name and by index, which makes tuple unpacking quite easy:

```
>>> x, y, z = point_a
>>> print('X: %d, Y: %d, Z: %d' % (x, y, z))
X: 1, Y: 2, Z: 3
>>> print('X: %d, Y: %d, Z: %d' % point_b)
X: 4, Y: 6, Z: 5
>>> print('X: %d' % point_a.x)
```

enum – a group of constants

The `enum` package is quite similar to `namedtuple` but has a completely different goal and interface. The basic `enum` object makes it really easy to have constants in your modules while still avoiding magic numbers. This is a basic example:

```
>>> import enum


>>> class Color(enum.Enum):
...     red = 1
...     green = 2
...     blue = 3


>>> Color.red
<Color.red: 1>
>>> Color['red']
<Color.red: 1>
>>> Color(1)
<Color.red: 1>
>>> Color.red.name
'red'
>>> Color.red.value
1
>>> isinstance(Color.red, Color)
True
>>> Color.red is Color['red']
```

```
True
>>> Color.red is Color(1)
True
```

A few of the handy features of the `enum` package are that the objects are iterable, accessible through both numeric and textual representation of the values, and, with proper inheritance, even comparable to other classes.

The following code shows the usage of a basic API:

```
>>> for color in Color:
...     color
<Color.red: 1>
<Color.green: 2>
<Color.blue: 3>


>>> colors = dict()
>>> colors[Color.green] = 0x00FF00
>>> colors
{<Color.green: 2>: 65280}
```

There is more though. One of the lesser known possibilities from the `enum` package is that you can make value comparisons work through inheritance of specific types, and this works for every type—not just integers but (your own) custom types as well.

This is the regular `enum`:

```
>>> import enum



>>> class Spam(enum.Enum):
...     EGGS = 'eggs'


>>> Spam.EGGS == 'eggs'
False
```

The following is `enum` with `str` inheritance:

```
>>> import enum



>>> class Spam(str, enum.Enum):
```

```
...        EGGS = 'eggs'

>>> Spam.EGGS == 'eggs'
True
```

OrderedDict – a dictionary where the insertion order matters

OrderdDict is a dict that keeps track of the order in which the items were inserted. Whereas a normal dict will return your keys in the order of hash, OrderedDict will return your keys by the order of insertion. So, it's not ordered by key or value, but that is easily possible too:

```
>>> import collections


>>> spam = collections.OrderedDict()
>>> spam['b'] = 2
>>> spam['c'] = 3
>>> spam['a'] = 1
>>> spam
OrderedDict([('b', 2), ('c', 3), ('a', 1)])

>>> for key, value in spam.items():
...        key, value
('b', 2)
('c', 3)
('a', 1)

>>> eggs = collections.OrderedDict(sorted(spam.items()))
>>> eggs
OrderedDict([('a', 1), ('b', 2), ('c', 3)])
```

While you can probably guess how this works, the internals might surprise you a little. I know I was expecting a different implementation.

Internally, OrderedDict uses a normal dict for key/value storage, and in addition to that, it uses a doubly linked list to keep track of the next/previous items. To keep track of the reverse relation (from the doubly linked list back to the keys), there is an extra dict stored internally.

Put simply, OrderedDict can be a very handy tool for keeping your dict sorted, but it does come at a cost. The system is structured in such a way that set and get are really fast O(1), but the object is still a lot heavier (double or more memory usage) when compared to a regular dict. In many cases, the memory usage of the objects inside will outweigh the memory usage of the dict itself, of course, but this is something to keep in mind.

heapq – the ordered list

The heapq module is a great little module that makes it very easy to create a priority queue in Python. A structure that will always make the smallest (or largest, depending on the implementation) item available with minimum effort. The API is quite simple, and one of the best examples of its usage can be seen in the OrderedDict object. You probably don't want to use heapq directly, but understanding the inner workings is important in order to analyze how classes such as OrderedDict work.

 If you are looking for a structure to keep your list always sorted, try the bisect module instead.

The basic usage is quite simple though:

```
>>> import heapq


>>> heap = [1, 3, 5, 7, 2, 4, 3]
>>> heapq.heapify(heap)
>>> heap
[1, 2, 3, 7, 3, 4, 5]

>>> while heap:
...      heapq.heappop(heap), heap
(1, [2, 3, 3, 7, 5, 4])
(2, [3, 3, 4, 7, 5])
(3, [3, 5, 4, 7])
(3, [4, 5, 7])
(4, [5, 7])
(5, [7])
(7, [])
```

One important thing to note here—something that you have probably already understood from the preceding example—is that the heapq module does not create a special object. It is simply a bunch of methods for treating a regular list as a heap. That doesn't make it less useful, but it is something to take into consideration. You may also wonder why the heap isn't sorted. Actually, it is sorted but not the way you expect it to be. If you view the heap as a tree, it becomes much more obvious:

```
    1
  2   3
 7 3 4 5
```

The smallest number is always at the top and the biggest numbers are always at the bottom of the tree. Because of that, it's really easy to find the smallest number, but finding the largest is not so easy. To get the sorted version of the heap, we simply need to keep removing the top of the tree until all items are gone.

bisect – the sorted list

We have seen the heapq module in the previous paragraph, which makes it really simple to always get the smallest number from a list, and therefore makes it easy to sort a list of objects. While the heapq module appends items to form a tree-like structure, the bisect module inserts items in such a way that they stay sorted. A big difference is that adding/removing items with the heapq module is very light whereas finding items is really light with the bisect module. If your primary purpose is searching, then bisect should be your choice.

As is the case with heapq, bisect does not really create a special data structure. It just works on a standard list and expects that list to always be sorted. It is important to understand the performance implications of this; simply adding items to the list using the bisect algorithm can be very slow because an insert on a list takes O(n). Effectively, creating a sorted list using bisect takes O(n*n), which is quite slow, especially because creating the same sorted list using heapq or sorted takes O(n * log(n)) instead.

The log(n) refers to the base 2 logarithm function. To calculate this value, the math.log2() function can be used. This results in an increase of 1 every time the number doubles in size. For n=2, the value of log(n) is 1, and consequently for n=4 and n=8, the log values are 2 and 3, respectively.

This means that a 32-bit number, which is 2**32 = 4294967296, has a log of 32.

If you have a sorted structure and you only need to add a single item, then the `bisect` algorithm can be used for insertion. Otherwise, it's generally faster to simply append the items and call a `.sort()` afterwards.

To illustrate, we have these lines:

```
>>> import bisect
```

```
Using the regular sort:
>>> sorted_list = []
>>> sorted_list.append(5)   # O(1)
>>> sorted_list.append(3)   # O(1)
>>> sorted_list.append(1)   # O(1)
>>> sorted_list.append(2)   # O(1)
>>> sorted_list.sort()  # O(n * log(n)) = O(4 * log(4)) = O(8)
>>> sorted_list
[1, 2, 3, 5]
```

```
Using bisect:
>>> sorted_list = []
>>> bisect.insort(sorted_list, 5)   # O(n) = O(1)
>>> bisect.insort(sorted_list, 3)   # O(n) = O(2)
>>> bisect.insort(sorted_list, 1)   # O(n) = O(3)
>>> bisect.insort(sorted_list, 2)   # O(n) = O(4)
>>> sorted_list
[1, 2, 3, 5]
```

For a small number of items, the difference is negligible, but it quickly grows to a point where the difference will be large. For n=4, the difference is just between `4 * 1 + 8 = 12` and `1 + 2 + 3 + 4 = 10` making the bisect solution faster. But if we were to insert 1,000 items, it would be `1000 + 1000 * log(1000) = 10966` versus `1 + 2 + ... 1000 = 1000 * (1000 + 1) / 2 = 500500`. So, be very careful while inserting many items.

Searching within the list is very fast though; because it is sorted, we can use a very simple binary search algorithm. For example, what if we want to check whether a few numbers exist within the list?

```
>>> import bisect
```

```
>>> sorted_list = [1, 2, 3, 5]
```

```
>>> def contains(sorted_list, value):
...         i = bisect.bisect_left(sorted_list, value)
...         return i < len(sorted_list) and sorted_list[i] == value

>>> contains(sorted_list, 2)
True
>>> contains(sorted_list, 4)
False
>>> contains(sorted_list, 6)
False
```

As you can see, the `bisect_left` function finds the position at which the number is supposed to be. This is actually what the `insort` function does as well; it inserts the number at the correct position by searching for the location of the number.

So how is this different from a regular value in `sorted_list`? The biggest difference is that `bisect` does a binary search internally, which means that it starts in the middle and jumps left or right depending on whether the value is bigger or smaller than the value. To illustrate, we will search for 4 in a list of numbers from 0 to 14:

```
sorted_list = [0, 1, 2, 3, 4, 5, 6, 7, 8, 9, 10, 11, 12, 13, 14]
Step 1: 4 > 7                    ^
Step 2: 4 > 3          ^
Step 3: 4 > 5               ^
Step 4: 4 > 5        ^
```

As you can see, after only four steps (actually three; the fourth is just for illustration), we have found the number we searched for. Depending on the number (7, for example), it may go faster, but it will never take more than $O(\log(n))$ steps to find a number.

With a regular list, a search would simply walk through all items until it finds the desired item. If you're lucky, it could be the first number you encounter, but if you're unlucky, it could be the last item. In the case of 1,000 items, that would be the difference between 1,000 steps and $\log(1000) = 10$ steps.

Summary

Python has quite a few very useful collections built in. Since more and more collections are added regularly, the best thing to do is simply keep track of the collections manual. And do you ever wonder how or why any of the structures works? Just look at the source here:

```
https://hg.python.org/cpython/file/default/Lib/collections/__init__.py
```

After finishing this chapter, you should be aware of both the core collections and the most important collections from the collections module, but more importantly the performance characteristics of these collections in several scenarios. Selecting the correct data structure within your applications is by far the most important performance factor that your code will ever experience, making this essential knowledge for any programmer.

Next, we will continue with functional programming which covers `lambda` functions, `list` comprehensions, `dict` comprehensions, `set` comprehensions and an array of related topics. This includes some background information on the mathematics involved which could be interesting but can safely be skipped.

4
Functional Programming – Readability Versus Brevity

Python is one of the few (or at least the earliest) nonfunctional languages to incorporate functional features. While Guido van Rossum has tried to remove some of them a few times, they have become ingrained in the Python community, and list comprehensions (`dict` and `set` comprehensions soon to follow) are widely used in all sorts of code. The most important thing about code shouldn't be how cool your `reduce` statement is or how you can fit the entire function in a single line with an incomprehensible list comprehension. Readability counts (once again, `PEP20`)!

This chapter will show you some of the cool tricks that functional programming in Python gives you, and it will explain some of the limitations of Python's implementation. While we will try to steer clear of lambda calculus (λ-calculus) as much as possible, the **Y combinator** will be discussed briefly.

The last few paragraphs will list (and explain) the usage of the `functools` and `itertools` libraries. If you are familiar with these libraries, feel free to skip them, but note that some of these will be used heavily in the later chapters about decorators (*Chapter 5, Decorators – Enabling Code Reuse by Decorating*), generators (*Chapter 6, Generators and Coroutines – Infinity, One Step at a Time*), and performance (*Chapter 12, Performance – Tracking and Reducing Your Memory and CPU Usage*).

These are the topics covered in this chapter:

- The theory behind functional programming
- `list` comprehensions
- `dict` comprehensions
- `set` comprehensions
- `lambda` functions
- `functools` (`partial`, and `reduce`)
- `itertools` (`accumulate`, `chain`, `dropwhile`, `starmap`, and so on)

Functional programming

Functional programming is a paradigm that originates from the lambda calculus. Without diving too much into the lambda calculus (λ-calculus), this roughly means that computation is performed through the use of mathematical functions, which avoids mutable data and changing state of surroundings. The idea of a strictly functional language is that all function outputs are dependent only on the input and not on any external state. Since Python is not strictly a programming language, this doesn't necessarily hold true, but it is a good idea to adhere to this paradigm as mixing these can cause unforeseen bugs as discussed in *Chapter 2, Pythonic Syntax, Common Pitfalls, and Style Guide.*

Even outside of functional programming, this is a good idea. Keeping functions purely functional (relying only on the given input) makes code clearer, easier to understand, and better to test as there are less dependencies. Well-known examples can be found within the `math` module. These functions (`sin`, `cos`, `pow`, `sqrt`, and so on) have an input and an output that is strictly dependent on the input.

list comprehensions

The Python `list` comprehensions are a very easy way to apply a function or filter to a list of items. List comprehensions can be very useful if used correctly but very unreadable if you're not careful.

Let's dive right into a few examples. The basic premise of a `list` comprehension looks like this:

```
>>> squares = [x ** 2 for x in range(10)]
>>> squares
[0, 1, 4, 9, 16, 25, 36, 49, 64, 81]
```

We can easily expand this with a filter:

```
>>> uneven_squares = [x ** 2 for x in range(10) if x % 2]
>>> uneven_squares
[1, 9, 25, 49, 81]
```

The syntax is pretty close to regular Python for loops, but the `if` statement and automatic storing of results makes it quite useful for some cases. The regular Python equivalent is not much longer, however:

```
>>> uneven_squares = []
>>> for x in range(10):
...     if x % 2:
...         uneven_squares.append(x ** 2)

>>> uneven_squares
[1, 9, 25, 49, 81]
```

Care must be taken though; because of the special list comprehension structure, some types of operations are not as obvious as you might expect. This time, we are looking for random numbers greater than `0.5`:

```
>>> import random
>>> [random.random() for _ in range(10) if random.random() >= 0.5]
[0.5211948104577864, 0.650010512129705, 0.021427316545174158]
```

See that last number? It's actually less than `0.5`. This happens because the first and the last random calls are actually separate calls and return different results.

One way to counter this is by creating the list separate from the filter:

```
>>> import random
>>> numbers = [random.random() for _ in range(10)]
>>> [x for x in numbers if x >= 0.5]
[0.715510247827078, 0.8426277505519564, 0.5071133900377911]
```

That obviously works, but it's not all that pretty. So what other options are there? Well, there are a few but the readability is a bit questionable, so these are not the solutions that I would recommend. It's good to see them at least once, however.

Here is a `list` comprehension in a list comprehension:

```
>>> import random
>>> [x for x in [random.random() for _ in range(10)] if x >= 0.5]
```

And here's one that quickly becomes an incomprehensible `list` comprehension:

```
>>> import random
>>> [x for _ in range(10) for x in [random.random()] if x >= 0.5]
```

Caution is needed with these options as the double list comprehension actually works like a nested `for` loop would, so it quickly generates a lot of results. To elaborate on this regard:

```
>>> [(x, y) for x in range(3) for y in range(3, 5)]
[(0, 3), (0, 4), (1, 3), (1, 4), (2, 3), (2, 4)]
```

This effectively does the following:

```
>>> results = []
>>> for x in range(3):
...         for y in range(3, 5):
...             results.append((x, y))
...
>>> results
[(0, 3), (0, 4), (1, 3), (1, 4), (2, 3), (2, 4)]
```

These can be useful for some cases, but I would recommend that you limit their usage, as they have a tendency to quickly become unreadable. I would strongly advise against using `list` comprehensions within `list` comprehensions for the sake of readability. It's still important to understand what is happening, so let's look at one more example. The following `list` comprehension swaps the column and row counts, so a 3 x 4 matrix becomes 4 x 3:

```
>>> matrix = [
...         [1, 2, 3, 4],
...         [5, 6, 7, 8],
...         [9, 10, 11, 12],
... ]

>>> reshaped_matrix = [
...     [
...         [y for x in matrix for y in x][i * len(matrix) + j]
...         for j in range(len(matrix))
...     ]
...     for i in range(len(matrix[0]))
```

```
... ]
```

```
>>> import pprint
>>> pprint.pprint(reshaped_matrix, width=40)
[[1, 2, 3],
 [4, 5, 6],
 [7, 8, 9],
 [10, 11, 12]]
```

Even with the extra indentation, the list comprehension just isn't all that readable. With four nested loops, that is expectedly so, of course. There are rare cases where nested list comprehensions might be justified, but generally I won't recommend their usage.

dict comprehensions

dict comprehensions are very similar to list comprehensions, but the result is a dict instead. Other than this, the only real difference is that you need to return both a key and a value, whereas a list comprehension accepts any type of value. The following is a basic example:

```
>>> {x: x ** 2 for x in range(10)}
{0: 0, 1: 1, 2: 4, 3: 9, 4: 16, 5: 25, 6: 36, 7: 49, 8: 64, 9: 81}
```

```
>>> {x: x ** 2 for x in range(10) if x % 2}
{1: 1, 3: 9, 9: 81, 5: 25, 7: 49}
```

 Since the output is a dictionary, the key needs to be hashable for the dict comprehension to work.

The funny thing is that you can mix these two, of course, for even more unreadable magic:

```
>>> {x ** 2: [y for y in range(x)] for x in range(5)}
{0: [], 1: [0], 4: [0, 1], 16: [0, 1, 2, 3], 9: [0, 1, 2]}
```

Obviously, you need to be careful with these. They can be very useful if used correctly, but the output quickly becomes unreadable, even with proper whitespace.

set comprehensions

Just as you can create a set using curly brackets ({ }), you can also create a set using set comprehensions. These work in a way similar to list comprehensions, but the values are unique (and without sort order):

```
>>> [x*y for x in range(3) for y in range(3)]
[0, 0, 0, 0, 1, 2, 0, 2, 4]


>>> {x*y for x in range(3) for y in range(3)}
{0, 1, 2, 4}
```

 As is the case with the regular set, set comprehensions support only hashable types.

lambda functions

The lambda statement in Python is simply an anonymous function. Due to the syntax, it is slightly more limited than regular functions, but a lot can be done through it. As always though, readability counts, so generally it is a good idea to keep it as simple as possible. One of the more common use cases is the sort key for the sorted function:

```
>>> class Spam(object):
...     def __init__(self, value):
...         self.value = value
...
...     def __repr__(self):
...         return '<%s: %s>' % (self.__class__.__name__, self.value)
...
>>> spams = [Spam(5), Spam(2), Spam(4), Spam(1)]
>>> sorted_spams = sorted(spams, key=lambda spam: spam.value)
>>> spams
[<Spam: 5>, <Spam: 2>, <Spam: 4>, <Spam: 1>]
>>> sorted_spams
[<Spam: 1>, <Spam: 2>, <Spam: 4>, <Spam: 5>]
```

While the function could have been written separately or the __cmp__ method of Spam could have been overwritten in this case, in many cases, this is an easy way to get a quick sort function as you would want it.

It's not that the regular function would be verbose, but by using an anonymous function, you have a small advantage; you are not contaminating your local scope with an extra function:

```
>>> def key_function(spam):
...         return spam.value

>>> spams = [Spam(5), Spam(2), Spam(4), Spam(1)]
>>> sorted_spams = sorted(spams, key=lambda spam: spam.value)
```

As for style, do note that PEP8 dictates that assigning a lambda to a variable is a bad idea. And logically, it is. The idea of an anonymous function is that it is just that—anonymous. If you are giving it an identity, you should define it as a normal function. It really isn't much longer if you want to keep it short. Note that both of the following statements are considered bad style and are for example purposes only:

```
>>> def key(spam): return spam.value

>>> key = lambda spam: spam.value
```

In my opinion, the only valid use case for lambda functions is as anonymous functions used as function parameters, and preferably only if they are short enough to fit on a single line.

The Y combinator

 Note that this paragraph can easily be skipped. It is mostly an example of the mathematical value of the lambda statement.

The Y combinator is probably the most famous example of the λ-calculus:

$$Y = \lambda f. \left(\lambda x. f(x\,x) \right) \left(\lambda x. f(x\,x) \right)$$

All this looks very complicated, but that's also because it has used the lambda calculus notation. You should read this syntax, $\lambda x. x^2$, as an anonymous (lambda) function that takes x as an input and returns x^2. In Python, this would be expressed almost exactly as it is in the original lambda calculus, except for replacing λ with lambda and . with :, so it results in lambda x: x^2.

With some algebra, this can be reduced to $Yf = f(Yf)$, or a function that takes the `f` function and applies it to itself. The λ-calculus notation of this function is as follows:

$$\lambda x. f(xx)$$

Here is the Python notation:

```
Y = lambda f: lambda *args: f(Y(f))(*args)
```

The following is the longer version:

```
def Y(f):
    def y(*args):
        y_function = f(Y(f))
        return y_function(*args)
    return y
```

This might still be a bit unclear to you, so let's look at an example that actually uses it:

```
>>> Y = lambda f: lambda *args: f(Y(f))(*args)

>>> def factorial(combinator):
...     def _factorial(n):
...         if n:
...             return n * combinator(n - 1)
...         else:
...             return 1
...     return _factorial
>>> Y(factorial)(5)
120
```

The following is the short version, where the power of the Y combinator actually appears, with a recursive but still anonymous function:

```
>>> Y = lambda f: lambda *args: f(Y(f))(*args)

>>> Y(lambda c: lambda n: n and n * c(n - 1) or 1)(5)
120
```

Note that the n and n * c(n - 1) or 1 part is short for the if statement used in the longer version of the function. Alternatively, this can be written using the Python ternary operator:

```
>>> Y = lambda f: lambda *args: f(Y(f))(*args)
```

```
>>> Y(lambda c: lambda n: n * c(n - 1) if n else 1)(5)
120
```

You might be wondering about the point of this entire exercise. Can't you write a factorial shorter/easier? Yes, you can. The importance of the Y combinator is that it can be applied to any function and is very close to the mathematical definition.

One final example of the Y combinator will be given by the definition of quicksort in a few lines:

```
>>> quicksort = Y(lambda f:
...     lambda x: (
...         f([item for item in x if item < x[0]])
...         + [y for y in x if x[0] == y]
...         + f([item for item in x if item > x[0]])
...     ) if x else [])
```

```
>>> quicksort([1, 3, 5, 4, 1, 3, 2])
[1, 1, 2, 3, 3, 4, 5]
```

While the Y combinator most likely doesn't have much practical use in Python, it does show the power of the lambda statement and how close Python is to the mathematical definition. Essentially, the difference is only in the notation and not in the functionality.

functools

In addition to the list/dict/set comprehensions, Python also has a few (more advanced) functions that can be really convenient when coding functionally. The functools library is a collection of functions that return callable objects. Some of these functions are used as decorators (we'll cover more about that in *Chapter 5, Decorators – Enabling Code Reuse by Decorating*), but the ones that we are going to talk about are used as straight-up functions to make your life easier.

partial – no need to repeat all arguments every time

The `partial` function is really convenient for adding some default arguments to a function that you use often but can't (or don't want to) redefine. With object-oriented code, you can usually work around cases similar to these, but with procedural code, you will often have to repeat your arguments. Let's take the `heapq` functions from *Chapter 3, Containers and Collections – Storing Data the Right Way*, as an example:

```
>>> import heapq
>>> heap = []
>>> heapq.heappush(heap, 1)
>>> heapq.heappush(heap, 3)
>>> heapq.heappush(heap, 5)
>>> heapq.heappush(heap, 2)
>>> heapq.heappush(heap, 4)
>>> heapq.nsmallest(3, heap)
[1, 2, 3]
```

Almost all the `heapq` functions require a `heap` argument, so why not make a shortcut for it? This is where `functools.partial` comes in:

```
>>> import functools
>>> import heapq
>>> heap = []
>>> push = functools.partial(heapq.heappush, heap)
>>> smallest = functools.partial(heapq.nsmallest, iterable=heap)

>>> push(1)
>>> push(3)
>>> push(5)
>>> push(2)
>>> push(4)
>>> smallest(3)
[1, 2, 3]
```

Seems a bit cleaner, right? In this case, both versions are fairly short and readable, but it's a convenient function to have.

Why should we use `partial` instead of writing a `lambda` argument? Well, it's mostly about convenience, but it also helps solve the late binding problem discussed in *Chapter 2, Pythonic Syntax, Common Pitfalls, and Style Guide*. Additionally, partial functions can be pickled whereas `lambda` statements cannot.

reduce – combining pairs into a single result

The `reduce` function implements a mathematical technique called `fold`. It basically applies a function to the first and second elements, uses that result to apply together with the third element, and continues until the list is exhausted.

The `reduce` function is supported by many languages but in most cases using different names such as `curry`, `fold`, `accumulate`, or `aggregate`. Python has actually supported `reduce` for a very long time, but since Python 3, it has been moved from the global scope to the `functools` library. Some code can be simplified beautifully using the `reduce` statement; whether it's readable or not is debatable, however.

Implementing a factorial function

One of the most used examples of `reduce` is for calculating factorials, which is indeed quite simple:

```
>>> import operator
>>> import functools
>>> functools.reduce(operator.mul, range(1, 6))
120
```

 The preceding code uses `operator.mul` instead of `lambda a, b: a * b`. While they produce the same results, the former can be quite faster.

Internally, the `reduce` function will do the following:

```
>>> import operator
>>> f = operator.mul
>>> f(f(f(f(1, 2), 3), 4), 5)
120
```

To clarify this further, let's look at it like this:

```
>>> iterable = range(1, 6)
>>> import operator
```

```
# The initial values:
>>> a, b, *iterable = iterable
>>> a, b, iterable
(1, 2, [3, 4, 5])

# First run
>>> a = operator.mul(a, b)
>>> b, *iterable = iterable
>>> a, b, iterable
(2, 3, [4, 5])

# Second run
>>> a = operator.mul(a, b)
>>> b, *iterable = iterable
>>> a, b, iterable
(6, 4, [5])

# Third run
>>> a = operator.mul(a, b)
>>> b, *iterable = iterable
>>> a, b, iterable
(24, 5, [])

# Fourth and last run
>>> a = operator.mul (a, b)
>>> a
120
```

Or with a simple `while` loop using the `deque` collection:

```
>>> import operator
>>> import collections
>>> iterable = collections.deque(range(1, 6))

>>> value = iterable.popleft()
>>> while iterable:
...     value = operator.mul(value, iterable.popleft())

>>> value
120
```

Processing trees

Trees are a case where the reduce function really shines. Remember the one-line tree definition using a defaultdict from *Chapter 3, Containers and Collections – Storing Data the Right Way*? What would be a good way to access the keys inside of that object? Given a path of a tree item, we can use reduce to easily access the items inside:

```
>>> import json
>>> import functools
>>> import collections

>>> def tree():
...     return collections.defaultdict(tree)

# Build the tree:
>>> taxonomy = tree()
>>> reptilia = taxonomy['Chordata']['Vertebrata']['Reptilia']
>>> reptilia['Squamata']['Serpentes']['Pythonidae'] = [
...     'Liasis', 'Morelia', 'Python']

# The actual contents of the tree
>>> print(json.dumps(taxonomy, indent=4))
{
    "Chordata": {
        "Vertebrata": {
            "Reptilia": {
                "Squamata": {
                    "Serpentes": {
                        "Pythonidae": [
                            "Liasis",
                            "Morelia",
                            "Python"
                        ]
                    }
                }
            }
        }
    }
}

# The path we wish to get
```

```
>>> path = 'Chordata.Vertebrata.Reptilia.Squamata.Serpentes'

# Split the path for easier access
>>> path = path.split('.')

# Now fetch the path using reduce to recursively fetch the items
>>> family = functools.reduce(lambda a, b: a[b], path, taxonomy)
>>> family.items()
dict_items([('Pythonidae', ['Liasis', 'Morelia', 'Python'])])

# The path we wish to get
>>> path = 'Chordata.Vertebrata.Reptilia.Squamata'.split('.')

>>> suborder = functools.reduce(lambda a, b: a[b], path, taxonomy)
>>> suborder.keys()
dict_keys(['Serpentes'])
```

And lastly, some people might be wondering why Python only has `fold_left` and no `fold_right`. In my opinion, you don't really need both of them as you can easily reverse the operation.

The regular `reduce` — the `fold left` operation:

```
fold_left = functools.reduce(
    lambda x, y: function(x, y),
    iterable,
    initializer,
)
```

The reverse — the `fold right` operation:

```
fold_right = functools.reduce(
    lambda x, y: function(y, x),
    reversed(iterable),
    initializer,
)
```

While this one is definitely very useful in purely functional languages — where these operations are used quite often — initially there were plans to remove the `reduce` function from Python with the introduction of Python 3. Luckily, that plan was modified, and instead of being removed, it has been moved from `reduce` to `functools.reduce`. There may not be many useful cases for `reduce`, but there are some cool use cases. Especially traversing recursive data structures is far more easily done using `reduce`, since it would otherwise involve more complicated loops or recursive functions.

itertools

The `itertools` library contains iterable functions inspired by those available in functional languages. All of these are iterable and have been constructed in such a way that only a minimal amount of memory is required to process even the largest of datasets. While you can easily write most of these functions yourself using a simple function, I would still recommend using the ones available in the `itertools` library. These are all fast, memory efficient, and — perhaps more importantly — tested.

 Even though the titles of the paragraphs are capitalized, the functions themselves are not. Be careful not to accidently type `Accumulate` instead of `accumulate`.

accumulate – reduce with intermediate results

The `accumulate` function is very similar to the `reduce` function, which is why some languages actually have `accumulate` instead of `reduce` as the folding operator.

The major difference between the two is that the `accumulate` function returns the immediate results. This can be useful when summing the results of a company's sales, for example:

```
>>> import operator
>>> import itertools


# Sales per month
>>> months = [10, 8, 5, 7, 12, 10, 5, 8, 15, 3, 4, 2]
>>> list(itertools.accumulate(months, operator.add))
[10, 18, 23, 30, 42, 52, 57, 65, 80, 83, 87, 89]
```

It should be noted that the `operator.add` function is actually optional in this case as the default behavior of accumulate is to sum the results. In some other languages and libraries, this function is called `cumsum` (cumulative sum).

chain – combining multiple results

The `chain` function is a simple but useful function that combines the results of multiple iterators. Very simple but also very useful if you have multiple lists, iterators, and so on — just combine them with a simple chain:

```
>>> import itertools
>>> a = range(3)
```

```
>>> b = range(5)
>>> list(itertools.chain(a, b))
[0, 1, 2, 0, 1, 2, 3, 4]
```

It should be noted that there is a small variant of `chain` that accepts an iterable containing iterables, namely `chain.from_iterable`. They work nearly identically, except for the fact that you need to pass along an iterable item instead of passing a list of arguments. Your initial response might be that this can be achieved simply by unpacking the (`*args`) tuple, as we will see in *Chapter 6, Generators and Coroutines – Infinity, One Step at a Time*. However, this is not always the case. For now, just remember that if you have a iterable containing iterables, the easiest method is to use `itertools.chain.from_iterable`.

combinations – combinatorics in Python

The `combinations` iterator produces results exactly as you would expect from the mathematical definition. All combinations with a specific length from a given list of items:

```
>>> import itertools
>>> list(itertools.combinations(range(3), 2))
[(0, 1), (0, 2), (1, 2)]
```

 The `combinations` function gives all possible combinations of the given items of a given length. The number of possible combinations is given by the binomial coefficient, the nCr button on many calculators. It is commonly denoted as follows:

$$\binom{n}{k}$$

We have n=2 and k=4 in this case.

Here is the variant with repetition of elements:

```
>>> import itertools
>>> list(itertools.combinations_with_replacement(range(3), 2))
[(0, 0), (0, 1), (0, 2), (1, 1), (1, 2), (2, 2)]
```

The combinations_with_repetitions function is very similar to the regular combinations function, except that the items can be combined with themselves as well. To calculate the number of results, the binomial coefficient described earlier can be used with the parameters as n=n+k-1 and k=k.

Let's look at a little combination of combinations and chain for generating a powerset:

```
>>> import itertools

>>> def powerset(iterable):
...     return itertools.chain.from_iterable(
...         itertools.combinations(iterable, i)
...         for i in range(len(iterable) + 1))
>>> list(powerset(range(3)))
[(), (0,), (1,), (2,), (0, 1), (0, 2), (1, 2), (0, 1, 2)]
```

 The powerset is essentially the combined result of all combinations from 0 to n, meaning that it also includes elements with zero items (the empty set, or ()), elements with 1 item, and all the way up to n. The number of items in the powerset is easily calculated using the power operator: 2**n.

permutations – combinations where the order matters

The permutations function is quite similar to the combinations function. The only real difference is that (a, b) is considered distinct from (b, a). In other words, the order matters:

```
>>> import itertools
>>> list(itertools.permutations(range(3), 2))
[(0, 1), (0, 2), (1, 0), (1, 2), (2, 0), (2, 1)]
```

compress – selecting items using a list of Booleans

The compress function is one of those that you won't need too often, but it can be very useful when you do need it. It applies a Boolean filter to your iterable, making it return only the ones you actually need. The most important thing to note here is that it's all executed lazily and that compress will stop if either the data or the selectors collection is exhausted. So, even with infinite ranges, it works without a hitch:

```
>>> import itertools
>>> list(itertools.compress(range(1000), [0, 1, 1, 1, 0, 1]))
[1, 2, 3, 5]
```

dropwhile/takewhile – selecting items using a function

The dropwhile function will drop all results until a given predicate evaluates to true. This can be useful if you are waiting for a device to finally return an expected result. That's a bit difficult to demonstrate here, so I'll just show an example with the basic usage—waiting for a number greater than 3:

```
>>> import itertools
>>> list(itertools.dropwhile(lambda x: x <= 3, [1, 3, 5, 4, 2]))
[5, 4, 2]
```

As you might expect, the takewhile function is the reverse of this. It will simply return all rows until the predicate turns false:

```
>>> import itertools
>>> list(itertools.takewhile(lambda x: x <= 3, [1, 3, 5, 4, 2]))
[1, 3]
```

Simply adding the two will give you the original result again.

count – infinite range with decimal steps

The count function is quite similar to the range function, but there are two significant differences.

The first is that this range is infinite, so don't even try to do list(itertools.count()). You'll definitely run out of memory immediately and it might even freeze your system.

The second difference is that unlike the range function, you can actually use floating-point numbers here, so there is no need of whole/integer numbers.

Since listing the entire range will kill our Python interpreter, we'll simply use zip both to limit the results and to compare the results of the regular range function. In a later paragraph, we will see a more convenient option using itertools.islice. The count function takes two optional parameters: a start parameter, which defaults to 0, and a step parameter, which defaults to 1:

```
>>> import itertools

# Except for being infinite, the standard version returns the same
# results as the range function does.
>>> for a, b in zip(range(3), itertools.count()):
...     a, b
(0, 0)
(1, 1)
(2, 2)

# With a different starting point the results are still the same
>>> for a, b in zip(range(5, 8), itertools.count(5)):
...     a, b
(5, 5)
(6, 6)
(7, 7)

# And a different step works the same as well
>>> for a, b in zip(range(5, 10, 2), itertools.count(5, 2)):
...     a, b
(5, 5)
(7, 7)
(9, 9)

# Unless you try to use floating point numbers
>>> range(5, 10, 0.5)
Traceback (most recent call last):
    ...
```

```
TypeError: 'float' object cannot be interpreted as an integer

# Which does work for count
>>> for a, b in zip(range(5, 10), itertools.count(5, 0.5)):
...     a, b
(5, 5)
(6, 5.5)
(7, 6.0)
(8, 6.5)
(9, 7.0)
```

The `itertools.islice` function is also very useful in conjunction with `itertools.count`, as we'll see in a later paragraph.

groupby – grouping your sorted iterable

The `groupby` function is a really convenient function for grouping results. The usage and use cases are probably clear, but there are some important things to keep in mind when using this function:

- The input needs to be sorted by the `group` parameter. Otherwise, it will be added as a separate group.

- The results are available for use only once. So, after processing a group, it will not be available anymore.

Here is an example of the proper use of `groupby`:

```
>>> import itertools
>>> items = [('a', 1), ('a', 2), ('b', 2), ('b', 0), ('c', 3)]

>>> for group, items in itertools.groupby(items, lambda x: x[0]):
...     print('%s: %s' % (group, [v for k, v in items]))
a: [1, 2]
b: [2, 0]
c: [3]
```

And then there are cases where you might get unexpected results:

```
>>> import itertools
>>> items = [('a', 1), ('b', 0), ('b', 2), ('a', 2), ('c', 3)]
>>> groups = dict()
```

```
>>> for group, items in itertools.groupby(items, lambda x: x[0]):
...     groups[group] = items
...     print('%s: %s' % (group, [v for k, v in items]))
a: [1]
b: [0, 2]
a: [2]
c: [3]

>>> for group, items in sorted(groups.items()):
...     print('%s: %s' % (group, [v for k, v in items]))
a: []
b: []
c: []
```

Now we see two groups containing a. So, make sure you sort by the grouping parameter before trying to group. Additionally, walking through the same group a second time offers no results. This can be fixed easily using `groups[group] = list(items)` instead, but it can give quite a few unexpected bugs if you are not aware of this.

islice – slicing any iterable

When working with the `itertools` functions, you might notice that you cannot slice these objects. That is because they are generators, a topic that we will discuss in *Chapter 6, Generators and Coroutines – Infinity, One Step at a Time*. Luckily, the `itertools` library has a function for slicing these objects as well—`islice`.

Let's take `itertools.counter` from before as an example:

```
>>> import itertools
>>> list(itertools.islice(itertools.count(), 2, 7))
[2, 3, 4, 5, 6]
```

So, instead of the regular `slice`:

```
itertools.count()[:10]
```

We enter the `slice` parameters to the function:

```
itertools.islice(itertools.count(), 10)
```

What you should note from this is actually more than the inability to slice the objects. It is not just that slicing doesn't work, but it is not possible to get the length either—at least not without counting all items separately—and with infinite iterators, even that is not possible. The only understanding you actually get from a generator is that you can fetch items one at a time. You won't even know in advance whether you're at the end of the generator or not.

Summary

For some reason, functional programming is a paradigm that scares many people, but really it shouldn't. The most important difference between functional and procedural programming (within Python) is the mindset. Everything is executed using simple (and often translations of the mathematical equivalent) functions without any storage of variables. Simply put, a functional program consists of many functions having a simple input and output, without using (or even having) any outside scope or context to access. Python is not a purely functional language, so it is easy to cheat and work outside of the local scope, but that is not recommended.

This chapter covered the basics of functional programming within Python and some of the mathematics behind it. In addition to this, some of the many useful libraries that can be used in a very convenient way by using functional programming were covered.

The most important outtakes should be the following:

- Lambda statements are not inherently bad but it would be best to make them use variables from the local scope only, and they should not be longer than a single line.

- Functional programming can be very powerful, but it has a tendency to quickly become unreadable. Care must be taken.

- list/dict/set comprehensions are very useful, but they should generally not be nested, and for the purpose of readability, they should be kept short as well.

Ultimately, it is a matter of preference. For the sake of readability, I recommend limiting the usage of the functional paradigm when there is no obvious benefit. Having said that, when executed correctly, it can be a thing of beauty.

Next up are decorators—methods to wrap your functions and classes in other functions and/or classes to modify their behavior and extend their functionality.

5
Decorators – Enabling Code Reuse by Decorating

In this chapter, you are going to learn about Python decorators. Decorators are essentially function/class wrappers that can be used to modify the input, output, or even the function/class itself before executing it. This type of wrapping can just as easily be achieved by having a separate function that calls the inner function, or via mixins. As is the case with many Python constructs, decorators are not the only way to reach the goal but are definitely convenient in many cases.

While you can live perfectly without knowing too much about decorators, they give you a lot of "reuse power" and are therefore used heavily in framework libraries such as web frameworks. Python actually comes bundled with some useful decorators, most notably the `property` decorator.

There are, however, some particularities to take note of: wrapping a function creates a new function and makes it harder to reach the inner function and its properties. One example of this is the `help(function)` functionality of Python; by default, you will lose function properties such as the help text and the module the function exists in.

This chapter will cover the usage of both function and class decorators as well as the intricate details you need to know when decorating functions within classes.

The following are the topics covered:

- Decorating functions
- Decorating class functions
- Decorating classes
- Using classes as decorators
- Useful decorators in the Python standard library

Decorating functions

Essentially, a decorator is nothing more than a function or class wrapper. If we have a function called spam and a decorator called eggs, then the following would decorate spam with eggs:

```
spam = eggs(spam)
```

To make the syntax easier to use, Python has a special syntax for this case. So, instead of adding a line such as the preceding one below the function, you can simply decorate a function using the @ operator:

```
@eggs
def spam():
    pass
```

The decorator simply receives the function and returns a — usually different — function. The simplest possible decorator is:

```
def eggs(function):
    return function
```

Looking at the earlier example, we realize that this gets spam as the argument for function and returns that function again, effectively changing nothing. Most decorators nest functions, however. The following decorator will print all arguments sent to spam and pass them to spam unmodified:

```
>>> import functools


>>> def eggs(function):
...     @functools.wraps(function)
...     def _eggs(*args, **kwargs):
...         print('%r got args: %r and kwargs: %r' % (
...             function.__name__, args, kwargs))
...         return function(*args, **kwargs)
...
...     return _eggs


>>> @eggs
... def spam(a, b, c):
```

```
...     return a * b + c
```

```
>>> spam(1, 2, 3)
'spam' got args: (1, 2, 3) and kwargs: {}
5
```

This should indicate how powerful decorators can be. By modifying `*args` and `**kwargs`, you can add, modify and remove arguments completely. Additionally, the return statement can be modified as well. Instead of `return function(...)`, you can return something completely different if you wish.

Why functools.wraps is important

Whenever you are writing a decorator, always be sure to add `functools.wraps` to wrap the inner function. Without wrapping it, you will lose all properties from the original function, which can lead to confusion. Take a look at the following code without `functools.wraps`:

```
>>> def eggs(function):
...     def _eggs(*args, **kwargs):
...         return function(*args, **kwargs)
...     return _eggs
```

```
>>> @eggs
... def spam(a, b, c):
...     '''The spam function Returns a * b + c'''
...     return a * b + c
```

```
>>> help(spam)
Help on function _eggs in module ...:
<BLANKLINE>
_eggs(*args, **kwargs)
<BLANKLINE>
```

```
>>> spam.__name__
'_eggs'
```

Now, our `spam` method has no documentation anymore and the name is gone. It has been renamed to `_eggs`. Since we are indeed calling `_eggs`, this is understandable, but it's very inconvenient for code that relies on this information. Now we will try the same code with the minor difference; we will use `functools.wraps`:

```
>>> import functools
```

```
>>> def eggs(function):
...     @functools.wraps(function)
...     def _eggs(*args, **kwargs):
...         return function(*args, **kwargs)
...     return _eggs
```

```
>>> @eggs
... def spam(a, b, c):
...     '''The spam function Returns a * b + c'''
...     return a * b + c
```

```
>>> help(spam)
Help on function spam in module ...:
<BLANKLINE>
spam(a, b, c)
    The spam function Returns a * b + c
<BLANKLINE>
```

```
>>> spam.__name__
'spam'
```

Without any further changes, we now have documentation and the expected function name. The working of `functools.wraps` is nothing magical though; it simply copies and updates several attributes. Specifically, the following attributes are copied:

- `__doc__`
- `__name__`
- `__module__`
- `__annotations__`
- `__qualname__`

Additionally, __dict__ is updated using _eggs.__dict__.update(spam.__dict__), and a new property called __wrapped__ is added, which contains the original (spam in this case) function. The actual wraps function is available in the functools.py file of your Python distribution.

How are decorators useful?

The use cases for decorators are plentiful, but some of the most useful cases are with debugging. More extensive examples of this will be covered in *Chapter 11, Debugging – Solving the Bugs* but I can give you a sneak preview of how to use decorators to keep track of what your code is doing.

Let's assume you have a bunch of functions that may or may not be called, and you're not entirely sure what kind of input and output each of these is getting. In this case, you could, of course, modify the function and add some print statements at the beginning and the end to print the output. This quickly gets tedious, however, and it's one of those cases where a simple decorator will make it easy to do the same thing.

For this example, we are using a very simple function, but we all know that in real life, we're not always that lucky:

```
>>> def spam(eggs):
...     return 'spam' * (eggs % 5)
...
>>> output = spam(3)
```

Let's take our simple spam function and add some output so that we can see what happens internally:

```
>>> def spam(eggs):
...     output = 'spam' * (eggs % 5)
...     print('spam(%r): %r' % (eggs, output))
...     return output
...
>>> output = spam(3)
spam(3): 'spamspamspam'
```

While this works, wouldn't it be far nicer to have a little decorator that takes care of this problem?

```
>>> def debug(function):
...     @functools.wraps(function)
...     def _debug(*args, **kwargs):
```

```
...            output = function(*args, **kwargs)
...            print('%s(%r, %r): %r' % (function.__name__, args, kwargs,
output))
...            return output
...        return _debug
...
>>>
>>> @debug
... def spam(eggs):
...        return 'spam' * (eggs % 5)
...
>>> output = spam(3)
spam((3,), {}): 'spamspamspam'
```

Now we have a decorator that we can easily reuse for any function that prints the input, output, and function name. This type of decorator can also be very useful for logging applications, as we will see in *Chapter 10, Testing and Logging – Preparing for Bugs*. It should be noted that you can use this example even if you are not able to modify the module containing the original code. We can wrap the function locally and even monkey-patch the module if needed:

```
import some_module


# Regular call
some_module.some_function()

# Wrap the function
debug_some_function = debug(some_module.some_function)

# Call the debug version
debug_some_function()

# Monkey patch the original module
some_module.some_function = debug_some_function

# Now this calls the debug version of the function
some_module.some_function()
```

Naturally, monkey-patching is not a good idea in production code, but it can be very useful when debugging.

Memoization using decorators

Memoization is a simple trick for making some code run a bit faster. The basic trick here is to store a mapping of the input and expected output so that you have to calculate a value only once. One of the most common examples of this technique is when demonstrating the naïve (recursive) Fibonacci function:

```
>>> import functools

>>> def memoize(function):
...     function.cache = dict()
...
...     @functools.wraps(function)
...     def _memoize(*args):
...         if args not in function.cache:
...             function.cache[args] = function(*args)
...         return function.cache[args]
...     return _memoize

>>> @memoize
... def fibonacci(n):
...     if n < 2:
...         return n
...     else:
...         return fibonacci(n - 1) + fibonacci(n - 2)

>>> for i in range(1, 7):
...     print('fibonacci %d: %d' % (i, fibonacci(i)))
fibonacci 1: 1
fibonacci 2: 1
fibonacci 3: 2
fibonacci 4: 3
fibonacci 5: 5
fibonacci 6: 8

>>> fibonacci.__wrapped__.cache
{(5,): 5, (0,): 0, (6,): 8, (1,): 1, (2,): 1, (3,): 2, (4,): 3}
```

While this example would work just fine without any memoization, for larger numbers, it would kill the system. For n=2, the function would execute fibonacci(n - 1) and fibonacci(n - 2) recursively, effectively giving an exponential time complexity. Also, effectively for n=30, the Fibonacci function is called 2,692,537 times which is still doable nonetheless. At n=40, it is going to take you quite a very long time to calculate.

The memoized version, however, doesn't even break a sweat and only needs to execute 31 times for n=30.

This decorator also shows how a context can be attached to a function itself. In this case, the cache property becomes a property of the internal (wrapped fibonacci) function so that an extra memoize decorator for a different object won't clash with any of the other decorated functions.

Note, however, that implementing the memoization function yourself is generally not that useful anymore since Python introduced lru_cache (least recently used cache) in Python 3.2. The lru_cache is similar to the preceding memoize function but a bit more advanced. It only maintains a fixed (128 by default) cache size to save memory and uses some statistics to check whether the cache size should be increased.

To demonstrate how lru_cache works internally, we will calculate fibonacci(100), which would keep our computer busy until the end of the universe without any caching. Moreover, to make sure that we can actually see how many times the fibonacci function is being called, we'll add an extra decorator that keeps track of the count, as follows:

```
>>> import functools


# Create a simple call counting decorator
>>> def counter(function):
...         function.calls = 0
...         @functools.wraps(function)
...         def _counter(*args, **kwargs):
...             function.calls += 1
...             return function(*args, **kwargs)
...         return _counter


# Create a LRU cache with size 3
>>> @functools.lru_cache(maxsize=3)
... @counter
... def fibonacci(n):
```

```
...       if n < 2:
...           return n
...       else:
...           return fibonacci(n - 1) + fibonacci(n - 2)

>>> fibonacci(100)
354224848179261915075


# The LRU cache offers some useful statistics
>>> fibonacci.cache_info()
CacheInfo(hits=98, misses=101, maxsize=3, currsize=3)


# The result from our counter function which is now wrapped both by
# our counter and the cache
>>> fibonacci.__wrapped__.__wrapped__.calls
101
```

You might wonder why we need only 101 calls with a cache size of 3. That's because we recursively require only n - 1 and n - 2, so we have no need of a larger cache in this case. With others, it would still be useful though.

Additionally, this example shows the usage of two decorators for a single function. You can see these as the layers of an onion. The first one is the outer layer and it works towards the inside. When calling fibonacci, lru_cache will be called first because it's the first decorator in the list. Assuming there is no cache available yet, the counter decorator will be called. Within the counter, the actual fibonacci function will be called.

Returning the values works in the reverse order, of course; fibonacci returns its value to counter, which passes the value along to lru_cache.

Decorators with (optional) arguments

The previous examples mostly used simple decorators without any arguments. As we have already seen with lru_cache, decorators can accept arguments as well since they are just regular functions, but this adds an extra layer to a decorator. This means that adding an argument can be as simple as the following:

```
>>> import functools


>>> def add(extra_n=1):
```

```
...         'Add extra_n to the input of the decorated function'
...
...         # The inner function, notice that this is the actual
...         # decorator
...         def _add(function):
...             # The actual function that will be called
...             @functools.wraps(function)
...             def __add(n):
...                 return function(n + extra_n)
...
...             return __add
...
...         return _add

>>> @add(extra_n=2)
... def eggs(n):
...     return 'eggs' * n

>>> eggs(2)
'eggseggseggseggs'
```

Optional arguments are a different matter, however, because they make the extra function layer optional. With arguments, you need three layers, but without arguments, you need only two layers. Since decorators are essentially regular functions that return functions, the difference would be to return the sub-function or the sub-sub-function, based on the parameters. This leaves just one issue—detecting whether the parameter is a function or a regular parameter. To illustrate, with the parameters the actual call looks like the following:

```
add(extra_n=2)(eggs)(2)
```

Whereas the call without arguments would look like this:

```
add(eggs)(2)
```

To detect whether the decorator was called with a function or a regular argument as a parameter, we have several options, none of which are completely ideal in my opinion:

- Using keyword arguments for decorator arguments so that the regular argument will always be the function
- Detecting whether the first and only argument is callable

In my opinion, the first one — using keyword arguments — is the better of the two options because it is somewhat more explicit and leaves less room for confusion. The second option could be problematic if, for some reason, your argument is callable as well.

Using the first method, the normal (non-keyword) argument has to be the decorated function and the other two checks can still apply. We can still check whether the function is indeed callable and whether there is only a single argument available. Here is an example using a modified version of the previous example:

```
>>> import functools

>>> def add(*args, **kwargs):
...     'Add n to the input of the decorated function'
...
...     # The default kwargs, we don't store this in kwargs
...     # because we want to make sure that args and kwargs
...     # can't both be filled
...     default_kwargs = dict(n=1)
...
...     # The inner function, notice that this is actually a
...     # decorator itself
...     def _add(function):
...         # The actual function that will be called
...         @functools.wraps(function)
...         def __add(n):
...             default_kwargs.update(kwargs)
...             return function(n + default_kwargs['n'])
...
...         return __add
...
...     if len(args) == 1 and callable(args[0]) and not kwargs:
...         # Decorator call without arguments, just call it
...         # ourselves
...         return _add(args[0])
...     elif not args and kwargs:
...         # Decorator call with arguments, this time it will
...         # automatically be executed with function as the
```

```
...                # first argument
...                default_kwargs.update(kwargs)
...                return _add
...        else:
...                raise RuntimeError('This decorator only supports '
...                                   'keyword arguments')

>>> @add
... def spam(n):
...        return 'spam' * n

>>> @add(n=3)
... def eggs(n):
...        return 'eggs' * n

>>> spam(3)
'spamspamspamspam'

>>> eggs(2)
'eggseggseggseggseggs'

>>> @add(3)
... def bacon(n):
...        return 'bacon' * n
Traceback (most recent call last):
    ...
RuntimeError: This decorator only supports keyword arguments
```

Whenever you have the choice available, I recommend that you either have a decorator with arguments or without them, instead of having optional arguments. However, if you have a really good reason for making the arguments optional, then you have a relatively safe method of making this possible.

Creating decorators using classes

Similar to how we create regular function decorators, it is also possible to create decorators using classes instead. After all, a function is just a callable object and a class can implement the callable interface as well. The following decorator works similarly to the `debug` decorator we used earlier, but uses a class instead of a regular function:

```
>>> import functools

>>> class Debug(object):
...
...     def __init__(self, function):
...         self.function = function
...         # functools.wraps for classes
...         functools.update_wrapper(self, function)
...
...     def __call__(self, *args, **kwargs):
...         output = self.function(*args, **kwargs)
...         print('%s(%r, %r): %r' % (
...             self.function.__name__, args, kwargs, output))
...         return output


>>> @Debug
... def spam(eggs):
...     return 'spam' * (eggs % 5)
...
>>> output = spam(3)
spam((3,), {}): 'spamspamspam'
```

The only notable difference between functions and classes is that `functools.wraps` is now replaced with `functools.update_wrapper` in the `__init__` method.

Decorating class functions

Decorating class functions is very similar to regular functions, but you need to be aware of the required first argument, `self`—the class instance. You have most likely already used a few class function decorators. The `classmethod`, `staticmethod`, and `property` decorators for example, are used in many different projects. To explain how all this works, we will build our own versions of the `classmethod`, `staticmethod`, and `property` decorators. First, let's look at a simple decorator for class functions to show the difference from regular decorators:

```
>>> import functools


>>> def plus_one(function):
...     @functools.wraps(function)
...     def _plus_one(self, n):
...         return function(self, n + 1)
...     return _plus_one


>>> class Spam(object):
...     @plus_one
...     def get_eggs(self, n=2):
...         return n * 'eggs'


>>> spam = Spam()
>>> spam.get_eggs(3)
'eggseggseggseggs'
```

As is the case with regular functions, the class function decorator now gets passed along `self` as the instance. Nothing unexpected!

Skipping the instance – classmethod and staticmethod

The difference between a `classmethod` and a `staticmethod` is fairly simple. The `classmethod` passes a class object instead of a class instance (`self`), and `staticmethod` skips both the class and the instance entirely. This effectively makes `staticmethod` very similar to a regular function outside of a class.

Before we recreate `classmethod` and `staticmethod`, we need to take a look at the expected behavior of these methods:

```
>>> import pprint


>>> class Spam(object):
...
...     def some_instancemethod(self, *args, **kwargs):
...         print('self: %r' % self)
...         print('args: %s' % pprint.pformat(args))
...         print('kwargs: %s' % pprint.pformat(kwargs))
...
...     @classmethod
...     def some_classmethod(cls, *args, **kwargs):
...         print('cls: %r' % cls)
...         print('args: %s' % pprint.pformat(args))
...         print('kwargs: %s' % pprint.pformat(kwargs))
...
...     @staticmethod
...     def some_staticmethod(*args, **kwargs):
...         print('args: %s' % pprint.pformat(args))
...         print('kwargs: %s' % pprint.pformat(kwargs))


# Create an instance so we can compare the difference between
# executions with and without instances easily
>>> spam = Spam()


# With an instance (note the lowercase spam)
>>> spam.some_instancemethod(1, 2, a=3, b=4)
self: <...Spam object at 0x...>
args: (1, 2)
kwargs: {'a': 3, 'b': 4}


# Without an instance (note the capitalized Spam)
>>> Spam.some_instancemethod()
```

```
Traceback (most recent call last):

    ...

TypeError: some_instancemethod() missing 1 required positional argument:
'self'

# But what if we add parameters? Be very careful with these!
# Our first argument is now used as an argument, this can give
# very strange and unexpected errors
>>> Spam.some_instancemethod(1, 2, a=3, b=4)
self: 1
args: (2,)
kwargs: {'a': 3, 'b': 4}


# Classmethods are expectedly identical
>>> spam.some_classmethod(1, 2, a=3, b=4)
cls: <class '...Spam'>
args: (1, 2)
kwargs: {'a': 3, 'b': 4}

>>> Spam.some_classmethod()
cls: <class '...Spam'>
args: ()
kwargs: {}

>>> Spam.some_classmethod(1, 2, a=3, b=4)
cls: <class '...Spam'>
args: (1, 2)
kwargs: {'a': 3, 'b': 4}


# Staticmethods are also identical
>>> spam.some_staticmethod(1, 2, a=3, b=4)
args: (1, 2)
kwargs: {'a': 3, 'b': 4}

>>> Spam.some_staticmethod()
```

```
args: ()
kwargs: {}
```

```
>>> Spam.some_staticmethod(1, 2, a=3, b=4)
args: (1, 2)
kwargs: {'a': 3, 'b': 4}
```

Note that calling `some_instancemethod` without an instance results in an error whereby `self` is missing. As expected (since we didn't instantiate the class in that case), for the version with the arguments, it seems to work but it is actually broken. This is because the first argument is now assumed to be `self`. This is obviously incorrect in this case, where you pass an integer, but if you had passed along some other class instance, this could be a source of very strange bugs. Both `classmethod` and `staticmethod` handle this correctly.

Before we can continue with decorators, you need to be aware of how Python descriptors function. Descriptors can be used to modify the binding behavior of object attributes. This means that if a descriptor is used as the value of an attribute, you can modify which value is being set, get, and deleted when these operations are called on the attribute. Here is a basic example of this behavior:

```
>>> class MoreSpam(object):
...
...     def __init__(self, more=1):
...         self.more = more
...
...     def __get__(self, instance, cls):
...         return self.more + instance.spam
...
...     def __set__(self, instance, value):
...         instance.spam = value - self.more
...

>>> class Spam(object):
...
...     more_spam = MoreSpam(5)
...
...     def __init__(self, spam):
...         self.spam = spam
```

```
>>> spam = Spam(1)
>>> spam.spam
1
>>> spam.more_spam
6

>>> spam.more_spam = 10
>>> spam.spam
5
```

As you can see, whenever we set or get values from more_spam, it actually calls __get__ or __set__ on MoreSpam. A very useful feat for automatic conversions and type checking, the property decorator we will see in the next paragraph is just a more convenient implementation of this technique.

Now that we know how descriptors work, we can continue with creating the classmethod and staticmethod decorators. For these two, we simply need to modify __get__ instead of __call__ so that we can control which type of instance (or none at all) is passed along:

```
import functools


class ClassMethod(object):

    def __init__(self, method):
        self.method = method

    def __get__(self, instance, cls):
        @functools.wraps(self.method)
        def method(*args, **kwargs):
            return self.method(cls, *args, **kwargs)
        return method


class StaticMethod(object):

    def __init__(self, method):
        self.method = method

    def __get__(self, instance, cls):
        return self.method
```

The `ClassMethod` decorator still features a sub-function to actually produce a working decorator. Looking at the function, you can most likely guess how it functions. Instead of passing `instance` as the first argument to `self.method`, it passes `cls`.

`StaticMethod` is even simpler, because it completely ignores both the `instance` and the `cls`. It can just return the original method unmodified. Because it returns the original method without any modifications, we have no need for the `functools.wraps` call either.

Properties – smart descriptor usage

The `property` decorator is probably the most used decorator in Python land. It allows you to add getters/setters to existing instance properties so that you can add validators and modify your values before setting them to your instance properties. The `property` decorator can be used both as an assignment and as a decorator. The following example shows both syntaxes so that we know what to expect from the `property` decorator:

```
>>> class Spam(object):
...
...     def get_eggs(self):
...         print('getting eggs')
...         return self._eggs
...
...     def set_eggs(self, eggs):
...         print('setting eggs to %s' % eggs)
...         self._eggs = eggs
...
...     def delete_eggs(self):
...         print('deleting eggs')
...         del self._eggs
...
...     eggs = property(get_eggs, set_eggs, delete_eggs)
...
...     @property
...     def spam(self):
...         print('getting spam')
...         return self._spam
...
```

```
...          @spam.setter
...          def spam(self, spam):
...              print('setting spam to %s' % spam)
...              self._spam = spam
...
...          @spam.deleter
...          def spam(self):
...              print('deleting spam')
...              del self._spam



>>> spam = Spam()
>>> spam.eggs = 123
setting eggs to 123
>>> spam.eggs
getting eggs
123
>>> del spam.eggs
deleting eggs
```

 Note that the `property` decorator works only if the class inherits `object`.

Similar to how we implemented the `classmethod` and `staticmethod` decorators, we need the Python descriptors again. This time, we require the full power of the descriptors, however—not just __get__ but __set__ and __delete__ as well:

```
class Property(object):
    def __init__(self, fget=None, fset=None, fdel=None,
                 doc=None):
        self.fget = fget
        self.fset = fset
        self.fdel = fdel
        # If no specific documentation is available, copy it
        # from the getter
        if fget and not doc:
            doc = fget.__doc__
        self.__doc__ = doc
```

```
def __get__(self, instance, cls):
    if instance is None:
        # Redirect class (not instance) properties to
        # self
        return self
    elif self.fget:
        return self.fget(instance)
    else:
        raise AttributeError('unreadable attribute')

def __set__(self, instance, value):
    if self.fset:
        self.fset(instance, value)
    else:
        raise AttributeError("can't set attribute")

def __delete__(self, instance):
    if self.fdel:
        self.fdel(instance)
    else:
        raise AttributeError("can't delete attribute")

def getter(self, fget):
    return type(self)(fget, self.fset, self.fdel)

def setter(self, fset):
    return type(self)(self.fget, fset, self.fdel)

def deleter(self, fdel):
    return type(self)(self.fget, self.fset, fdel)
```

As you can see, most of the `Property` implementation is simply an implementation of the descriptor methods. The `getter`, `setter`, and `deleter` functions are simply shortcuts for making the usage of the decorator possible, which is why we have to `return self` if no `instance` is available.

Naturally, there are more methods of achieving this effect. In the previous paragraph, we saw the bare descriptor implementation, and in our previous example, we saw the property decorator. A somewhat more generic solution for a class is to implement `__getattr__` or `__getattribute__`. Here's a simple demonstration:

```
>>> class Spam(object):
...     def __init__(self):
...         self.registry = {}
```

```
...
...         def __getattr__(self, key):
...             print('Getting %r' % key)
...             return self.registry.get(key, 'Undefined')
...
...         def __setattr__(self, key, value):
...             if key == 'registry':
...                 object.__setattr__(self, key, value)
...             else:
...                 print('Setting %r to %r' % (key, value))
...                 self.registry[key] = value
...
...         def __delattr__(self, key):
...             print('Deleting %r' % key)
...             del self.registry[key]


>>> spam = Spam()

>>> spam.a
Getting 'a'
'Undefined'

>>> spam.a = 1
Setting 'a' to 1

>>> spam.a
Getting 'a'
1

>>> del spam.a
Deleting 'a'
```

The __getattr__ method looks for the key in instance.__dict__ first and is called only if it does not exist. That's why we never see a __getattr__ for the registry attribute. The __getattribute__ method is called in all cases, which makes it a bit more dangerous to use. With the __getattribute__ method, you will need a specific exclusion for registry since it will be executed recursively if you try to access self.registry.

There is rarely a need to look at descriptors, but they are used by several internal Python processes, such as the `super()` method when inheriting classes.

Decorating classes

Python 2.6 introduced the class decorator syntax. As is the case with the function decorator syntax, this is not really a new technique either. Even without the syntax, a class can be decorated simply by executing `DecoratedClass = decorator(RegularClass)`. After the previous paragraphs, you should be familiar with writing decorators. Class decorators are no different from regular ones, except for the fact that they take a class instead of a function. As is the case with functions, this happens at declaration time and *not* at instantiating/calling time.

Because there are quite a few alternative ways to modify how classes work, such as standard inheritance, mixins, and metaclasses (more about that in *Chapter 8, Metaclasses – Making Classes (Not Instances) Smarter*), class decorators are never strictly needed. This does not reduce their usefulness, but it does offer an explanation of why you will most likely not see too many examples of class decorating in the wild.

Singletons – classes with a single instance

Singletons are classes that always allow only a single instance to exist. So, instead of getting an instance specifically for your call, you always get the same one. These can be very useful for things such as a database connection pool, where you don't want to keep opening connections all of the time but want to reuse the original ones:

```
>>> import functools


>>> def singleton(cls):
...     instances = dict()
...     @functools.wraps(cls)
...     def _singleton(*args, **kwargs):
...         if cls not in instances:
...             instances[cls] = cls(*args, **kwargs)
...         return instances[cls]
...     return _singleton

>>> @singleton
... class Spam(object):
...     def __init__(self):
```

```
...                print('Executing init')


>>> a = Spam()
Executing init
>>> b = Spam()


>>> a is b
True


>>> a.x = 123
>>> b.x
123
```

As you can see in the `a is b` comparison, both objects have the same identity, so we can conclude that they are indeed the same object. As is the case with regular decorators, due to the `functools.wraps` functionality, we can still access the original class through `Spam.__wrapped__` if needed.

 The `is` operator compares objects by identity, which is implemented as the memory address in CPython. If `a is b` returns `True`, we can conclude that both a and b are the same instance.

Total ordering – sortable classes the easy way

At some point or the other, you have probably needed to sort data structures. While this is easily achievable using the key parameter to the `sorted` function, there is a more convenient way if you need to do this often—by implementing the `__gt__`, `__ge__`, `__lt__`, `__le__`, and `__eq__` functions. That seems a bit verbose, doesn't it? If you want the best performance, it's still a good idea, but if you can take a tiny performance hit and some slightly more complicated stack traces, then `total_ordering` might be a nice alternative. The `total_ordering` class decorator can implement all required sort functions based on a class that possesses an `__eq__` function and one of the comparison functions (`__lt__`, `__le__`, `__gt__`, or `__ge__`). This means you can seriously shorten your function definitions. Let's compare the regular one and the one using the `total_ordering` decorator:

```
>>> import functools


>>> class Value(object):
```

```
...         def __init__(self, value):
...             self.value = value
...
...         def __repr__(self):
...             return '<%s[%d]>' % (self.__class__, self.value)


>>> class Spam(Value):
...         def __gt__(self, other):
...             return self.value > other.value
...
...         def __ge__(self, other):
...             return self.value >= other.value
...
...         def __lt__(self, other):
...             return self.value < other.value
...
...         def __le__(self, other):
...             return self.value <= other.value
...
...         def __eq__(self, other):
...             return self.value == other.value


>>> @functools.total_ordering
... class Egg(Value):
...         def __lt__(self, other):
...             return self.value < other.value
...
...         def __eq__(self, other):
...             return self.value == other.value


>>> numbers = [4, 2, 3, 4]
>>> spams = [Spam(n) for n in numbers]
>>> eggs = [Egg(n) for n in numbers]

>>> spams
```

```
[<<class 'H05.Spam'>[4]>, <<class 'H05.Spam'>[2]>,
<<class 'H05.Spam'>[3]>, <<class 'H05.Spam'>[4]>]

>>> eggs
[<<class 'H05.Egg'>[4]>, <<class 'H05.Egg'>[2]>,
<<class 'H05.Egg'>[3]>, <<class 'H05.Egg'>[4]>]

>>> sorted(spams)
[<<class 'H05.Spam'>[2]>, <<class 'H05.Spam'>[3]>,
<<class 'H05.Spam'>[4]>, <<class 'H05.Spam'>[4]>]

>>> sorted(eggs)
[<<class 'H05.Egg'>[2]>, <<class 'H05.Egg'>[3]>,
<<class 'H05.Egg'>[4]>, <<class 'H05.Egg'>[4]>]

# Sorting using key is of course still possible and in this case
# perhaps just as easy:
>>> values = [Value(n) for n in numbers]
>>> values
[<<class 'H05.Value'>[4]>, <<class 'H05.Value'>[2]>,
<<class 'H05.Value'>[3]>, <<class 'H05.Value'>[4]>]

>>> sorted(values, key=lambda v: v.value)
[<<class 'H05.Value'>[2]>, <<class 'H05.Value'>[3]>,
<<class 'H05.Value'>[4]>, <<class 'H05.Value'>[4]>]
```

Now, you might be wondering, "Why isn't there a class decorator to make a class sortable using a specified key property?" Well, that might indeed be a good idea for the functools library but it isn't there yet. So let's see how we would implement something like it:

```
>>> def sort_by_attribute(attr, keyfunc=getattr):
...     def _sort_by_attribute(cls):
...         def __gt__(self, other):
...             return getattr(self, attr) > getattr(other, attr)
...
...         def __ge__(self, other):
...             return getattr(self, attr) >= getattr(other, attr)
...
```

```
...             def __lt__(self, other):
...                 return getattr(self, attr) < getattr(other, attr)
...
...             def __le__(self, other):
...                 return getattr(self, attr) <= getattr(other, attr)
...
...             def __eq__(self, other):
...                 return getattr(self, attr) <= getattr(other, attr)
...
...             cls.__gt__ = __gt__
...             cls.__ge__ = __ge__
...             cls.__lt__ = __lt__
...             cls.__le__ = __le__
...             cls.__eq__ = __eq__
...
...             return cls
...         return _sort_by_attribute


>>> class Value(object):
...     def __init__(self, value):
...         self.value = value
...
...     def __repr__(self):
...         return '<%s[%d]>' % (self.__class__, self.value)


>>> @sort_by_attribute('value')
... class Spam(Value):
...     pass


>>> numbers = [4, 2, 3, 4]
>>> spams = [Spam(n) for n in numbers]
>>> sorted(spams)
[<<class '...Spam'>[2]>, <<class '...Spam'>[3]>,
<<class '...Spam'>[4]>, <<class '...Spam'>[4]>]
```

Certainly, this greatly simplifies the making of a sortable class. And if you would rather have your own key function instead of `getattr`, it's even easier. Simply replace the `getattr(self, attr)` call with `key_function(self)`, do that for `other` as well, and change the argument for the decorator to your function. You can even use that as the base function and implement `sort_by_attribute` by simply passing a wrapped `getattr` function.

Useful decorators

In addition to the ones already mentioned in this chapter, Python comes bundled with a few other useful decorators. There are some that aren't in the standard library (yet?).

Single dispatch – polymorphism in Python

If you've used C++ or Java before, you're probably used to having ad hoc polymorphism available—different functions being called depending on the argument types. Python being a dynamically typed language, most people would not expect the possibility of a single dispatch pattern. Python, however, is a language that is not only dynamically typed but also strongly typed, which means we can rely on the type we receive.

A dynamically typed language does not require strict type definitions. On the other hand, a language such as C would require the following to declare an integer:

```
int some_integer = 123;
```

Python simply accepts that your value has a type:

```
some_integer = 123
```

As opposed to languages such as JavaScript and PHP, however, Python does very little implicit type conversion. In Python, the following will return an error, whereas JavaScript would execute it without any problems:

```
'spam' + 5
```

In Python, the result is a `TypeError`. In Javascript, it's `'spam5'`.

The idea of single dispatch is that depending on the type you pass along, the correct function is called. Since `str + int` results in an error in Python, this can be very convenient to automatically convert your arguments before passing them to your function. This can be useful to separate the actual workings of your function from the type conversions.

Since Python 3.4, there is a decorator that makes it easily possible to implement the single dispatch pattern in Python. For one of those cases that you need to handle a specific type different from the normal execution. Here is the basic example:

```python
>>> import functools


>>> @functools.singledispatch
... def printer(value):
...     print('other: %r' % value)

>>> @printer.register(str)
... def str_printer(value):
...     print(value)

>>> @printer.register(int)
... def int_printer(value):
...     printer('int: %d' % value)

>>> @printer.register(dict)
... def dict_printer(value):
...     printer('dict:')
...     for k, v in sorted(value.items()):
...         printer('    key: %r, value: %r' % (k, v))


>>> printer('spam')
spam

>>> printer([1, 2, 3])
other: [1, 2, 3]

>>> printer(123)
```

```
int: 123
```

```
>>> printer({'a': 1, 'b': 2})
dict:
    key: 'a', value: 1
    key: 'b', value: 2
```

See how, depending on the type, the other functions were called? This pattern can be very useful for reducing the complexity of a single function that takes several types of argument.

 When naming the functions, make sure that you do not overwrite the original `singledispatch` function. If we had named `str_printer` as just `printer`, it would overwrite the initial `printer` function. This would make it impossible to access the original `printer` function and make all `register` operations after that fail as well.

Now, a slightly more useful example—differentiating between a filename and a file handler:

```
>>> import json
>>> import functools



>>> @functools.singledispatch
... def write_as_json(file, data):
...     json.dump(data, file)



>>> @write_as_json.register(str)
... @write_as_json.register(bytes)
... def write_as_json_filename(file, data):
...     with open(file, 'w') as fh:
...         write_as_json(fh, data)



>>> data = dict(a=1, b=2, c=3)
```

```
>>> write_as_json('test1.json', data)
>>> write_as_json(b'test2.json', 'w')
>>> with open('test3.json', 'w') as fh:
...     write_as_json(fh, data)
```

So now we have a single `write_as_json` function; it calls the right code depending on the type. If it's an `str` or `bytes` object, it will automatically open the file and call the regular version of `write_as_json`, which accepts file objects.

Writing a decorator that does this is not that hard to do, of course, but it's still quite convenient to have it in the base library. It most certainly beats a couple of `isinstance` calls in your function. To see which function will be called, you can use the `write_as_json.dispatch` function with a specific type. When passing along an `str`, you will get the `write_as_json_filename` function. It should be noted that the name of the dispatched functions is completely arbitrary. They are accessible as regular functions, of course, but you can name them anything you like.

To check the registered types, you can access the registry, which is a dictionary, through `write_as_json.registry`:

```
>>> write_as_json.registry.keys()
dict_keys([<class 'bytes'>, <class 'object'>, <class 'str'>])
```

Contextmanager, with statements made easy

Using the `contextmanager` class, we can make the creation of a context wrapper very easy. Context wrappers are used whenever you use a `with` statement. One example is the `open` function, which works as a context wrapper as well, allowing you to use the following code:

```
with open(filename) as fh:
    pass
```

Let's just assume for now that the `open` function is not usable as a context manager and that we need to build our own function to do this. The standard method of creating a context manager is by creating a class that implements the `__enter__` and `__exit__` methods, but that's a bit verbose. We can have it shorter and simpler:

```
>>> import contextlib


>>> @contextlib.contextmanager
... def open_context_manager(filename, mode='r'):
...     fh = open(filename, mode)
```

```
...        yield fh
...        fh.close()
```

```
>>> with open_context_manager('test.txt', 'w') as fh:
...        print('Our test is complete!', file=fh)
```

Simple, right? However, I should mention that for this specific case — the closing of objects — there is a dedicated function in `contextlib`, and it is even easier to use. Let's demonstrate it:

```
>>> import contextlib
```

```
>>> with contextlib.closing(open('test.txt', 'a')) as fh:
...        print('Yet another test', file=fh)
```

For a `file` object, this is of course not needed since it already functions as a context manager. However, some objects such as requests made by `urllib` don't support automatic closing in that manner and benefit from this function.

But wait; there's more! In addition to being usable in a `with` statement, the results of a `contextmanager` are actually usable as decorators since Python 3.2. In older Python versions, it was simply a small wrapper, but since Python 3.2 it's based on the `ContextDecorator` class, which makes it a decorator. The previous decorator isn't really suitable for that task since it yields a result (more about that in *Chapter 6, Generators and Coroutines – Infinity, One Step at a Time*), but we can think of other functions:

```
>>> @contextlib.contextmanager
... def debug(name):
...        print('Debugging %r:' % name)
...        yield
...        print('End of debugging %r' % name)
```

```
>>> @debug('spam')
... def spam():
...        print('This is the inside of our spam function')
```

```
>>> spam()
Debugging 'spam':
This is the inside of our spam function
End of debugging 'spam'
```

There are quite a few nice use cases for this, but at the very least, it's just a convenient way to wrap a function in a context without all the (nested) `with` statements.

Validation, type checks, and conversions

While checking for types is usually not the best way to go in Python, at times it can be useful if you know that you will need a specific type (or something that can be cast to that type). To facilitate this, Python 3.5 introduces a type hinting system so that you can do the following:

```
def spam(eggs: int):
    pass
```

Since Python 3.5 is not that common yet, here's a decorator that achieves the same with more advanced type checking. To allow for this type of checking, some magic has to be used, specifically the usage of the `inspect` module. Personally, I am not a great fan of inspecting code to perform tricks like these, as they are easy to break. This piece of code actually breaks when a regular decorator (one that doesn't copy `argspec`) is used between the function and this decorator, but it's a nice example nonetheless:

```
>>> import inspect
>>> import functools


>>> def to_int(name, minimum=None, maximum=None):
...     def _to_int(function):
...         # Use the method signature to map *args to named
...         # arguments
...         signature = inspect.signature(function)
...
...         # Unfortunately functools.wraps doesn't copy the
...         # signature (yet) so we do it manually.
...         # For more info: http://bugs.python.org/issue23764
...         @functools.wraps(function, ['__signature__'])
...         @functools.wraps(function)
...         def __to_int(*args, **kwargs):
...             # Bind all arguments to the names so we get a single
...             # mapping of all arguments
...             bound = signature.bind(*args, **kwargs)
...
```

```
...                 # Make sure the value is (convertible to) an integer
...                 default = signature.parameters[name].default
...                 value = int(bound.arguments.get(name, default))
...
...                 # Make sure it's within the allowed range
...                 if minimum is not None:
...                     assert value >= minimum, (
...                         '%s should be at least %r, got: %r' %
...                         (name, minimum, value))
...
...                 if maximum is not None:
...                     assert value <= maximum, (
...                         '%s should be at most %r, got: %r' %
...                         (name, maximum, value))
...
...                 return function(*args, **kwargs)
...             return __to_int
...         return _to_int

>>> @to_int('a', minimum=10)
... @to_int('b', maximum=10)
... @to_int('c')
... def spam(a, b, c=10):
...     print('a', a)
...     print('b', b)
...     print('c', c)

>>> spam(10, b=0)
a 10
b 0
c 10

>>> spam(a=20, b=10)
a 20
b 10
c 10

>>> spam(1, 2, 3)
```

```
Traceback (most recent call last):
    ...
AssertionError: a should be at least 10, got: 1

>>> spam()
Traceback (most recent call last):
    ...
TypeError: 'a' parameter lacking default value

>>> spam('spam', {})
Traceback (most recent call last):
    ...
ValueError: invalid literal for int() with base 10: 'spam'
```

Because of the inspect magic, I'm still not sure whether I would recommend using the decorator like this. Instead, I would opt for a simpler version that uses no inspect whatsoever and simply parses the arguments from kwargs:

```
>>> import functools



>>> def to_int(name, minimum=None, maximum=None):
...     def _to_int(function):
...         @functools.wraps(function)
...         def __to_int(**kwargs):
...             value = int(kwargs.get(name))
...
...             # Make sure it's within the allowed range
...             if minimum is not None:
...                 assert value >= minimum, (
...                     '%s should be at least %r, got: %r' %
...                     (name, minimum, value))
...
...             if maximum is not None:
...                 assert value <= maximum, (
...                     '%s should be at most %r, got: %r' %
...                     (name, maximum, value))
...
```

```
...                 return function(**kwargs)
...             return __to_int
...         return _to_int

>>> @to_int('a', minimum=10)
... @to_int('b', maximum=10)
... def spam(a, b):
...     print('a', a)
...     print('b', b)

>>> spam(a=20, b=10)
a 20
b 10

>>> spam(a=1, b=10)
Traceback (most recent call last):
    ...
AssertionError: a should be at least 10, got: 1
```

However, as demonstrated, supporting both args and kwargs is not impossible as long as you keep in mind that __signature__ is not copied by default. Without __signature__, the inspect module won't know which parameters are allowed and which aren't.

The missing __signature__ issue is currently being discussed and might be solved in a future Python version: http://bugs.python.org/issue23764.

Useless warnings – how to ignore them

Generally when writing Python, warnings are very useful the first time when you're actually writing the code. When executing it, however, it is not useful to get that same message every time you run your script/application. So, let's create some code that allows easy hiding of the expected warnings, but not all of them so that we can easily catch new ones:

```
import warnings
import functools


def ignore_warning(warning, count=None):
```

```python
def _ignore_warning(function):
    @functools.wraps(function)
    def __ignore_warning(*args, **kwargs):
        # Execute the code while recording all warnings
        with warnings.catch_warnings(record=True) as ws:
            # Catch all warnings of this type
            warnings.simplefilter('always', warning)
            # Execute the function
            result = function(*args, **kwargs)

            # Now that all code was executed and the warnings
            # collected, re-send all warnings that are beyond our
            # expected number of warnings
            if count is not None:
                for w in ws[count:]:
                    warnings.showwarning(
                        message=w.message,
                        category=w.category,
                        filename=w.filename,
                        lineno=w.lineno,
                        file=w.file,
                        line=w.line,
                    )

        return result
    return __ignore_warning
return _ignore_warning


@ignore_warning(DeprecationWarning, count=1)
def spam():
    warnings.warn('deprecation 1', DeprecationWarning)
    warnings.warn('deprecation 2', DeprecationWarning)
```

Using this method, we can catch the first (expected) warning and still see the second (not expected) warning.

Summary

This chapter showed us some of the places where decorators can be used to make our code simpler and add some fairly complex behavior to very simple functions. Truthfully, most decorators are more complex than the regular function would have been by simply adding the functionality directly, but the added advantage of applying the same pattern to many functions and classes is generally well worth it.

Decorators have so many uses to make your functions and classes smarter and more convenient to use:

- Debugging
- Validation
- Argument convenience (pre-filling or converting arguments)
- Output convenience (converting the output to a specific type)

The most important takeaway of this chapter should be to never forget `functools.wraps` when wrapping a function. Debugging decorated functions can be rather difficult because of (unexpected) behavior modification, but losing attributes as well can make that problem much worse.

The next chapter will show us how and when to use `generators` and `coroutines`. This chapter has already shown us the usage of the `with` statement slightly, but `generators` and `coroutines` go much further with this. We will still be using decorators often though, so make sure you have a good understanding of how they work.

6
Generators and Coroutines – Infinity, One Step at a Time

A generator is a specific type of iterator that generates values through a function. While traditional methods build and return a `list` of items, a generator will simply `yield` every value separately at the moment when they are requested by the caller. This method has several benefits:

- Generators pause execution completely until the next value is yielded, which makes them completely lazy. If you fetch five items from a generator, only five items will be generated, so no other computation is needed.

- Generators have no need to save values. Whereas a traditional function would require creating a `list` and storing all results until they are returned, a generator only needs to store a single value.

- Generators can have infinite size. There is no requirement to stop at a certain point.

These benefits come at a price, however. The immediate results of these benefits are a few disadvantages:

- Until you are done processing, you never know how many values are left; it could even be infinite. This makes usage dangerous in some cases; executing `list(some_infinite_generator)` will run out of memory.

- You cannot slice generators.

- You cannot get specific items without yielding all values before that index.

- You cannot restart a generator. All values are yielded exactly once.

In addition to generators, there is a variation to the generator's syntax that creates coroutines. Coroutines are functions that allow for multitasking without requiring multiple threads or processes. Whereas generators can only yield values to the caller, coroutines actually receive values from the caller while it is still running. While this technique has a few limitations, if it suits your purpose, it can result in great performance at a very little cost.

In short, the topics covered in this chapter are:

- The characteristics and uses of generators
- Generator comprehensions
- Generator functions
- Generator classes
- Bundled generators
- Coroutines

What are generators?

A generator, in its simplest form, is a function that returns elements one at a time instead of returning a collection of items. The most important advantage of this is that it requires very little memory and that it doesn't need to have a predefined size. Creating an endless generator (such as the `itertools.count` iterator discussed in *Chapter 4, Functional Programming – Readability Versus Brevity*) is actually quite easy, but it does come with a cost, of course. Not having the size of an object available makes certain patterns difficult to achieve.

The basic trick in writing generators (as functions) is using the `yield` statement. Let's use the `itertools.count` generator as an example and extend it with a `stop` variable:

```
>>> def count(start=0, step=1, stop=10):
...     n = start
...     while n <= stop:
...         yield n
...         n += step

>>> for x in count(10, 2.5, 20):
...     print(x)
10
12.5
```

```
15.0

17.5

20.0
```

Due to the potentially infinite nature of generators, caution is required. Without
the `stop` variable, simply doing `list(count())` would result in an out-of-memory
situation quite fast.

So how does this work? It's just a normal `for` loop, but the big difference between
this and the regular method of returning a list of items is that the `yield` statement
returns the items one at a time. An important thing to note here is that the `return`
statement results in a `StopIteration` and passing something along to `return`
will be the argument to the `StopIteration`. It should be noted that this behavior
changed in Python 3.3; in Python 3.2 and earlier versions, it was simply not possible
to return anything other than `None`. Here is an example:

```
>>> def generator():
...     yield 'this is a generator'
...     return 'returning from a generator'


>>> g = generator()
>>> next(g)
'this is a generator'
>>> next(g)
Traceback (most recent call last):

    ...

StopIteration: returning from a generator
```

Of course, as always, there are multiple ways of creating generators with Python.
Other than functions, there are also generator comprehensions and classes that
can do the same thing. Generator comprehensions are pretty much identical to list
comprehensions but use parentheses instead of brackets, like this for example:

```
>>> generator = (x ** 2 for x in range(4))


>>> for x in generator:
...     print(x)
0
1
4
9
```

For completeness, the class version of the count function is as follows:

```
>>> class Count(object):
...     def __init__(self, start=0, step=1, stop=10):
...         self.n = start
...         self.step = step
...         self.stop = stop
...
...     def __iter__(self):
...         return self
...
...     def __next__(self):
...         n = self.n
...         if n > self.stop:
...             raise StopIteration()
...
...         self.n += self.step
...         return n

>>> for x in Count(10, 2.5, 20):
...     print(x)
10
12.5
15.0
17.5
20.0
```

The biggest difference between the class and the function-based approach is that you are required to raise a StopIteration explicitly instead of just returning it. Beyond that, they are quite similar, although the class-based version obviously adds some verbosity.

Advantages and disadvantages of generators

You have seen a few examples of generators and know the basics of what you can do with them. However, it is important to keep their advantages and disadvantages in mind.

The following are most important pros:

- Memory usage. Items can be processed one at a time, so there is generally no need to keep the entire list in memory.

- The results can depend on outside factors, instead of having a static list. Think of processing a queue/stack for example.

- Generators are lazy. This means that if you're using only the first five results of a generator, the rest won't even be calculated.

- Generally, it is simpler to write than list generating functions.

The most important cons:

- The results are available only once. After processing the results of a generator, it cannot be used again.

- The size is unknown until you are done processing, which can be detrimental to certain algorithms.

- Generators are not indexable, which means that `some_generator[5]` will not work.

Considering all the advantages and disadvantages, my general advice would be to use generators if possible and only return a `list` or `tuple` when you actually need to. Converting a generator to a `list` is as simple as `list(some_generator)`, so that shouldn't stop you since generator functions tend to be simpler than the equivalents that produce `list`.

The memory usage advantage is understandable; one item requires less memory than many items. The lazy part, however, needs some additional explanation as it has a small snag:

```
>>> def generator():
...     print('Before 1')
...     yield 1
...     print('After 1')
...     print('Before 2')
...     yield 2
...     print('After 2')
```

```
...         print('Before 3')
...         yield 3
...         print('After 3')

>>> g = generator()
>>> print('Got %d' % next(g))
Before 1
Got 1

>>> print('Got %d' % next(g))
After 1
Before 2
Got 2
```

As you can see, the generator effectively freezes right after the `yield` statement, so even the `After 2` won't print until 3 is yielded.

This has important advantages, but it's definitely something you need to take into consideration. You can't have your cleanup right after the `yield` as it won't be executed until the next `yield`.

Pipelines – an effective use of generators

The theoretical possibilities of generators are infinite (no pun intended), but their practical uses can be difficult to find. If you are familiar with the Unix/Linux shell, you must have probably used pipes before, something like `ps aux | grep python'` for example to list all Python processes. There are many ways to do this, of course, but let's emulate something similar in Python to see a practical example. To create an easy and consistent output, we will create a file called `lines.txt` with the following lines:

```
spam
eggs
spam spam
eggs eggs
spam spam spam
eggs eggs eggs
```

Now, let's take the following Linux/Unix/Mac shell command to read the file with some modifications:

```
# cat lines.txt | grep spam | sed 's/spam/bacon/g'
bacon
bacon bacon
bacon bacon bacon
```

This reads the file using `cat`, outputs all lines that contain `spam` using `grep`, and replaces `spam` with `bacon` using the `sed` command. Now let's see how we can recreate this with the use of Python generators:

```
>>> def cat(filename):
...     for line in open(filename):
...         yield line.rstrip()
...
>>> def grep(sequence, search):
...     for line in sequence:
...         if search in line:
...             yield line
...
>>> def replace(sequence, search, replace):
...     for line in sequence:
...         yield line.replace(search, replace)
...
>>> lines = cat('lines.txt')
>>> spam_lines = grep(lines, 'spam')
>>> bacon_lines = replace(spam_lines, 'spam', 'bacon')

>>> for line in bacon_lines:
...     print(line)
...
bacon
bacon bacon
bacon bacon bacon
```

```
# Or the one-line version, fits within 78 characters:
>>> for line in replace(grep(cat('lines.txt'), 'spam'),
...                       'spam', 'bacon'):
...     print(line)
...
bacon
bacon bacon
bacon bacon bacon
```

That's the big advantage of generators. You can wrap a list or sequence multiple times with very little performance impact. Not a single one of the functions involved executes anything until a value is requested.

tee – using an output multiple times

As mentioned before, one of the biggest disadvantages of generators is that the results are usable only once. Luckily, Python has a function that allows you to copy the output to several generators. The name tee might be familiar to you if you are used to working in a command-line shell. The tee program allows you to write outputs to both the screen and a file, so you can store an output while still maintaining a live view of it.

The Python version, itertools.tee, does a similar thing except that it returns several iterators, allowing you to process the results separately.

By default, tee will split your generator into a tuple containing two different generators, which is why tuple unpacking works nicely here. By passing along the n parameter, this can easily be changed to support more than 2 generators. Here is an example:

```
>>> import itertools

>>> def spam_and_eggs():
...     yield 'spam'
...     yield 'eggs'

>>> a, b = itertools.tee(spam_and_eggs())
>>> next(a)
'spam'
>>> next(a)
'eggs'
```

```
>>> next(b)
'spam'
>>> next(b)
'eggs'
>>> next(b)
Traceback (most recent call last):
    ...
StopIteration
```

After seeing this code, you might be wondering about the memory usage of tee. Does it need to store the entire list for you? Luckily, no. The tee function is pretty smart in handling this. Assume you have a generator that contains 1,000 items, and you read the first 100 items from a and the first 75 items from b simultaneously. Then tee will only keep the difference (100 - 75 = 25 items) in the memory and drop the rest while you are iterating the results.

Whether tee is the best solution in your case or not depends, of course. If instance a is read from the beginning to (nearly) the end before instance b is read, then it would not be a great idea to use tee. Simply converting the generator to a list would be faster since it involves much fewer operations.

Generating from generators

As we have seen before, we can use generators to filter, modify, add, and remove items. In many cases, however, you'll notice that when writing generators, you'll be returning from sub-generators and/or sequences. An example of this is when creating a powerset using the itertools library:

```
>>> import itertools

>>> def powerset(sequence):
...     for size in range(len(sequence) + 1):
...         for item in itertools.combinations(sequence, size):
...             yield item

>>> for result in powerset('abc'):
...     print(result)
()
('a',)
('b',)
```

```
('c',)
('a', 'b')
('a', 'c')
('b', 'c')
('a', 'b', 'c')
```

This pattern was so common that the yield syntax was actually enhanced to make this even easier. Instead of manually looping over the results, Python 3.3 introduced the `yield from` syntax, which makes this common pattern even simpler:

```
>>> import itertools

>>> def powerset(sequence):
...     for size in range(len(sequence) + 1):
...         yield from itertools.combinations(sequence, size)

>>> for result in powerset('abc'):
...     print(result)
()
('a',)
('b',)
('c',)
('a', 'b')
('a', 'c')
('b', 'c')
('a', 'b', 'c')
```

And that's how you create a powerset in only three lines of code.

Perhaps, a more useful example of this is flattening a sequence recursively:

```
>>> def flatten(sequence):
...     for item in sequence:
...         try:
...             yield from flatten(item)
...         except TypeError:
...             yield item
...
>>> list(flatten([1, [2, [3, [4, 5], 6], 7], 8]))
[1, 2, 3, 4, 5, 6, 7, 8]
```

Note that this code uses `TypeError` to detect non-iterable objects. The result is that if the sequence (which could be a generator) returns a `TypeError`, it will silently hide it.

Also note that this is a very basic flattening function that has no type checking whatsoever. An iterable containing an `str` for example will be flattened recursively until the maximum recursion depth is reached, since every item in an `str` also returns an `str`.

Context managers

As with most of the techniques described in this book, Python also comes bundled with a few useful generators. Some of these (`itertools` and `contextlib.contextmanager` for example) have already been discussed in *Chapter 4, Functional Programming – Readability Versus Brevity* and *Chapter 5, Decorators – Enabling Code Reuse by Decorating* but we can use some extra examples to demonstrate how simple and powerful they can be.

The Python context managers do not appear to be directly related to generators, but that's a large part of what they use internally:

```
>>> import datetime
>>> import contextlib


# Context manager that shows how long a context was active
>>> @contextlib.contextmanager
... def timer(name):
...     start_time = datetime.datetime.now()
...     yield
...     stop_time = datetime.datetime.now()
...     print('%s took %s' % (name, stop_time - start_time))


# The write to log function writes all stdout (regular print data) to
# a file. The contextlib.redirect_stdout context wrapper
# temporarily redirects standard output to a given file handle, in
# this case the file we just opened for writing.
>>> @contextlib.contextmanager
... def write_to_log(name):
...     with open('%s.txt' % name, 'w') as fh:
...         with contextlib.redirect_stdout(fh):
```

```
...            with timer(name):
...                yield


# Use the context manager as a decorator
>>> @write_to_log('some function')
... def some_function():
...     print('This function takes a bit of time to execute')
...     ...
...     print('Do more...')


>>> some_function()
```

While all this works just fine, the three levels of context managers tend to get a bit unreadable. Generally, decorators can solve this. In this case, however, we need the output from one context manager as the input for the next.

That's where ExitStack comes in. It allows easy combining of multiple context managers:

```
>>> import contextlib


>>> @contextlib.contextmanager
... def write_to_log(name):
...     with contextlib.ExitStack() as stack:
...         fh = stack.enter_context(open('stdout.txt', 'w'))
...         stack.enter_context(contextlib.redirect_stdout(fh))
...         stack.enter_context(timer(name))
...
...         yield


>>> @write_to_log('some function')
... def some_function():
...     print('This function takes a bit of time to execute')
...     ...
...     print('Do more...')


>>> some_function()
```

Looks at least a bit simpler, doesn't it? While the necessity is limited in this case, the convenience of ExitStack becomes quickly apparent when you need to do specific teardowns. In addition to the automatic handling as seen before, it's also possible to transfer the contexts to a new ExitStack and manually handle the closing:

```
>>> import contextlib


>>> with contextlib.ExitStack() as stack:
...        spam_fh = stack.enter_context(open('spam.txt', 'w'))
...        eggs_fh = stack.enter_context(open('eggs.txt', 'w'))
...        spam_bytes_written = spam_fh.write('writing to spam')
...        eggs_bytes_written = eggs_fh.write('writing to eggs')
...        # Move the contexts to a new ExitStack and store the
...        # close method
...        close_handlers = stack.pop_all().close


>>> spam_bytes_written = spam_fh.write('still writing to spam')
>>> eggs_bytes_written = eggs_fh.write('still writing to eggs')


# After closing we can't write anymore
>>> close_handlers()
>>> spam_bytes_written = spam_fh.write('cant write anymore')
Traceback (most recent call last):

    ...

ValueError: I/O operation on closed file.
```

Most of the contextlib functions have extensive documentation available in the Python manual. ExitStack in particular is documented using many examples at https://docs.python.org/3/library/contextlib.html#contextlib. ExitStack. I recommend keeping an eye on the contextlib documentation as it is improving greatly with every Python version.

Coroutines

Coroutines are subroutines that offer non-pre-emptive multitasking through multiple entry points. The basic premise is that coroutines allow two functions to communicate with each other while running. Normally, this type of communication is reserved only for multitasking solutions, but coroutines offer a relatively simple way of achieving this at almost no added performance cost.

Since generators are lazy by default, the working of coroutines is fairly obvious. Until a result is consumed, the generator sleeps; but while consuming a result, the generator becomes active. The difference between regular generators and coroutines is that coroutines don't simply return values to the calling function but can receive values as well.

A basic example

In the previous paragraphs, we saw how regular generators can yield values. But that's not all that generators can do. They can actually receive values as well. The basic usage is fairly simple:

```
>>> def generator():
...     value = yield 'spam'
...     print('Generator received: %s' % value)
...     yield 'Previous value: %r' % value


>>> g = generator()
>>> print('Result from generator: %s' % next(g))
Result from generator: spam
>>> print(g.send('eggs'))
Generator received: eggs
Previous value: 'eggs'
```

And that's all there is to it. The function is frozen until the `send` method is called, at which point it will process up to the next `yield` statement.

Priming

Since generators are lazy, you can't just send a value to a brand new generator. Before a value can be sent to the generator, either a result must be fetched using `next()` or a `send(None)` has to be issued so that the code is actually reached. The need for this is understandable but a bit tedious at times. Let's create a simple decorator to omit the need for this:

```
>>> import functools
```

```
>>> def coroutine(function):
...     @functools.wraps(function)
...     def _coroutine(*args, **kwargs):
...         active_coroutine = function(*args, **kwargs)
...         next(active_coroutine)
...         return active_coroutine
...     return _coroutine
```

```
>>> @coroutine
... def spam():
...     while True:
...         print('Waiting for yield...')
...         value = yield
...         print('spam received: %s' % value)

>>> generator = spam()
Waiting for yield...

>>> generator.send('a')
spam received: a
Waiting for yield...

>>> generator.send('b')
spam received: b
Waiting for yield...
```

As you've probably noticed, even though the generator is still lazy, it now automatically executes all of the code until it reaches the `yield` statement again. At that point, it will stay dormant until new values are sent.

 Note that the `coroutine` decorator will be used throughout this chapter from this point onwards. For brevity, we will omit it from the following examples.

Closing and throwing exceptions

Unlike regular generators, which simply exit as soon as the input sequence is exhausted, coroutines generally employ infinite `while` loops, which means that they won't be torn down the normal way. That's why coroutines also support both `close` and `throw` methods, which will exit the function. The important thing here is not the closing but the possibility of adding a teardown method. Essentially, it is very comparable to how context wrappers function with an __enter__ and __exit__ method, but with coroutines in this case:

```python
@coroutine
def simple_coroutine():
    print('Setting up the coroutine')
    try:
        while True:
            item = yield
            print('Got item: %r' % item)
    except GeneratorExit:
        print('Normal exit')
    except Exception as e:
        print('Exception exit: %r' % e)
        raise
    finally:
        print('Any exit')


print('Creating simple coroutine')
active_coroutine = simple_coroutine()
print()

print('Sending spam')
active_coroutine.send('spam')
print()
```

```
print('Close the coroutine')
active_coroutine.close()
print()


print('Creating simple coroutine')
active_coroutine = simple_coroutine()
print()

print('Sending eggs')
active_coroutine.send('eggs')
print()

print('Throwing runtime error')
active_coroutine.throw(RuntimeError, 'Oops...')
print()
```

This generates the following output, which should be as expected—no strange behavior but simply two methods of exiting a coroutine:

```
# python3 H06.py
Creating simple coroutine
Setting up the coroutine

Sending spam
Got item: 'spam'

Close the coroutine
Normal exit
Any exit

Creating simple coroutine
Setting up the coroutine

Sending eggs
Got item: 'eggs'

Throwing runtime error
Exception exit: RuntimeError('Oops...',)
Any exit
```

```
Traceback (most recent call last):
...
  File ... in <module>
    active_coroutine.throw(RuntimeError, 'Oops...')
  File ... in simple_coroutine
    item = yield
RuntimeError: Oops...
```

Bidirectional pipelines

In the previous paragraphs, we saw pipelines; they process the output sequentially and one-way. However, there are cases where this is simply not enough—times where you need a pipe that not only sends values to the next pipe but also receives information back from the sub-pipe. Instead of always having a single list that is processed, we can maintain the state of the generator between executions this way. So, let's start by converting the earlier pipelines to coroutines. First, the lines.txt file again:

```
spam
eggs
spam spam
eggs eggs
spam spam spam
eggs eggs eggs
```

Now, the coroutine pipeline. The functions are the same as before but using coroutines instead:

```
>>> @coroutine
... def replace(search, replace):
...     while True:
...         item = yield
...         print(item.replace(search, replace))


>>> spam_replace = replace('spam', 'bacon')
>>> for line in open('lines.txt'):
...     spam_replace.send(line.rstrip())
bacon
eggs
```

```
bacon bacon
eggs eggs
bacon bacon bacon
eggs eggs eggs
```

Given this example, you might be wondering why we are now printing the value instead of yielding it. Well! We can, but remember that generators freeze until a value is yielded. Let's see what would happen if we simply `yield` the value instead of calling `print`. By default, you might be tempted to do this:

```
>>> @coroutine
... def replace(search, replace):
...     while True:
...         item = yield
...         yield item.replace(search, replace)


>>> spam_replace = replace('spam', 'bacon')
>>> spam_replace.send('spam')
'bacon'
>>> spam_replace.send('spam spam')
>>> spam_replace.send('spam spam spam')
'bacon bacon bacon'
```

Half of the values have disappeared now, so the question is, "Where did they go?" Notice that the second `yield` isn't storing the results. That's where the values are disappearing. We need to store those as well:

```
>>> @coroutine
... def replace(search, replace):
...     item = yield
...     while True:
...         item = yield item.replace(search, replace)


>>> spam_replace = replace('spam', 'bacon')
>>> spam_replace.send('spam')
```

```
'bacon'
>>> spam_replace.send('spam spam')
'bacon bacon'
>>> spam_replace.send('spam spam spam')
'bacon bacon bacon'
```

But even this is far from optimal. We are essentially using coroutines to mimic the behavior of generators right now. Although it works, it's just a tad silly and not all that clear. Let's make a real pipeline this time where the coroutines send the data to the next coroutine (or coroutines) and actually show the power of coroutines by sending the results to multiple coroutines:

```
# Grep sends all matching items to the target
>>> @coroutine
... def grep(target, pattern):
...     while True:
...         item = yield
...         if pattern in item:
...             target.send(item)


# Replace does a search and replace on the items and sends it to
# the target once it's done
>>> @coroutine
... def replace(target, search, replace):
...     while True:
...         target.send((yield).replace(search, replace))


# Print will print the items using the provided formatstring
>>> @coroutine
... def print_(formatstring):
...     while True:
...         print(formatstring % (yield))


# Tee multiplexes the items to multiple targets
>>> @coroutine
... def tee(*targets):
...     while True:
```

```
...             item = yield
...             for target in targets:
...                 target.send(item)


# Because we wrap the results we need to work backwards from the
# inner layer to the outer layer.

# First, create a printer for the items:
>>> printer = print_('%s')

# Create replacers that send the output to the printer
>>> replacer_spam = replace(printer, 'spam', 'bacon')
>>> replacer_eggs = replace(printer, 'spam spam', 'sausage')

# Create a tee to send the input to both the spam and the eggs
# replacers
>>> branch = tee(replacer_spam, replacer_eggs)

# Send all items containing spam to the tee command
>>> grepper = grep(branch, 'spam')

# Send the data to the grepper for all the processing
>>> for line in open('lines.txt'):
...     grepper.send(line.rstrip())
bacon
spam
bacon bacon
sausage
bacon bacon bacon
sausage spam
```

This makes the code much simpler and more readable, but more importantly, it shows how a single source can be split into multiple destinations. While this might not look too exciting, it most certainly is. If you look closely, you will see that the `tee` method splits the input into two different outputs, but both of those outputs write back to the same `print_` instance. This means that it's possible to route your data along whichever way is convenient for you while still having it end up at the same endpoint with no effort whatsoever.

Regardless, the example is still not that useful, as these functions still don't use all of the coroutine's power. The most important feature, a consistent state, is not really used in this case.

The most important lesson to learn from these lines is that mixing generators and coroutines is not a good idea in most cases since it can have very strange side effects if used incorrectly. Even though both use the `yield` statement, they are significantly different creatures with different behavior. The next paragraph will show one of the few cases where mixing coroutines and generators can be useful.

Using the state

Now that we know how to write basic coroutines and which pitfalls we have to take care of, how about writing a function where remembering the state is required? That is, a function that always gives you the average value of all sent values. This is one of the few cases where it is still relatively safe and useful to combine the coroutine and generator syntax:

```
>>> @coroutine
... def average():
...     count = 1
...     total = yield
...     while True:
...         total += yield total / count
...         count += 1

>>> averager = average()
>>> averager.send(20)
20.0
>>> averager.send(10)
15.0
>>> averager.send(15)
15.0
>>> averager.send(-25)
5.0
```

It still requires some extra logic to work properly though. To make sure we don't divide by zero, we initialize the `count` to 1. After that, we fetch our first item using `yield`, but we don't send any data at that point because the first `yield` is the primer and is executed before we get the value. Once that's all set up, we can easily yield the average value while summing. Not all that bad, but the pure coroutine version is slightly simpler to understand since we don't have to worry about priming:

```
>>> @coroutine
... def print_(formatstring):
...     while True:
...         print(formatstring % (yield))


>>> @coroutine
... def average(target):
...     count = 0
...     total = 0
...     while True:
...         count += 1
...         total += yield
...         target.send(total / count)

>>> printer = print_('%.1f')
>>> averager = average(printer)
>>> averager.send(20)
20.0
>>> averager.send(10)
15.0
>>> averager.send(15)
15.0
>>> averager.send(-25)
5.0
```

As simple as it should be, just keeping the count and the total value and simply send the new average for every new value.

Another nice example is `itertools.groupby`, also quite simple to do with coroutines. For comparison, we will once again show both the generator coroutine and the pure coroutine version:

```
>>> @coroutine
... def groupby():
...         # Fetch the first key and value and initialize the state
...         # variables
...         key, value = yield
...         old_key, values = key, []
...         while True:
...             # Store the previous value so we can store it in the
...             # list
...             old_value = value
...             if key == old_key:
...                 key, value = yield
...             else:
...                 key, value = yield old_key, values
...                 old_key, values = key, []
...             values.append(old_value)


>>> grouper = groupby()
>>> grouper.send(('a', 1))
>>> grouper.send(('a', 2))
>>> grouper.send(('a', 3))
>>> grouper.send(('b', 1))
('a', [1, 2, 3])
>>> grouper.send(('b', 2))
>>> grouper.send(('a', 1))
('b', [1, 2])
>>> grouper.send(('a', 2))
>>> grouper.send((None, None))
('a', [1, 2])
```

As you can see, this function uses a few tricks. We store the previous `key` and `value` so that we can detect when the group (`key`) changes. And that is the second issue; we obviously cannot recognize a group until the group has changed, so only after the group has changed will the results be returned. This means that the last group will be sent only if a different group is sent after it, hence the (`None`, `None`). And now, here is the pure coroutine version:

```
>>> @coroutine
... def print_(formatstring):
...     while True:
...         print(formatstring % (yield))


>>> @coroutine
... def groupby(target):
...     old_key = None
...     while True:
...         key, value = yield
...         if old_key != key:
...             # A different key means a new group so send the
...             # previous group and restart the cycle.
...             if old_key and values:
...                 target.send((old_key, values))
...             values = []
...             old_key = key
...         values.append(value)


>>> grouper = groupby(print_('group: %s, values: %s'))
>>> grouper.send(('a', 1))
>>> grouper.send(('a', 2))
>>> grouper.send(('a', 3))
>>> grouper.send(('b', 1))
group: a, values: [1, 2, 3]
>>> grouper.send(('b', 2))
>>> grouper.send(('a', 1))
group: b, values: [1, 2]
>>> grouper.send(('a', 2))
>>> grouper.send((None, None))
group: a, values: [1, 2]
```

While the functions are fairly similar, the pure coroutine version is, once again, quite a bit simpler. This is because we don't have to think about priming and values that might get lost.

Summary

This chapter showed us how to create generators and both the strengths and weaknesses that they possess. Additionally, it should now be clear how to work around their limitations and the implications of doing so.

While the paragraphs about coroutines should have provided some insights into what they are and how they can be used, not everything has been shown yet. We saw the constructs of both pure coroutines and coroutines that are generators at the same time, but they are still all synchronous. The coroutines allow sending the results to many other coroutines, therefore effectively executing many functions at once, but they can still freeze Python completely if an operation turns out to be blocking. That's where our next chapter will help.

Python 3.5 introduced a few useful features, such as the `async` and `await` statements. These make it possible to make coroutines fully asynchronous and non-blocking, whereas this chapter uses the basic coroutine features that have been available since Python 2.5.

The next chapter will expand on the newer features, including the `asyncio` module. This module makes it almost simple to use coroutines for asynchronous I/O to endpoints such as TCP, UDP, files, and processes.

7
Async IO – Multithreading without Threads

The previous chapter showed us the basic implementation of synchronous coroutines. Whenever you are dealing with external resources, however, synchronous coroutines are a bad idea. Just a single stalling remote connection can cause your entire process to hang, unless you are using multiprocessing (explained in *Chapter 13*, *Multiprocessing – When a Single CPU Core Is Not Enough*) or asynchronous functions that is.

Asynchronous IO makes it possible to access external resources without having to worry about slowing down or stalling your application. Instead of actively waiting for results, the Python interpreter can simply continue with other tasks until it is needed again. This is very similar to the functioning of Node.js and AJAX calls in JavaScript. Within Python, we have seen libraries such as `asyncore`, `gevent`, and `eventlet` that have made this possible for years. With the introduction of the `asyncio` module, however, it has become significantly easier to use.

This chapter will explain how asynchronous functions can be used in Python (particularly 3.5 and above) and how code can be restructured in such a way that it still functions even though it doesn't follow the standard procedural coding pattern of returning values.

The following topics will be covered in this chapter:

- Functions using:
    - `async def`
    - `async for`
    - `async with`
    - `await`

- Parallel execution
- Servers
- Clients
- Eventual results using `Future`

Introducing the asyncio library

The `asyncio` library was created to make asynchronous processing much easier and results more predictable. It was introduced with the purpose of replacing the `asyncore` module, which has been available for a very long time (since Python 1.5 in fact). The `asyncore` module was never very usable, which prompted the creation of the `gevent` and `eventlet` third-party libraries. Both `gevent` and `eventlet` make asynchronous programming much easier than `asyncore` ever did, but I feel that both have been made largely obsolete with the introduction of `asyncio`. Even though I have to admit that `asyncio` still has quite a few rough edges, it is in very active development, which makes me think that all the rough edges will soon be fixed by either the core Python library or third-party wrappers.

The `asyncio` library was officially introduced for Python 3.4, but a back port for Python 3.3 is available through the Python Package Index. With that in mind, while some portions of this chapter will be able to run on Python 3.3, most of it has been written with Python 3.5 and the newly introduced `async` and `await` keywords in mind.

The async and await statements

Before we continue with any example, it is important to know how the Python 3.4 and Python 3.5 code syntaxes relate. Even though the `asyncio` library was introduced only in Python 3.4, a large portion of the generic syntax has already been replaced in Python 3.5. Not forcefully, but the easier and therefore recommended syntax using `async` and `await` has been introduced.

Python 3.4

For the traditional Python 3.4 usage, a few things need to be considered:

- Functions should be declared using the `asyncio.coroutine` decorator
- Asynchronous results should be fetched using `yield from coroutine()`
- Asynchronous loops are not directly supported but can be emulated using `while True: yield from coroutine()`

Here is an example:

```python
import asyncio


@asyncio.coroutine
def sleeper():
    yield from asyncio.sleep(1)
```

Python 3.5

In Python 3.5, a new syntax was introduced to mark a function as asynchronous. Instead of the `asyncio.coroutine` decorator, the `async` keyword can be used. Also, instead of the confusing `yield from` syntax, Python now supports the `await` statement. The `yield from` statement was slightly confusing because it might give someone the idea that a value is being exchanged, which is not always the case.

The following is the `async` statement:

```python
async def some_coroutine():
    pass
```

It can be used instead of the decorator:

```python
import asyncio


@asyncio.coroutine
def some_coroutine():
    pass
```

Within Python 3.5, and most likely in future versions as well, the `coroutine` decorator will still be supported, but if backwards compatibility is not an issue, I strongly recommend the new syntax.

Additionally, instead of the `yield from` statement, we can use the much more logical `await` statement. So, the example from the previous paragraph becomes as simple as the following:

```
import asyncio


async def sleeper():
    await asyncio.sleep(1)
```

The `yield from` statement originated from the original coroutines implementation in Python and was a logical extension from the `yield` statement used within synchronous coroutines. Actually, the `yield from` statement still works and the `await` statement is just a wrapper for it, with some added checks. While using `await`, the interpreter checks whether the object is an awaitable object, meaning it needs to be one of the following:

- A native coroutine created with the `async def` statement
- A coroutine created with the `asyncio.coroutine` decorator
- An object that implements the __await__ method

This check alone makes the `await` statement preferable over the `yield from` statement, but I personally think that `await` conveys the meaning of the statement much better as well.

To summarize, to convert to the new syntax, make the following changes:

- Functions should be declared using `async def` instead of `def`
- Asynchronous results should be fetched using `await coroutine()`
- Asynchronous loops can be created using `async for ... in ...`
- Asynchronous `with` statements can be created using `async with ...`

Choosing between the 3.4 and 3.5 syntax

Unless you really need Python 3.3 or 3.4 support, I would strongly recommend the Python 3.5 syntax. The new syntax is clearer and supports more features, such as asynchronous `for` loops and `with` statements. Unfortunately, they are not fully compatible, so you need to make a choice. Within an `async def` (3.5), we cannot use `yield from`, but all we need to do to fix that is replace `yield from` with `await`.

A simple example of single-threaded parallel processing

Parallel processing has many uses: a server taking care of multiple requests at the same time, speeding up heavy tasks, waiting for external resources, and much more. Generic coroutines can help with handling multiple requests and external resources in some cases, but they are still synchronous and therefore limited. With `asyncio`, we can transcend the limitations of generic coroutines and easily handle stalling resources without having to worry about blocking the main thread. Let's see a quick example of how the code does not stall with multiple parallel functions:

```
>>> import asyncio


>>> async def sleeper(delay):
...     await asyncio.sleep(delay)
...     print('Finished sleeper with delay: %d' % delay)


>>> loop = asyncio.get_event_loop()
>>> results = loop.run_until_complete(asyncio.wait((
...     sleeper(1),
...     sleeper(3),
...     sleeper(2),
... )))
Finished sleeper with delay: 1
Finished sleeper with delay: 2
Finished sleeper with delay: 3
```

Even though we started the sleepers with the order of 1, 3, 2, which sleeps for that amount of time, `asyncio.sleep` combined with the `await` statement actually tells Python that it should just continue with a task that needs actual processing at this time. A regular `time.sleep` would actually stall the Python task, meaning they would execute sequentially. This makes it somewhat more obviously transparent what these can be used for, as it handles any type of wait, which we can hand off to `asyncio` instead of keeping the entire Python thread busy. So, instead of `while True: fh.read()`, we can just respond whenever there is new data.

Let's analyze the components used in this example:

- `asyncio.coroutine`: This decorator enables yielding from `async def` coroutines. Unless you are using this syntax, there is no real need for the decorator, but it's a good default if only used as documentation.

- `asyncio.sleep`: This is the asynchronous version of `time.sleep`. The big difference between these two is that `time.sleep` will keep the Python process busy while it is sleeping, whereas `asyncio.sleep` will allow switching to a different task within the event loop. This process is very similar to the workings of task switching in most operating systems.

- `asyncio.get_event_loop`: The default event loop is effectively the `asyncio` task switcher; we'll explain more about these in the next paragraph.

- `asyncio.wait`: This is the coroutine for wrapping a sequence of coroutines or futures and waiting for the results. The wait time is configurable, as is the manner of waiting (first done, all done, or the first exception).

That should explain the basic workings of the example: the `sleeper` function is the asynchronous coroutine, which exits after the given delay. The `wait` function waits for all coroutines to finish before exiting, and the `event` loop is used for switching between the three coroutines.

Concepts of asyncio

The `asyncio` library has several basic concepts, which have to be explained before we venture further into examples and uses. The example shown in the previous paragraph actually used most of them, but a little explanation about the how and the why might still be useful.

The main concepts of `asyncio` are *coroutines* and *event loops*. Within them, there are several helper classes available, such as `Streams`, `Futures`, and `Processes`. The next few paragraphs will explain the basics so that you can understand the implementations in the examples in the later paragraphs.

Futures and tasks

The `asyncio.Future` class is essentially a promise of a result; it returns the results if they are available, and once it receives results, it will pass them along to all the registered callbacks. It maintains a state variable internally, which allows an outside party to mark a future as canceled. The API is very similar to the `concurrent.futures.Future` class, but since they are not fully compatible, make sure you do not confuse the two.

The `Future` class by itself is not that convenient to use though, so that is where `asyncio.Task` comes in. The `Task` class wraps a coroutine and automatically handles the execution, results, and state for you. The coroutine will be executed through the given event loop, or the default event loop if none was given.

The creation of these classes is not something you need to worry about directly. This is because instead of creating the class yourself, the recommended way is through either `asyncio.ensure_future` or `loop.create_task`. The former actually executes `loop.create_task` internally but it is more convenient if you simply want to execute it on the main/default event loop without having to specify it first. The usage is simple enough. To create your own future manually, you simply tell the event loop to execute `create_task` for you. The following example is a bit complicated because of all the setup code but the usage of C should be clear enough. The most important aspect to note is that the event loop should be linked so that the task knows how/where to run:

```
>>> import asyncio


>>> async def sleeper(delay):
...         await asyncio.sleep(delay)
...         print('Finished sleeper with delay: %d' % delay)


# Create an event loop
>>> loop = asyncio.get_event_loop()


# Create the task
>>> result = loop.call_soon(loop.create_task, sleeper(1))


# Make sure the loop stops after 2 seconds
>>> result = loop.call_later(2, loop.stop)


# Start the loop and make it run forever. Or at least until the loop.stop gets
# called in 2 seconds.
>>> loop.run_forever()
Finished sleeper with delay: 1
```

Now, a little bit about debugging asynchronous functions. Debugging asynchronous functions used to be very difficult if not impossible, as there was no good way to see where and how the functions were stalling. Luckily, that has changed. In the case of the `Task` class, it is as simple as calling `task.get_stack` or `task.print_stack` to see where it is currently. The usage can be as simple as the following:

```
>>> import asyncio


>>> async def stack_printer():
...        for task in asyncio.Task.all_tasks():
...            task.print_stack()

# Create an event loop
>>> loop = asyncio.get_event_loop()

# Create the task
>>> result = loop.run_until_complete(stack_printer())
```

Event loops

The concept of event loops is actually the most important one within `asyncio`. You might have suspected that the coroutines themselves are what everything is about, but without the event loop, they are useless. Event loops function as task switchers, just the way operating systems switch between active tasks on the CPU. Even with multicore processors, there is still a need for a main process to tell the CPU which tasks have to run and which need to wait/sleep for a while. This is exactly what the event loop does: it decides which task to run.

Event loop implementations

So far, we have only seen `asyncio.get_event_loop`, which returns the default event loop with the default event loop policy. Currently, there are two bundled event loop implementations: the `async.SelectorEventLoop` and `async.ProactorEventLoop` implementations. Which of the two is available depends on your operating system. The latter event loop is available only on Windows machines and uses I/O Completion Ports, which is a system that is supposedly faster and more efficient than the `Select` implementation of `asyncio.SelectorEventLoop`. This is something to consider if performance is an issue. The usage is simple enough, luckily:

```
import asyncio


loop = asyncio.ProActorEventLoop()
asyncio.set_event_loop(loop)
```

The alternative event loop is based on selectors, which, since Python 3.4, are available through the `selectors` module in the core Python installation. The `selectors` module was introduced in Python 3.4 to enable easy access to low-level asynchronous I/O operations. Basically, it allows you to open and read from many files by using I/O multiplexing. Since `asyncio` handles all complexities for you, there is generally no need to use the module directly, but the usage is simple enough if you need it. Here's an example of binding a function to the read event (EVENT_READ) on the standard input. The code will simply wait until one of the registered files provides new data:

```
import sys
import selectors


def read(fh):
    print('Got input from stdin: %r' % fh.readline())


if __name__ == '__main__':
    # Create the default selector
    selector = selectors.DefaultSelector()

    # Register the read function for the READ event on stdin
    selector.register(sys.stdin, selectors.EVENT_READ, read)

    while True:
        for key, mask in selector.select():
            # The data attribute contains the read function here
            callback = key.data
            # Call it with the fileobj (stdin here)
            callback(key.fileobj)
```

There are several selectors available, such as the traditional `selectors.SelectSelector` (which uses `select.select` internally), but there are also more modern solutions such as `selectors.KqueueSelector`, `selectors.EpollSelector`, and `selectors.DevpollSelector`. Even though it should select the most efficient selector by default, there are cases where the most efficient one is not suitable in some way or another. In those cases, the selector event loop allows you to specify a different selector:

```
import asyncio
import selectors


selector = selectors.SelectSelector()
loop = asyncio.SelectorEventLoop(selector)
asyncio.set_event_loop(loop)
```

It should be noted that the differences between these selectors are generally too small to notice in most real-world applications. The only situation I have come across where such an optimization makes a difference is when building a server that has to handle a lot of simultaneous connections. With "a lot," I am referring to over 100,000 concurrent connections on a single server, which is a problem only a few people on this planet have had to deal with.

Event loop policies

Event loop policies are objects that create and store the actual event loops for you. They have been written with maximum flexibility in mind but are not objects that you often need to modify. The only reason I can think of modifying the event loop policy is if you want to make specific event loops run on specific processors and/ or systems, or if you wish to change the default event loop type. Beyond that, it offers more flexibility than most people will ever need. Making your own event loop (`ProActorEventLoop` in this case) the default is simply possible through this code:

```
import asyncio


class ProActorEventLoopPolicy(
        asyncio.events.BaseDefaultEventLoopPolicy):
    _loop_factory = asyncio.SelectorEventLoop


policy = ProActorEventLoopPolicy()
asyncio.set_event_loop_policy(policy)
```

Event loop usage

So far, we have only seen the `loop.run_until_complete` method. Naturally, there are a few others as well. The one you will most likely use most often is `loop.run_forever`. This method, as you might expect, keeps running forever, or at least until `loop.stop` has been run.

So, assuming we have an event loop running forever now, we need to add tasks to it. This is where things get interesting. There are quite a few choices available within the default event loops:

- `call_soon`: Add an item to the end of the (FIFO) queue so that the functions will be executed in the order in which they were inserted.

- `call_soon_threadsafe`: This is the same as `call_soon` except for being thread safe. The `call_soon` method is not thread safe because thread safety requires the usage of the global interpreter lock (GIL), which effectively makes your program single threaded at the moment of thread safety. The performance chapter will explain this more thoroughly.

- `call_later`: Call the function after the given number of seconds. If two jobs would run at the same time, they will run in an undefined order. Note that the delay is a minimum. If the event loop is locked/busy, it can run later.

- `call_at`: Call a function at a specific time related to the output of `loop.time`. Every integer after `loop.time` adds a second.

All of these functions return `asyncio.Handle` objects. These objects allow the cancellation of the task through the `handle.cancel` function as long as it has not been executed yet. Be careful with canceling from other threads, however, as cancellation is not thread safe either. To execute it in a thread-safe way, we have to execute the cancellation function as a task as well: `loop.call_soon_threadsafe(handle.cancel)`. The following is an example usage:

```
>>> import time
>>> import asyncio


>>> t = time.time()


>>> def printer(name):
...     print('Started %s at %.1f' % (name, time.time() - t))
...     time.sleep(0.2)
...     print('Finished %s at %.1f' % (name, time.time() - t))



>>> loop = asyncio.get_event_loop()
>>> result = loop.call_at(loop.time() + .2, printer, 'call_at')
>>> result = loop.call_later(.1, printer, 'call_later')
>>> result = loop.call_soon(printer, 'call_soon')
>>> result = loop.call_soon_threadsafe(printer, 'call_soon_threadsafe')

>>> # Make sure we stop after a second
>>> result = loop.call_later(1, loop.stop)

>>> loop.run_forever()
Started call_soon at 0.0
Finished call_soon at 0.2
Started call_soon_threadsafe at 0.2
```

```
Finished call_soon_threadsafe at 0.4

Started call_later at 0.4

Finished call_later at 0.6

Started call_at at 0.6

Finished call_at at 0.8
```

You might be wondering why we are not using the coroutine decorator here. The reason is that the loop won't allow running of coroutines directly. To run a coroutine through these call functions, we need to make sure that it is wrapped in an `asyncio.Task`. As we have seen in the previous paragraph, this is easy enough—luckily:

```
>>> import time
>>> import asyncio


>>> t = time.time()


>>> async def printer(name):
...     print('Started %s at %.1f' % (name, time.time() - t))
...     await asyncio.sleep(0.2)
...     print('Finished %s at %.1f' % (name, time.time() - t))


>>> loop = asyncio.get_event_loop()


>>> result = loop.call_at(
...     loop.time() + .2, loop.create_task, printer('call_at'))
>>> result = loop.call_later(.1, loop.create_task,
...     printer('call_later'))
>>> result = loop.call_soon(loop.create_task,
...     printer('call_soon'))

>>> result = loop.call_soon_threadsafe(
...     loop.create_task, printer('call_soon_threadsafe'))

>>> # Make sure we stop after a second
>>> result = loop.call_later(1, loop.stop)
```

```
>>> loop.run_forever()
Started call_soon at 0.0
Started call_soon_threadsafe at 0.0
Started call_later at 0.1
Started call_at at 0.2
Finished call_soon at 0.2
Finished call_soon_threadsafe at 0.2
Finished call_later at 0.3
Finished call_at at 0.4
```

These call methods might appear slightly different but the internals actually boil down to two queues that are implemented through `heapq`. The `loop._scheduled` is used for scheduled operations and `loop._ready` is for immediate execution. When the `_run_once` method is called (the `run_forever` method wraps this method in a `while True` loop), the loop will first try to process all items in the `loop._ready` heap with the specific loop implementation (for example, `SelectorEventLoop`). Once everything in `loop._ready` is processed, the loop will continue to move items from the `loop._scheduled` heap to the `loop._ready` heap if they are due.

Both `call_soon` and `call_soon_threadsafe` write to the `loop._ready` heap. And the `call_later` method is simply a wrapper for `call_at` with the current value of `asyncio.time` added to the scheduled time, which writes to the `loop._scheduled` heap.

The result of this method of processing is that everything added through the `call_soon*` methods will always execute after everything that is added through the `call_at`/`call_later` methods.

As for the `ensure_futures` function, it will call `loop.create_task` internally to wrap the coroutine in a `Task` object, which is, of course, a subclass of a `Future` object. If you need to extend the `Task` class for some reason, that is easily possible through the `loop.set_task_factory` method.

Depending on the type of event loop, there are actually many other methods for creating connections, file handlers, and more. Those will be explained by example in later paragraphs, since they have less to do with the event loop and are more about programming with coroutines.

Processes

So far, we have simply executed specifically asynchronous Python functions, but some things are a tad more difficult to run asynchronously within Python. For example, let's assume we have a long-running external application that we wish to run. The subprocess module would be the standard approach for running external applications, and it works quite well. With a bit of care, one could even make sure that these do not block the main thread by polling the output. That still requires polling, however. Yet, won't events be better so that we can do other things while we are waiting for the results? Luckily, this is easily arranged through asyncio.Process. Similar to the Future and Task classes, this class is meant to be created through the event loop. In terms of usage, the class is very similar to the subprocess.Popen class, except that the functions have been made asynchronous. This results in the removal of the polling function, of course.

First, let's look at the traditional sequential version:

```
>>> import time
>>> import subprocess
>>>
>>>
>>> t = time.time()
>>>
>>>
>>> def process_sleeper():
...     print('Started sleep at %.1f' % (time.time() - t))
...     process = subprocess.Popen(['sleep', '0.1'])
...     process.wait()
...     print('Finished sleep at %.1f' % (time.time() - t))
...
>>>
>>> for i in range(3):
...     process_sleeper()
Started sleep at 0.0
Finished sleep at 0.1
Started sleep at 0.1
Finished sleep at 0.2
Started sleep at 0.2
Finished sleep at 0.3
```

Since everything is executed sequentially, it takes three times the 0.1 seconds that the sleep command is sleeping. So, instead of waiting for all of them at the same time, let's run them in parallel this time:

```
>>> import time
>>> import subprocess


>>> t = time.time()


>>> def process_sleeper():
...     print('Started sleep at %.1f' % (time.time() - t))
...     return subprocess.Popen(['sleep', '0.1'])
...
>>>
>>> processes = []
>>> for i in range(5):
...     processes.append(process_sleeper())
Started sleep at 0.0
Started sleep at 0.0
Started sleep at 0.0
Started sleep at 0.0
Started sleep at 0.0

>>> for process in processes:
...     returncode = process.wait()
...     print('Finished sleep at %.1f' % (time.time() - t))
Finished sleep at 0.1
Finished sleep at 0.1
Finished sleep at 0.1
Finished sleep at 0.1
Finished sleep at 0.1
```

While this looks a lot better in terms of runtime, our program structure is a bit messy now. We needed two loops, one to start the processes and one to measure the finish time. Moreover, we had to move the print statement outside of the function, which is generally not desirable either. This time, we will try the `asyncio` version:

```
>>> import time
>>> import asyncio


>>> t = time.time()


>>> async def async_process_sleeper():
...     print('Started sleep at %.1f' % (time.time() - t))
...     process = await asyncio.create_subprocess_exec('sleep', '0.1')
...     await process.wait()
...     print('Finished sleep at %.1f' % (time.time() - t))


>>> loop = asyncio.get_event_loop()
>>> for i in range(5):
...     task = loop.create_task(async_process_sleeper())

>>> future = loop.call_later(.5, loop.stop)

>>> loop.run_forever()
Started sleep at 0.0
Started sleep at 0.0
Started sleep at 0.0
Started sleep at 0.0
Started sleep at 0.0
Finished sleep at 0.1
Finished sleep at 0.1
Finished sleep at 0.1
Finished sleep at 0.1
Finished sleep at 0.1
```

As you can see, it is easy to run multiple applications at the same time this way. But that is the easy part; the difficult part with processes is interactive input and output. The `asyncio` module has several measures to make it easier, but it can still be difficult when actually working with the results. Here's an example of calling the Python interpreter, executing some code, and exiting again:

```python
import asyncio


async def run_script():
    process = await asyncio.create_subprocess_shell(
        'python3',
        stdout=asyncio.subprocess.PIPE,
        stdin=asyncio.subprocess.PIPE,
    )

    # Write a simple Python script to the interpreter
    process.stdin.write(b'\n'.join((
        b'import math',
        b'x = 2 ** 8',
        b'y = math.sqrt(x)',
        b'z = math.sqrt(y)',
        b'print("x: %d" % x)',
        b'print("y: %d" % y)',
        b'print("z: %d" % z)',
        b'for i in range(int(z)):',
        b'    print("i: %d" % i)',
    )))
    # Make sure the stdin is flushed asynchronously
    await process.stdin.drain()
    # And send the end of file so the Python interpreter will
    # start processing the input. Without this the process will
    # stall forever.
    process.stdin.write_eof()

    # Fetch the lines from the stdout asynchronously
    async for out in process.stdout:
        # Decode the output from bytes and strip the whitespace
        # (newline) at the right
        print(out.decode('utf-8').rstrip())

    # Wait for the process to exit
```

```
        await process.wait()


    if __name__ == '__main__':
        loop = asyncio.get_event_loop()
        loop.run_until_complete(run_script())
        loop.close()
```

The code is simple enough, but there are a few parts of this code that are not obvious to us and yet required to function. While the creation of the subprocess and the writing code is quite obvious, you might be wondering about the `process.stdin.write_eof()` line. The problem here is buffering. To improve performance, most programs will buffer input and output by default. In the case of the Python program, the result is that unless we send the **end of file** (**eof**), the program will keep waiting for more input. An alternative solution would be to close the `stdin` stream or somehow communicate with the Python program that we will not send any more input. However, it is certainly something to take into consideration. Another option is to use `yield` from `process.stdin.drain()`, but that only takes care of the sending side of the code; the receiving side might still be waiting for more input. Let's see the output though:

```
# python3 processes.py

x: 256

y: 16

z: 4

i: 0

i: 1

i: 2

i: 3
```

With this implementation, we still need a loop to get all the results from the `stdout` stream. Unfortunately, the `asyncio.StreamReader` (which `process.stdout` is) class does not support the `async for` syntax yet. If it did, a simple `async for out in process.stdout` would have worked. A simple `yield from process.stdout.read()` would have worked as well, but reading per line is generally more convenient to use.

If possible, I recommend that you abstain from using `stdin` to send data to subprocesses and instead use some network, pipe, or file communication. As we will see in the next paragraphs, these are much more convenient to handle.

Asynchronous servers and clients

One of the most common reason for stalling scripts and applications is the usage of remote resources. With `asyncio`, at least a large portion of that is easily fixable. Fetching multiple remote resources and serving to multiple clients is quite a bit easier and more lightweight than it used to be. While both multithreading and multiprocessing can be used for these cases as well, `asyncio` is a much lighter alternative and it is actually easier to manage. There are two main methods of creating clients and servers. The coroutine way is to use `asyncio.open_connection` and `asyncio.start_server`. The class-based approach requires you to inherit the `asyncio.Protocol` class. While these are essentially the same thing, the workings are slightly different.

Basic echo server

The basic client and server versions are simple enough to write. The `asyncio` module takes care of all the low-level connection handling, leaving us with only the requirement of connecting the correct methods. For the server, we need a method to handle the incoming connections, and for the client, we need a function to create connections. And to illustrate what is happening and at which point in time, we will add a dedicated print function that prints both the time since the server process was started and the given arguments:

```python
import time
import sys
import asyncio


HOST = '127.0.0.1'
PORT = 1234


start_time = time.time()


def printer(start_time, *args, **kwargs):
    '''Simple function to print a message prefixed with the
    time relative to the given start_time'''
    print('%.1f' % (time.time() - start_time), *args, **kwargs)


async def handle_connection(reader, writer):
    client_address = writer.get_extra_info('peername')
    printer(start_time, 'Client connected', client_address)

    # Send over the server start time to get consistent
    # timestamps
    writer.write(b'%.2f\n' % start_time)
    await writer.drain()
```

```
        repetitions = int((await reader.readline()))
        printer(start_time, 'Started sending to', client_address)

        for i in range(repetitions):
            message = 'client: %r, %d\n' % (client_address, i)
            printer(start_time, message, end='')
            writer.write(message.encode())
            await writer.drain()

        printer(start_time, 'Finished sending to', client_address)
        writer.close()


    async def create_connection(repetitions):
        reader, writer = await asyncio.open_connection(
            host=HOST, port=PORT)

        start_time = float((await reader.readline()))

        writer.write(repetitions.encode() + b'\n')
        await writer.drain()

        async for line in reader:
            # Sleeping a little to emulate processing time and make
            # it easier to add more simultaneous clients
            await asyncio.sleep(1)

            printer(start_time, 'Got line: ', line.decode(),
                    end='')

        writer.close()


    if __name__ == '__main__':
        loop = asyncio.get_event_loop()

        if sys.argv[1] == 'server':
            server = asyncio.start_server(
                handle_connection,
                host=HOST,
                port=PORT,
            )
            running_server = loop.run_until_complete(server)

            try:
                result = loop.call_later(5, loop.stop)
                loop.run_forever()
            except KeyboardInterrupt:
                pass
```

```
        running_server.close()
        loop.run_until_complete(running_server.wait_closed())
    elif sys.argv[1] == 'client':
        loop.run_until_complete(create_connection(sys.argv[2]))

    loop.close()
```

Now we will run the server and two simultaneous clients. Since these run in parallel, the server output is a bit strange, of course. Because of that, we synchronize the start time from the server to the clients and prefix all print statements with the number of seconds since the server was started.

The server:

```
# python3 simple_connections.py server
0.4 Client connected ('127.0.0.1', 59990)
0.4 Started sending to ('127.0.0.1', 59990)
0.4 client: ('127.0.0.1', 59990), 0
0.4 client: ('127.0.0.1', 59990), 1
0.4 client: ('127.0.0.1', 59990), 2
0.4 Finished sending to ('127.0.0.1', 59990)
2.0 Client connected ('127.0.0.1', 59991)
2.0 Started sending to ('127.0.0.1', 59991)
2.0 client: ('127.0.0.1', 59991), 0
2.0 client: ('127.0.0.1', 59991), 1
2.0 Finished sending to ('127.0.0.1', 59991)
```

The first client:

```
# python3 simple_connections.py client 3
1.4 Got line:  client: ('127.0.0.1', 59990), 0
2.4 Got line:  client: ('127.0.0.1', 59990), 1
3.4 Got line:  client: ('127.0.0.1', 59990), 2
```

The second client:

```
# python3 simple_connections.py client 2
3.0 Got line:  client: ('127.0.0.1', 59991), 0
4.0 Got line:  client: ('127.0.0.1', 59991), 1
```

Since both the input and output have buffers, we need to manually drain the input after writing and use `yield from` when reading the output from the other party. That is exactly the reason that communication with regular external processes is more difficult than network interaction. The standard input for processes is more focused towards user input than computer input, which makes it less convenient to use.

If you wish to use `reader.read(BUFFER)` instead of `reader.readline()`, that's also possible. Just note that you need to specifically separate the data because it might accidently get appended otherwise. All write operations write to the same buffer, resulting in one long return stream. On the other hand, trying to write without a new line (\n) for `reader.readline()` to recognize will cause the client to wait forever.

Summary

In this chapter, we saw how to use asynchronous I/O in Python using `asyncio`. For many scenarios, the `asyncio` module is still a bit raw and unfinished, but there should not be any obstacles in using it. Creating a fully functional server/client setup is still a tad complicated, but the most obvious use of `asyncio` is the handling of basic network I/O such as database connections and external resources such as websites. Especially, the latter takes only a few lines to implement with the use of `asyncio`, removing some very important bottlenecks from your code.

The point of this chapter is understanding how to tell Python to wait for results in the background instead of simply waiting or polling for them as usual. In *Chapter 13, Multiprocessing – When a Single CPU Core Is Not Enough* you will learn about multiprocessing, which is also an option for handling stalling resources. However, the goal of multiprocessing is actually to use multiple processors instead of handling stalling resources. When it comes to potentially slow external resources, I recommend that you always use `asyncio`, if at all possible.

When building utilities based on the `asyncio` library, make sure you search for premade libraries to solve your problems, as many of them are currently being developed. While writing this chapter, Python 3.5 was not officially out yet, so the odds are that a lot more documentation and libraries using the `async/await` syntax will pop up soon. To make sure you do not repeat work that others have done, search the Internet thoroughly before writing your own code extending on `asyncio`.

The next chapter will explain a completely different topic—the construction of classes using metaclasses. Regular classes are created using the type class, but now we will see how we can extend and modify the default behavior to make a class do pretty much anything we want. Metaclasses even make it possible to have automatically registering plugins and add features to classes in a very magical way—in short, how to customize not just the class instances but the class definitions themselves.

8
Metaclasses – Making Classes (Not Instances) Smarter

The previous chapters have already shown us how to modify classes and functions using decorators. But that's not the only option to modify or extend a class. An even more advanced technique of modifying your classes before creation is the usage of **metaclasses**. The name already gives a hint to what it could be; a metaclass is a class containing meta information about a class.

The basic premise of a metaclass is a class that generates another class for you at definition time, so generally you wouldn't use it to change the class instances but only the class definitions. By changing the class definitions, it is possible to automatically add some properties to a class, validate whether certain properties are set, change inheritance, automatically register the class at a manager, and do many other things.

Although metaclasses are generally considered to be a more powerful technique than (class) decorators, effectively they don't differ too much in possibilities. The choice usually comes down to either convenience or personal preference.

The following topics are covered in this chapter:

- Basic dynamic class creation
- Metaclasses with arguments
- Internals of class creation, the order of operations
- Abstract base classes, examples and inner workings
- Automatic plugin system using metaclasses
- Storing definition order of class attributes

Dynamically creating classes

Metaclasses are the factories that create new classes in Python. In fact, even though you may not be aware of it, Python will always execute the `type` metaclass whenever you create a class.

When creating classes in a procedural way, the `type` metaclass is used as a function. This function takes three arguments: `name`, `bases`, and `dict`. The name will become the `__name__` attribute, the `bases` is the list of inherited base classes and will be stored in `__bases__` and `dict` is the namespace dictionary that contains all variables and will be stored in `__dict__`.

It should be noted that the `type()` function has another use as well. Given the arguments documented earlier, it creates a class given those specifications. Given a single argument with the instance of a class, it will return the class as well but from the instance. Your next question might be, "What happens if I call `type()` on a class definition instead of a class instance?" Well, that returns the metaclass for the class which is `type` by default.

Let's clarify this using a few examples:

```
>>> class Spam(object):
>>>     eggs = 'my eggs'


>>> Spam = type('Spam', (object,), dict(eggs='my eggs'))
```

The preceding two definitions of `Spam` are completely identical; they both create a class with an instantiated property of `eggs` and `object` as a base. Let's test if this actually works as you would expect:

```
>>> class Spam(object):
...     eggs = 'my eggs'


>>> spam = Spam()
>>> spam.eggs
'my eggs'
>>> type(spam)
<class '...Spam'>
>>> type(Spam)
<class 'type'>
```

```
>>> Spam = type('Spam', (object,), dict(eggs='my eggs'))

>>> spam = Spam()
>>> spam.eggs
'my eggs'
>>> type(spam)
<class '...Spam'>
>>> type(Spam)
<class 'type'>
```

As expected, the results for the two are the same. When creating a class, Python silently adds the `type` metaclass and `custom` metaclasses are simply classes that inherit `type`. A simple class definition has a silent metaclass making a simple definition such as:

```
class Spam(object):
    pass
```

Essentially identical to:

```
class Spam(object, metaclass=type):
    pass
```

This raises the question that if every class is created by a (silent) metaclass, what is the metaclass of `type`? This is actually a recursive definition; the metaclass of `type` is `type`. This is the essence of what a custom metaclass is: a class that inherits type to allow class modification without needing to modify the class definition itself.

A basic metaclass

Since metaclasses can modify any class attribute, you can do absolutely anything you wish. Before we continue with more advanced metaclasses, let's look at a basic example:

```
# The metaclass definition, note the inheritance of type instead
# of object
>>> class MetaSpam(type):
...
...     # Notice how the __new__ method has the same arguments
...     # as the type function we used earlier?
...     def __new__(metaclass, name, bases, namespace):
...         name = 'SpamCreatedByMeta'
```

```
...             bases = (int,) + bases
...             namespace['eggs'] = 1
...             return type.__new__(metaclass, name, bases, namespace)


# First, the regular Spam:
>>> class Spam(object):
...     pass


>>> Spam.__name__
'Spam'
>>> issubclass(Spam, int)
False
>>> Spam.eggs
Traceback (most recent call last):
    ...
AttributeError: type object 'Spam' has no attribute 'eggs'


# Now the meta-Spam
>>> class Spam(object, metaclass=MetaSpam):
...     pass


>>> Spam.__name__
'SpamCreatedByMeta'
>>> issubclass(Spam, int)
True
>>> Spam.eggs
1
```

As you can see, everything about the class definition can easily be modified using metaclasses. This makes it both a very powerful and a very dangerous tool, as you can easily cause very unexpected behavior.

Arguments to metaclasses

The possibility of adding arguments to a metaclass is a little-known feature, but very useful nonetheless. In many cases, simply adding attributes or methods to a class definition is enough to detect what to do, but there are cases where it is useful to be more specific.

```
>>> class MetaWithArguments(type):
...     def __init__(metaclass, name, bases, namespace, **kwargs):
...         # The kwargs should not be passed on to the
...         # type.__init__
...         type.__init__(metaclass, name, bases, namespace)
...
...     def __new__(metaclass, name, bases, namespace, **kwargs):
...         for k, v in kwargs.items():
...             namespace.setdefault(k, v)
...
...         return type.__new__(metaclass, name, bases, namespace)


>>> class WithArgument(metaclass=MetaWithArguments, spam='eggs'):
...     pass


>>> with_argument = WithArgument()
>>> with_argument.spam
'eggs'
```

This simplistic example may not be useful but the possibilities are. The only thing you need to keep in mind is that both the __new__ and __init__ methods need to be extended for this to work.

Accessing metaclass attributes through classes

When using metaclasses, it might be confusing to note that the class actually does more than simply construct the class, it actually inherits the class during the creation. To illustrate:

```
>>> class Meta(type):
...
...     @property
```

```
...        def spam(cls):
...            return 'Spam property of %r' % cls
...
...        def eggs(self):
...            return 'Eggs method of %r' % self


>>> class SomeClass(metaclass=Meta):
...        pass


>>> SomeClass.spam
"Spam property of <class '...SomeClass'>"
>>> SomeClass().spam
Traceback (most recent call last):
    ...
AttributeError: 'SomeClass' object has no attribute 'spam'

>>> SomeClass.eggs()
"Eggs method of <class '...SomeClass'>"
>>> SomeClass().eggs()
Traceback (most recent call last):
    ...
AttributeError: 'SomeClass' object has no attribute 'eggs'
```

As can be seen in the preceding example, these methods are only available for the `class` objects and not the instances. The `spam` attribute and the `eggs` method are not accessible through the instance while they are accessible through the class. I personally don't see any useful cases for this behavior but it is definitely noteworthy.

Abstract classes using collections.abc

The abstract base classes module is one of the most useful and most used examples of metaclasses in Python, as it makes it easy to ensure that a class adheres to a certain interface without a lot of manual checks. We have already seen some examples of abstract base classes in the previous chapters, but now we will look at the inner workings of these and the more advanced features, such as custom ABCs.

Internal workings of the abstract classes

First, let's demonstrate the usage of the regular abstract base class:

```
>>> import abc

>>> class Spam(metaclass=abc.ABCMeta):
...
...     @abc.abstractmethod
...     def some_method(self):
...         raise NotImplemented()


>>> class Eggs(Spam):
...     def some_new_method(self):
...         pass


>>> eggs = Eggs()
Traceback (most recent call last):
    ...
TypeError: Can't instantiate abstract class Eggs with abstract
methods some_method


>>> class Bacon(Spam):
...     def some_method():
...         pass


>>> bacon = Bacon()
```

As you can see, the abstract base class blocks us from instantiating the classes until all the abstract methods have been inherited. In addition to the regular methods, `property`, `staticmethod`, and `classmethod` are also supported.

```
>>> import abc

>>> class Spam(object, metaclass=abc.ABCMeta):
...     @property
```

```
...         @abc.abstractmethod
...         def some_property(self):
...             raise NotImplemented()
...
...         @classmethod
...         @abc.abstractmethod
...         def some_classmethod(cls):
...             raise NotImplemented()
...
...         @staticmethod
...         @abc.abstractmethod
...         def some_staticmethod():
...             raise NotImplemented()
...
...         @abc.abstractmethod
...         def some_method():
...             raise NotImplemented()
```

So what does Python do internally? You could, of course, read the `abc.py` source code but I think a simple explanation would be better.

First, `abc.abstractmethod` sets the `__isabstractmethod__` property on the function to `True`. So if you don't want to use the decorator, you can simply emulate the behavior by doing something along the lines of:

```
some_method.__isabstractmethod__ = True
```

After that, the `abc.ABCMeta` metaclass walks through all the items in a namespace and looks for objects where the `__isabstractmethod__` attribute evaluates to `True`. In addition to that, it walks through all bases and checks the `__abstractmethods__` set for every base class, in case the class inherits an `abstract` class. All the items where `__isabstractmethod__` still evaluates to `True` get added to the `__abstractmethods__` set which is stored in the class as `frozenset`.

> Note that we don't use `abc.abstractproperty`, `abc.abstractclassmethod`, and `abc.abstractstaticmethod`. Since Python 3.3 these have been deprecated as the `classmethod`, `staticmethod`, and `property` decorators are recognized by `abc.abstractmethod` so a simple `property` decorator followed by a `abc.abstractmethod` is recognized as well. Take care when ordering the decorators; `abc.abstractmethod` needs to be the innermost decorator for this to work properly.

The next question now is about where the actual checks come in; the checks to see if the classes are completely implemented. This actually functions through a few Python internals:

```
>>> class AbstractMeta(type):
...     def __new__(metaclass, name, bases, namespace):
...         cls = super().__new__(metaclass, name, bases, namespace)
...         cls.__abstractmethods__ = frozenset(('something',))
...         return cls


>>> class Spam(metaclass=AbstractMeta):
...     pass


>>> eggs = Spam()
Traceback (most recent call last):
    ...
TypeError: Can't instantiate abstract class Spam with ...
```

We can easily emulate the same behavior with a `metaclass` ourselves, but it should be noted that `abc.ABCMeta` actually does more, which we will demonstrate in the next section. To mimic the behavior of the built-in abstract base class support, take a look at the following example:

```
>>> import functools


>>> class AbstractMeta(type):
...     def __new__(metaclass, name, bases, namespace):
...         # Create the class instance
...         cls = super().__new__(metaclass, name, bases, namespace)
...
...         # Collect all local methods marked as abstract
...         abstracts = set()
...         for k, v in namespace.items():
...             if getattr(v, '__abstract__', False):
...                 abstracts.add(k)
...
...         # Look for abstract methods in the base classes and add
```

```
...                  # them to the list of abstracts
...                  for base in bases:
...                      for k in getattr(base, '__abstracts__', ()):
...                          v = getattr(cls, k, None)
...                          if getattr(v, '__abstract__', False):
...                              abstracts.add(k)
...
...                  # store the abstracts in a frozenset so they cannot be
...                  # modified
...                  cls.__abstracts__ = frozenset(abstracts)
...
...                  # Decorate the __new__ function to check if all abstract
...                  # functions were implemented
...                  original_new = cls.__new__
...                  @functools.wraps(original_new)
...                  def new(self, *args, **kwargs):
...                      for k in self.__abstracts__:
...                          v = getattr(self, k)
...                          if getattr(v, '__abstract__', False):
...                              raise RuntimeError(
...                                  '%r is not implemented' % k)
...
...                      return original_new(self, *args, **kwargs)
...
...                  cls.__new__ = new
...                  return cls


>>> def abstractmethod(function):
...     function.__abstract__ = True
...     return function


>>> class Spam(metaclass=AbstractMeta):
...     @abstractmethod
...     def some_method(self):
```

```
...          pass


# Instantiating the function, we can see that it functions as the
# regular ABCMeta does
>>> eggs = Spam()
Traceback (most recent call last):

    ...

RuntimeError: 'some_method' is not implemented
```

The actual implementation is a bit more complicated as it still needs to take care of the old style classes and the `property`, `classmethod`, and `staticmethod` types of methods. Additionally, it features caching, but this code covers the most useful part of the implementation. One of the most important tricks to note here is that the actual check is executed by decorating the __new__ function of the actual class. This method is only executed once within a class so we can avoid the overhead of these checks for multiple instantiations.

 The actual implementation of the abstract methods can be found by looking for __isabstractmethod__ in the Python source code in the following files: `Objects/descrobject.c`, `Objects/funcobject.c`, and `Objects/object.c`. The Python part of the implementation can be found in `Lib/abc.py`.

Custom type checks

Defining your own interfaces using abstract base classes is great, of course. But it can also be very convenient to tell Python what your class actually resembles and what kind of types are similar. For that, `abc.ABCMeta` offers a register function which allows you to specify which types are similar. For example, a custom list that sees the list type as similar:

```
>>> import abc


>>> class CustomList(abc.ABC):
...      'This class implements a list-like interface'
...      pass


>>> CustomList.register(list)
<class 'list'>
```

```
>>> issubclass(list, CustomList)
True
>>> isinstance([], CustomList)
True
>>> issubclass(CustomList, list)
False
>>> isinstance(CustomList(), list)
False
```

As demonstrated with the last four lines, this is a one-way relationship. The other way around would generally be easy enough to realize through inheriting list, but that won't work in this case. abc.ABCMeta refuses to create inheritance cycles.

```
>>> import abc

>>> class CustomList(abc.ABC, list):
...     'This class implements a list-like interface'
...     pass

>>> CustomList.register(list)
Traceback (most recent call last):
    ...
RuntimeError: Refusing to create an inheritance cycle
```

To be able to handle cases like these, there is another useful feature in abc.ABCMeta. When subclassing abc.ABCMeta, the __subclasshook__ method can be extended to customize the behavior of issubclass and with that, isinstance.

```
>>> import abc

>>> class UniversalClass(abc.ABC):
...     @classmethod
...     def __subclasshook__(cls, subclass):
...         return True


>>> issubclass(list, UniversalClass)
True
>>> issubclass(bool, UniversalClass)
```

```
True
>>> isinstance(True, UniversalClass)
True
>>> issubclass(UniversalClass, bool)
False
```

The __subclasshook__ should return True, False, or NotImplemented, which would result in issubclass returning True, False, or the usual behavior when NotImplemented is raised.

Using abc.ABC before Python 3.4

The abc.ABC class we have used in this paragraph is only available in Python versions 3.4 and higher, but it's trivial to implement it in older versions. It's little more than syntactic sugar for metaclass=abc.ABCMeta. To implement it yourself, you can simply use the following snippet:

```
import abc

class ABC(metaclass=abc.ABCMeta):
    pass
```

Automatically registering a plugin system

One of the most common uses of metaclasses is to have classes automatically register themselves as plugins/handlers. Examples of these can be seen in many projects, such as web frameworks. Those codebases are too extensive to usefully explain here though. Hence, we'll show a simpler example showing the power of metaclasses as a self-registering plugin system:

```
>>> import abc


>>> class Plugins(abc.ABCMeta):
...     plugins = dict()
...
...     def __new__(metaclass, name, bases, namespace):
...         cls = abc.ABCMeta.__new__(metaclass, name, bases,
...                                   namespace)
...         if isinstance(cls.name, str):
...             metaclass.plugins[cls.name] = cls
```

```
...             return cls
...
...         @classmethod
...         def get(cls, name):
...             return cls.plugins[name]


>>> class PluginBase(metaclass=Plugins):
...         @property
...         @abc.abstractmethod
...         def name(self):
...             raise NotImplemented()


>>> class SpamPlugin(PluginBase):
...         name = 'spam'


>>> class EggsPlugin(PluginBase):
...         name = 'eggs'


>>> Plugins.get('spam')
<class '...SpamPlugin'>
>>> Plugins.plugins
{'spam': <class '...SpamPlugin'>,
 'eggs': <class '...EggsPlugin'>}
```

This example is a tad simplistic of course, but it's the basis for many plugin systems. Which is a very important thing to note while implementing systems like these; however, while metaclasses run at definition time, the module still needs to be imported to work. There are several options to do this; loading on-demand through the get method has my vote as that also doesn't add load time if the plugin is not used.

The following examples will use the following file structure to get reproducible results. All files will be contained in a plugins directory.

The __init__.py file is used to create shortcuts, so a simple import plugins will result in having plugins.Plugins available, instead of requiring importing plugins.base explicitly.

```
# plugins/__init__.py
from .base import Plugin
from .base import Plugins


__all__ = ['Plugin', 'Plugins']
```

The base.py file containing the Plugins collection and the Plugin base class:

```
# plugins/base.py
import abc


class Plugins(abc.ABCMeta):
    plugins = dict()

    def __new__(metaclass, name, bases, namespace):
        cls = abc.ABCMeta.__new__(
            metaclass, name, bases, namespace)
        if isinstance(cls.name, str):
            metaclass.plugins[cls.name] = cls
        return cls

    @classmethod
    def get(cls, name):
        return cls.plugins[name]


class Plugin(metaclass=Plugins):
    @property
    @abc.abstractmethod
    def name(self):
        raise NotImplemented()
```

And two simple plugins, spam.py:

```
from . import base


class Spam(base.Plugin):
    name = 'spam'
```

And `eggs.py`:

```
from . import base


class Eggs(base.Plugin):
    name = 'eggs'
```

Importing plugins on-demand

The first of the solutions for the import problem is simply taking care of it in the `get` method of the `Plugins` metaclass. Whenever the plugin is not found in the registry, it should automatically load the module from the `plugins` directory.

The advantages of this approach are that not only the plugins don't explicitly need to be preloaded but also that the plugins are only loaded when the need is there. Unused plugins are not touched, so this method can help in reducing your applications' load times.

The downside is that the code will not be run or tested, so it might be completely broken and you won't know about it until it is finally loaded. Solutions for this problem will be covered in the testing chapter, *Chapter 10, Testing and Logging – Preparing for Bugs*. The other problem is that if the code self-registers itself into other parts of an application then that code won't be executed either.

Modifying the `Plugins.get` method, we get the following:

```
import abc
import importlib


class Plugins(abc.ABCMeta):
    plugins = dict()

    def __new__(metaclass, name, bases, namespace):
        cls = abc.ABCMeta.__new__(
            metaclass, name, bases, namespace)
        if isinstance(cls.name, str):
            metaclass.plugins[cls.name] = cls
        return cls

    @classmethod
    def get(cls, name):
        if name not in cls.plugins:
            print('Loading plugins from plugins.%s' % name)
            importlib.import_module('plugins.%s' % name)
        return cls.plugins[name]
```

This results in the following when executing:

```
>>> import plugins
>>> plugins.Plugins.get('spam')
Loading plugins from plugins.spam
<class 'plugins.spam.Spam'>

>>> plugins.Plugins.get('spam')
<class 'plugins.spam.Spam'>
```

As you can see, this approach only results in running `import` once. The second time, the plugin will be available in the plugins dictionary so no loading will be necessary.

Importing plugins through configuration

While only loading the needed plugins is generally a better idea, there is something to be said to preload the plugins you will likely need. As explicit is better than implicit, an explicit list of plugins to load is generally a good solution. The added advantages of this method are that firstly you are able to make the registration a bit more advanced as you are guaranteed that it is run and secondly you can load plugins from multiple packages.

Instead of importing in the `get` method, we will add a `load` method this time; a `load` method that imports all the given module names:

```python
import abc
import importlib


class Plugins(abc.ABCMeta):
    plugins = dict()

    def __new__(metaclass, name, bases, namespace):
        cls = abc.ABCMeta.__new__(
            metaclass, name, bases, namespace)
        if isinstance(cls.name, str):
            metaclass.plugins[cls.name] = cls
        return cls

    @classmethod
    def get(cls, name):
        return cls.plugins[name]
```

```
    @classmethod
    def load(cls, *plugin_modules):
        for plugin_module in plugin_modules:
            plugin = importlib.import_module(plugin_module)
```

Which can be called using the following code:

```
>>> import plugins


>>> plugins.Plugins.load(
...     'plugins.spam',
...     'plugins.eggs',
... )


>>> plugins.Plugins.get('spam')
<class 'plugins.spam.Spam'>
```

A fairly simple and straightforward system to load the plugins based on settings, this can easily be combined with any type of settings system to fill the load method.

Importing plugins through the file system

Whenever possible, it is best to avoid having systems depend on automatic detection of modules on a filesystem as it goes directly against PEP8. Specifically, "explicit is better than implicit". While these systems can work fine in specific cases, they often make debugging much more difficult. Similar automatic import systems in Django have caused me a fair share of headaches as they tend to obfuscate the errors. Having said that, automatic plugin loading based on all the files in a plugins directory is still a possibility warranting a demonstration.

```
import os
import re
import abc
import importlib

MODULE_NAME_RE = re.compile('[a-z][a-z0-9_]*', re.IGNORECASE)

class Plugins(abc.ABCMeta):
    plugins = dict()

    def __new__(metaclass, name, bases, namespace):
        cls = abc.ABCMeta.__new__(
            metaclass, name, bases, namespace)
```

```
        if isinstance(cls.name, str):
            metaclass.plugins[cls.name] = cls
        return cls

    @classmethod
    def get(cls, name):
        return cls.plugins[name]

    @classmethod
    def load_directory(cls, module, directory):
        for file_ in os.listdir(directory):
            name, ext = os.path.splitext(file_)
            full_path = os.path.join(directory, file_)
            import_path = [module]
            if os.path.isdir(full_path):
                import_path.append(file_)
            elif ext == '.py' and MODULE_NAME_RE.match(name):
                import_path.append(name)
            else:
                # Ignoring non-matching files/directories
                continue

            plugin = importlib.import_module('.'.join(import_path))

    @classmethod
    def load(cls, **plugin_directories):
        for module, directory in plugin_directories.items():
            cls.load_directory(module, directory)
```

If possible, I would try to avoid using a fully automatic import system as it's very prone to accidental errors and can make debugging more difficult, not to mention that the import order cannot easily be controlled this way. To make this system a bit smarter (even importing packages outside of your Python path), you can create a plugin loader using the abstract base classes in `importlib.abc`. Note that you will most likely still need to list the directories through `os.listdir` or `os.walk` though.

Order of operations when instantiating classes

The order of operations during class instantiation is very important to keep in mind when debugging issues with dynamically created and/or modified classes. The instantiation of a class happens in the following order.

Finding the metaclass

The metaclass comes from either the explicitly given metaclass on the class or `bases`, or by using the default `type` metaclass.

For every class, the class itself and the bases, the first matching of the following will be used:

- Explicitly given metaclass
- Explicit metaclass from bases
- `type()`

 Note that if no metaclass is found that is a subtype of all the candidate metaclasses, a `TypeError` will be raised. This scenario is not that likely to occur but certainly a possibility when using multiple inheritance/mixins with metaclasses.

Preparing the namespace

The class namespace is prepared through the metaclass selected previously. If the metaclass has a `__prepare__` method, it will be called `namespace = metaclass.__prepare__(names, bases, **kwargs)`, where `**kwargs` originates from the class definition. If no `__prepare__` method is available, the result will be `namespace = dict()`.

Note that there are multiple ways of achieving custom namespaces, as we saw in the previous paragraph, the `type()` function call also takes a `dict` argument which can be used to alter the namespace as well.

Executing the class body

The body of the class is executed very similarly to normal code execution with one key difference, the separate namespace. Since a class has a separate namespace, which shouldn't pollute the `globals()`/`locals()` namespaces, it is executed within that context. The resulting call looks something like this: `exec(body, globals(), namespace)` where `namespace` is the previously produced namespace.

Creating the class object (not instance)

Now that we have all the components ready, the actual class object can be produced. This is done through the `class_ = metaclass(name, bases, namespace, **kwargs)` call. This is, as you can see, actually identical to the `type()` call previously discussed. `**kwargs` here are the same as the ones passed to the `__prepare__` method earlier.

It might be useful to note that this is also the object that will be referenced from the `super()` call without arguments.

Executing the class decorators

Now that the class object is actually done already, the class decorators will be executed. Since this is only executed after everything else in the class object has already been constructed, it becomes difficult to modify class attributes, such as which classes are being inherited, and the name of the class. By modifying the `__class__` object you can still modify or overwrite these, but it is, at the very least, more difficult.

Creating the class instance

From the class object produced previously, we can now finally create the actual instances as you normally would with a class. It should be noted that this step and the class decorators steps, unlike the earlier steps, are the only ones that are executed every time you instantiate a class. The steps before these two are only executed once per class definition.

Example

Enough theory! Let's illustrate the creation and instantiation of the class objects so we can check the order of operations:

```
>>> import functools
```

```
>>> def decorator(name):
...     def _decorator(cls):
...         @functools.wraps(cls)
...         def __decorator(*args, **kwargs):
...             print('decorator(%s)' % name)
...             return cls(*args, **kwargs)
```

```
...            return __decorator
...        return _decorator


>>> class SpamMeta(type):
...
...        @decorator('SpamMeta.__init__')
...        def __init__(self, name, bases, namespace, **kwargs):
...            print('SpamMeta.__init__()')
...            return type.__init__(self, name, bases, namespace)
...
...        @staticmethod
...        @decorator('SpamMeta.__new__')
...        def __new__(cls, name, bases, namespace, **kwargs):
...            print('SpamMeta.__new__()')
...            return type.__new__(cls, name, bases, namespace)
...
...        @classmethod
...        @decorator('SpamMeta.__prepare__')
...        def __prepare__(cls, names, bases, **kwargs):
...            print('SpamMeta.__prepare__()')
...            namespace = dict(spam=5)
...            return namespace


>>> @decorator('Spam')
... class Spam(metaclass=SpamMeta):
...
...        @decorator('Spam.__init__')
...        def __init__(self, eggs=10):
...            print('Spam.__init__()')
...            self.eggs = eggs
decorator(SpamMeta.__prepare__)
SpamMeta.__prepare__()
decorator(SpamMeta.__new__)
SpamMeta.__new__()
```

```
decorator(SpamMeta.__init__)
SpamMeta.__init__()



# Testing with the class object
>>> spam = Spam
>>> spam.spam
5
>>> spam.eggs
Traceback (most recent call last):
    ...
AttributeError: ... object has no attribute 'eggs'



# Testing with a class instance
>>> spam = Spam()
decorator(Spam)
decorator(Spam.__init__)
Spam.__init__()
>>> spam.spam
5
>>> spam.eggs
10
```

The example clearly shows the creation order of the class:

1. Preparing the namespace through __prepare__.
2. Creating the class body using __new__.
3. Initializing the metaclass using __init__ (note that this is not the class __init__).
4. Initializing the class through the class decorator.
5. Initializing the class through the class __init__ function.

One thing we can note from this is that the class decorators are executed each and every time the class is actually instantiated and not before that. This can be both an advantage and a disadvantage of course, but if you wish to build a register of all subclasses, it is definitely more convenient to use a metaclass since the decorator will not register until you instantiate the class.

In addition to this, having the power to modify the namespace before actually creating the class object (not the instance) can be very powerful as well. It can be convenient for sharing a certain scope between several class objects for example, or for easily ensuring that certain items are always available in the scope.

Storing class attributes in definition order

There are cases where the definition order makes a difference. For example, let's assume we are creating a class that represents a CSV (Comma Separated Values) format. The CSV format expects the fields to have a particular order. In some cases this will be indicated by a header but it's still useful to have a consistent field order. Similar systems are using in ORM systems such as SQLAlchemy to store the column order for table definitions and for the input field order within forms in Django.

The classic solution without metaclasses

An easy way to store the order of the fields is by giving the field instances a special __init__ method which increments for every definition, so the fields have an incrementing index property. This solution can be considered the classic solution as it also works in Python 2.

```
>>> import itertools

>>> class Field(object):
...     counter = itertools.count()
...
...     def __init__(self, name=None):
...         self.name = name
...         self.index = next(Field.counter)
...
...     def __repr__(self):
...         return '<%s[%d] %s>' % (
...             self.__class__.__name__,
...             self.index,
...             self.name,
...         )


>>> class FieldsMeta(type):
```

```
...         def __new__(metaclass, name, bases, namespace):
...             cls = type.__new__(metaclass, name, bases, namespace)
...             fields = []
...             for k, v in namespace.items():
...                 if isinstance(v, Field):
...                     fields.append(v)
...                     v.name = v.name or k
...
...             cls.fields = sorted(fields, key=lambda f: f.index)
...             return cls


>>> class Fields(metaclass=FieldsMeta):
...     spam = Field()
...     eggs = Field()

>>> Fields.fields
[<Field[0] spam>, <Field[1] eggs>]

>>> fields = Fields()
>>> fields.eggs.index
1
>>> fields.spam.index
0
>>> fields.fields
[<Field[0] spam>, <Field[1] eggs>]
```

For convenience, and to make things prettier, we have added the `FieldsMeta` class. It is not strictly required here, but it automatically takes care of filling in the name if needed, and adds the `fields` list which contains a sorted list of fields.

Using metaclasses to get a sorted namespace

The previous solution is a bit more straightforward and supports Python 2 as well, but with Python 3 we have more options. As you have seen in the previous paragraphs, since Python 3 we have the `__prepare__` method, which returns the namespace. From the previous chapters you might also remember `collections.OrderedDict`, so let's see what happens when we combine them.

```
>>> import collections

>>> class Field(object):
```

```
...         def __init__(self, name=None):
...             self.name = name
...
...         def __repr__(self):
...             return '<%s %s>' % (
...                 self.__class__.__name__,
...                 self.name,
...             )


>>> class FieldsMeta(type):
...         @classmethod
...         def __prepare__(metaclass, name, bases):
...             return collections.OrderedDict()
...
...         def __new__(metaclass, name, bases, namespace):
...             cls = type.__new__(metaclass, name, bases, namespace)
...             cls.fields = []
...             for k, v in namespace.items():
...                 if isinstance(v, Field):
...                     cls.fields.append(v)
...                     v.name = v.name or k
...
...             return cls


>>> class Fields(metaclass=FieldsMeta):
...         spam = Field()
...         eggs = Field()

>>> Fields.fields
[<Field spam>, <Field eggs>]
>>> fields = Fields()
>>> fields.fields
[<Field spam>, <Field eggs>]
```

As you can see, the fields are indeed in the order we defined them. `Spam` first and
`eggs` after that. Since the class namespace is now a `collections.OrderedDict`
instance, we know that the order is guaranteed. Instead of the regular not
predetermined order of the Python `dict`. This demonstrates how convenient
metaclasses can be to extend your classes in a generic way. Another big advantage
of metaclasses, instead of a custom __init__ method, is that the users won't lose the
functionality if they forget to call the parent __init__ method. The metaclass will
always be executed, unless a different metaclass is added, that is.

Summary

The Python metaclass system is something every Python programmer uses all the time, perhaps without even knowing about it. Every class should be created through some (subclass of) `type`, which allows for endless customization and magic. Instead of statically defining your class, you can now have it created as you normally would and dynamically add, modify, or remove attributes from your class during definition; very magical but very useful. The magic component, however, is also the reason it should be used with a lot of caution. While metaclasses can be used to make your life much easier, they are also amongst the easiest ways of producing completely incomprehensible code.

Regardless, there are some great use-cases for metaclasses and many libraries such as `SQLAlchemy` and `Django` use metaclasses to make your code work much easier and arguably better. Actually comprehending the magic that is used inside is generally not needed for the usage of these libraries, which makes the cases defendable. The question becomes whether a much better experience for beginners is worth some dark magic internally, and looking at the success of these libraries, I would say yes in this case.

To conclude, when thinking about using metaclasses, keep in mind what Tim Peters once said: "Metaclasses are deeper magic than 99% of users should ever worry about. If you wonder whether you need them, you don't."

Now we will continue with a solution to remove some of the magic that metaclasses generate: documentation. The next chapter will show us how your code can be documented, how that documentation can be tested, and most importantly, how the documentation can be made smarter by annotating types in your documentation.

Documentation – How to Use Sphinx and reStructuredText

9

Documenting code can be both fun and useful! I will admit that many programmers have a strong dislike for documenting code and understandably so. Writing documentation can be a boring job and traditionally only others reap the benefits of that effort. The tools available for Python, however, make it almost trivial to generate useful and up-to-date documentation with little to no effort at all. Generating documentation has actually become so easy that I create and generate documentation before using a Python package. Assuming it wasn't available already, that is.

In addition to simple text documentation explaining what a function does, it is also possible to add metadata, such as type hints. These type hints can be used to make the arguments and return types of a function or class clickable in the documentation. But more importantly, many modern IDEs and editors, such as VIM, have plugins available that parse the type hints and use them for intelligent auto-completion. So if you type `Spam.eggs`, your editor will automatically complete the specific attributes and methods of the eggs object; something that is traditionally only viable with statically typed languages such as Java, C, and C++.

This chapter will explain the types of documentation available in Python and how easily a full set of documentation can be created. With the amazing tools that Python provides, you can have fully functioning documentation within minutes.

Topics covered in this chapter are as follows:

- The reStructuredText syntax
- Setting up documentation using Sphinx
- Sphinx style docstrings
- Google style docstrings
- NumPy style docstrings

The reStructuredText syntax

The **reStructuredText** format (also known as **RST**, **ReST**, or **reST**) was developed in 2002 as a simple language that implements enough markup to be usable, but is simple enough to be readable as plain text. These two features make it readable enough to use in code, yet still versatile enough to generate pretty and useful documentation.

The greatest thing about reStructuredText is that it is very intuitive. Even without knowing anything about the standard, you can easily write documentation in this style without ever knowing that it would be recognized as a language. However, more advanced techniques, such as images and links, do require some explanation.

Next to reStructuredText, there are also languages such as **Markdown** which are quite similar in usage. Within the Python community, reStructuredText has been the standard documentation language for over 10 years, making it the recommended solution.

 To easily convert between formats such as reStructuredText and Markdown, use the Pandoc tool, available at `http://pandoc.org/`.

The basic syntax reads just like text and the next few paragraphs will show some of the more advanced features. However, let us start with a simple example demonstrating how simple a reStructuredText file can be.

```
Documentation, how to use Sphinx and reStructuredText
#####################################################################

Documenting code can be both fun and useful! ...

Additionally, adding ...

... So that typing `Spam.eggs.` will automatically ...

Topics covered in this chapter are as follows:

  - The reStructuredText syntax
  - Setting up documentation using Sphinx
  - Sphinx style docstrings
  - Google style docstrings
  - NumPy style docstrings
```

```
The reStructuredText syntax
****************************************************************
```

```
The reStructuredText format (also known as ...
```

That's how easy it is to convert the text of this chapter so far to reStructuredText. The following paragraphs will cover the following features:

1. Inline markup (italic, bold, code, and links)
2. Lists
3. Headers
4. Advanced links
5. Images
6. Substitutions
7. Blocks containing code, math, and others

Getting started with reStructuredText

To quickly convert a reStructuredText file to HTML, we can use the `docutils` library. The `sphinx` library discussed later in this chapter actually uses the `docutils` library internally, but has some extra features that we won't need initially. To get started, we just need to install `docutils`:

```
pip install docutils
```

After that we can easily convert reStructuredText into PDF, LaTeX, HTML, and other formats. For the examples in this paragraph, we'll use the HTML format which is easily generated using the following command:

```
rst2html.py file.rst file.html
```

The basic components of reStructuredText are roles, which are used for inline modifications of the output and directives to generate markup blocks. Within pure reStructuredText, the directives are the most important, but we will see many uses for the roles in the section about Sphinx.

Inline markup

Inline markup is the markup that is used within a regular line of text. Examples of these are emphasis, in-line code examples, links, images, and bullet lists.

Emphasis, for example, can be added by encapsulating the words between one or two asterisk signs. This sentence for example could add a little bit of `*emphasis*` by adding a single asterisk on both sides or a lot of `**emphasis**` by adding two asterisks at both sides. There are many different inline markup directives so we will list only the most common ones. A full list can always be found through the reStructuredText homepage at `docutils.sourceforge.net`.

Following are some examples:

- Emphasis (italic) text: `*emphasis for this phrase*`.
- Extra emphasis (bold) text: `**extra emphasis for this phrase**`.
- For lists without numbers, a simple dash with spaces after it:

```
- item 1
- item 2
```

 The space after the dash is required for reStructuredText to recognize the list.

- For lists with numbers, the number followed by a period and a space:

```
1. item 1
2. item 2
```

- For numbered lists, the period after the number is required.
- Interpreted text: These are domain specific. Within Python documentation, the default role is code which means that surround text with back ticks will convert your code to use code tags. For example, `` `if spam and eggs:` ``.

  Different roles can be set through either a role prefix or suffix depending on your preference. For example, `:math:`E=mc^2`` to show mathematical equations.

- Inline literals: This is formatted with a mono-space font, which makes it ideal for inline code. Just add two back ticks to ` ``add some code`` `.
- References: These can be created through a trailing underscore. They can point to headers, links, labels, and more. The next section will cover more about these, but the basic syntax is simply `reference_` or enclosed in back ticks when the reference contains spaces, `` `some reference link`_ ``.
- To escape the preceding characters, the backslash can be used. So if you wish to have an asterisk with emphasis, it's possible to use `*\**`, quite similar to escaping in Python strings.

There are many more available, but these are the ones you will use the most when writing reStructuredText.

Headers

The headers are used to indicate the start of a document, section, chapter, or paragraph. It is therefore the first structure you need in a document. While not strictly needed, its usage is highly recommended as it serves several purposes:

1. The headers are consistently formatted according to their level.
2. Sphinx can generate a Table Of Contents (TOC) tree from the headers.
3. All headers automatically function as labels, which means you can create links towards them.

When creating headers, consistency is one of the few constraints; the character used is fairly arbitrary as is the amount of levels.

Personally, I default to a simple system with a fixed-size header, but I recommend at least following the default of the Python documentation in terms of the parts, chapters, sections, subsections, subsubsections, and paragraphs. Something along the lines of the following:

```
Part
################################################################

Chapter
****************************************************************

Section
================================================================

Subsection
----------------------------------------------------------------

Subsubsection
^^^^^^^^^^^^^^^^^^^^^^^^^^^^^^^^^^^^^^^^^^^^^^^^^^^^^^^^^^^^^^^^^^

Paragraph
""""""""""""""""""""""""""""""""""""""""""""""""""""""""""""""""

Content
```

Output:

> **Part**
>
> **Chapter**
>
> ## Section
>
> **Subsection**
>
> **Subsubsection**
>
> Paragraph
>
> Content

That is just the common usage of the headers, but the main idea of reStructuredText is that you can use just about anything that feels natural to you, which means that you can use any of the following characters: = - ` : ' " ~ ^ _ * + # <>. It also supports both underlines and overlines, so if you prefer that, they are options as well:

```
####################################################################
Part
####################################################################


********************************************************************
Chapter
********************************************************************


====================================================================
Section
====================================================================


--------------------------------------------------------------------
Subsection
--------------------------------------------------------------------


^^^^^^^^^^^^^^^^^^^^^^^^^^^^^^^^^^^^^^^^^^^^^^^^^^^^^^^^^^^^^^^^^^^^^^
Subsubsection
^^^^^^^^^^^^^^^^^^^^^^^^^^^^^^^^^^^^^^^^^^^^^^^^^^^^^^^^^^^^^^^^^^^^^^


""""""""""""""""""""""""""""""""""""""""""""""""""""""""""""""""""""
Paragraph
""""""""""""""""""""""""""""""""""""""""""""""""""""""""""""""""""""

Content
```

While I try to keep the number of characters fixed to 78 characters as PEP8 (*Chapter 2, Pythonic Syntax, Common Pitfalls, and Style Guide*) recommends for Python, the number of characters used is mostly arbitrary, but it does have to be at least as long as the text of the header. This allows it to get the following result:

```
Section
=======
```

But not this:

```
Section
====
```

Lists

The reStructuredText format has several styles of lists:

1. Enumerated
2. Bulleted
3. Options
4. Definitions

The simplest forms of lists were already displayed in the introduction section, but it's actually possible to use many different characters, such as letters, Roman numerals, and others, for enumeration. After demonstrating the basic list types, we will continue with the nesting of lists and structures which makes them even more powerful. Care must be taken with the amount of whitespace, as a space too many can cause a structure to be recognized as regular text instead of a structure.

Enumerated list

Enumerated lists are convenient for all sorts of enumerations. The basic premise for enumerated lists is an alphanumeric character followed by a period, a right parenthesis, or parentheses on both sides. Additionally, the # character functions as an automatic enumeration. For example:

```
1. With
2. Numbers

a. With
#. letters
```

```
i. Roman
#. numerals
```

```
(1) With
(2) Parenthesis
```

The output is perhaps a bit simpler than you would expect. The reason is that it depends on the output format. These were generated with the HTML output format which has no support for parentheses. If you output LaTeX for example, the difference can be made visible. Following is the rendered HTML output:

1. With
2. Numbers

   a. With
   b. letters

      i. Roman
      ii. numerals

      1. With
      2. Parenthesis

Bulleted list

If the order of the list is not relevant and you simply need a list of items without enumeration, then the bulleted list is what you need. To create a simple list using bullets only, the bulleted items need to start with a *, +, -, •, ⊠, or ⊠. This list is mostly arbitrary and can be modified by extending Sphinx or Docutils. For example:

```
- dashes
- and more dashes
```

```
* asterisk
* stars
```

```
+ plus
+ and plus
```

As you can see, with the HTML output again all bullets look identical. When generating documentation as LaTeX (and consecutively, PDF or Postscript), these can differ. Since web-based documentation is by far the most common output format for Sphinx, we default to that output instead. The rendered HTML output is as follows:

- dashes
- and more dashes

- asterisk
- stars

- plus
- and plus

Option list

The `option` list is one meant specifically for documenting the command line arguments of a program. The only special thing about the syntax is that the comma-space is recognized as a separator for options.

```
-s, --spam  This is the spam option
--eggs      This is the eggs option
```

Following is the output:

-s, --spam	This is the spam option
--eggs	This is the eggs option

Definition list

The definition list is a bit more obscure than the other types of lists, since the actual structure consists of whitespace only. It's therefore pretty straightforward to use, but not always as easy to identify in a file.

```
spam
    Spam is a canned pork meat product
eggs
    Is, similar to spam, also food
```

Following is the output:

```
spam
        Spam is a canned pork meat product

eggs
        Is, similar to spam, also food
```

Nested lists

Nesting items is actually not limited to lists and can be done with multiple types of blocks, but the idea is the same. Just be careful to keep the indenting at the correct level. If you don't, it either won't be recognized as a separate level or you will get an error.

```
1. With

2. Numbers


    (food) food

    spam
        Spam is a canned pork meat product


    eggs
        Is, similar to spam, also food


    (other) non-food stuff
```

Following is the output:

```
1. With

2. Numbers

    (food) food

        spam
            Spam is a canned pork meat product

        eggs
            Is, similar to spam, also food

    (other) non-food stuff
```

Links, references, and labels

There are many types of links supported in reStructuredText, the simplest of which is just a link with the protocol such as `http://python.org`, which will automatically be recognized by most parsers. However, custom labels are also an option by using the interpreted text syntax we saw earlier: `` `Python <http://python.org>`_ ``.

Both of these are nice for simple links, which won't be repeated too often, but generally it's more convenient to attach labels to links so they can be reused and don't clog up the text too much.

For example, refer to the following:

```
The switch to reStructuredText and Sphinx was made with the
`Python 2.6 <https://docs.python.org/whatsnew/2.6.html>`_
release.
```

Now compare it with the following:

```
The switch to reStructuredText and Sphinx was made with the
`python 2.6`_ release.

.. _`Python 2.6`: https://docs.python.org/whatsnew/2.6.html
```

The output is as follows:

> The switch to reStructuredText and Sphinx was made with the Python 2.6 release.

Using labels, you can easily have a list of references at a designated location without making the actual text harder to read. These labels can be used for more than external links however; similar to the GOTO statements found in older programming languages, you can create labels and refer to them from other parts of the documentation:

```
.. _label:
```

Within HTML or PDF output, this can be used to create a clickable link from anywhere in the text using the underscore links. Creating a clickable link to the label is as simple as having `label_` in the text. Note that reStructuredText ignores case differences so both uppercase and lowercase links work just fine. Even though it's not likely to make this mistake, having the same label in a single document with only case differences results in an error to make sure duplicates never occur.

The usage of references in conjunction with the headers works in a very natural way; you can just refer to them as you normally would and add an underscore to make it a link:

```
The introduction section
======================================================================


This section contains:

- `chapter 1`_
- :ref:`chapter2`

  1. my_label_


  2. `And a label link with a custom title <my_label>`_


Chapter 1
----------------------------------------------------------------------


Jumping back to the beginning of `chapter 1`_ is also possible.
Or jumping to :ref:`Chapter 2 <chapter2>`


.. _chapter2:


Chapter 2 With a longer title
----------------------------------------------------------------------


The next chapter.


.. _my_label:


The label points here.


Back to `the introduction section`_
```

The output is as follows:

The introduction section

This section contains:

* chapter 1
* Chapter 2 With a longer title

    1. my_label
    2. And a label link with a custom title

Chapter 1

Jumping back to the beginning of chapter 1 is also possible. Or jumping to Chapter 2

Chapter 2 With a longer title

The next chapter.

The label points here.

Back to the introduction section

Images

The image directive looks very similar to the label syntax. They're actually a bit different but the pattern is quite similar. The image directive is just one of the many directives that is supported by reStructuredText. We will see more about that later on when we cover Sphinx and reStructuredText extensions. For the time being, it is enough to know that the directives start with two periods followed by a space, the name of the directive, and two colons:

```
.. name_of_directive::
```

In the case of the image, the directive is called `image` of course:

```
.. image:: python.png
```

Scaled output as the actual image is much larger:

 Note the double colon after the directives.

But how about specifying the size and other properties? The image directive has many other options (as do most other directives) which can be used: `http://docutils.sourceforge.net/docs/ref/rst/directives.html#images`, they are mostly fairly obvious however. To specify the width and height or the scale (in percent) of the image:

```
.. image:: python.png
   :width: 150
   :height: 100


.. image:: python.png
   :scale: 10
```

Following is the output:

With a scaled image:

 The `scale` option uses the `width` and `height` options if available and falls back to the PIL (Python Imaging Library) or Pillow library to detect the image. If both width/height and PIL/Pillow are not available, the `scale` option will be ignored silently.

In addition to the `image` directive, there is also the `figure` directive. The difference is that `figure` adds a caption to the image. Beyond that, the usage is the same as `image`:

```
.. figure:: python.png
   :scale: 10


   The Python logo
```

The output is as follows:

The Python logo

Substitutions

When writing documentation, it often happens that constructs are being repeated, the links have their own labelling system but there are more ways within reStructuredText. The substitution definitions make it possible to shorten directives so they can easily be re-used.

Let's assume we have a logo that we use quite often within a bit of text. Instead of typing the entire `.. image:: <url>` it would be very handy to have a shorthand to make it easier. That's where the substitutions are very useful:

```
.. |python| image:: python.png
   :scale: 1
```

```
The Python programming language uses the logo: |python|
```

The output is as follows:

> The Python programming language uses the logo: 🐍

These substitutions can be used with many directives, though they are particularly useful for outputting a variable in many places of a document. For example:

```
.. |author| replace:: Rick van Hattem
```

```
This book was written by |author|
```

Following is the output:

> This book was written by Rick van Hattem

Blocks, code, math, comments, and quotes

When writing documentation, a common scenario is the need for blocks that contain different type of content, explanations with mathematical formulas, code examples, and more. The usage of these directives is similar to the image directive. Following is an example of a code block:

```
.. code:: python

    def spam(*args):
        print('spam got args', args)
```

The output is as follows:

```
def spam(*args):
        print('spam got args', args)
```

Or math using LaTeX syntax, the fundamental theorem of calculus:

```
.. math::

    \int_a^b f(x)\,dx = F(b) - F(a)
```

Following is the output:

$$\int_a^b f(x)\,dx = F(b) - F(a)$$

Commenting a bunch of text/commands is easily achieved by using the "empty" directive followed by an indent:

```
Before comments

.. Everything here will be commented

   And this as well

   .. code:: python

      def even_this_code_sample():
          pass  # Will be commented

After comments
```

The output is as follows:

Before comments

After comments

The simplest ones are the block quotes. A block quote requires nothing but just a simple bit of indentation.

```
Normal text

    Quoted text
```

The output is as follows:

Normal text
        Quoted text

Conclusion

reStructuredText is both a very simple and a very extensive language; a large portion of the syntax comes naturally when writing plain-text notes. A full guide to all the intricacies, however, could fill a separate book. The previous demonstrations should have given enough of an introduction to do at least 90 percent of the work you will need when documenting your projects. Beyond that, Sphinx will help a lot as we will see in the next sections.

The Sphinx documentation generator

The Sphinx documentation generator was created in 2008 for the Python 2.6 release to replace the old LaTeX documentation for Python. It's a generator that makes it almost trivial to generate documentation for programming projects, but even outside of the programming world it can be easily used. Within programming projects, there is specific support for the following domains (programming languages):

- Python
- C
- C++
- Javascript
- reStructuredText

Outside of these languages, there are extensions available for many other languages such as CoffeeScript, MATLAB, PHP, Ruby Lisp, Go, and Scala. And if you're simply looking for snippet code highlighting, the Pygments highlighter which is used internally supports over 120 languages and is easily extendible for new languages if needed.

The most important advantage of Sphinx is that almost everything can be automatically generated from your source code. So the documentation is always up to date.

Getting started with Sphinx

First of all, we have to make sure we install Sphinx. Even though the Python core documentation is written using Sphinx, it is still a separately maintained project and must be installed separately. Luckily, that's easy enough using pip:

```
pip install sphinx
```

After installing Sphinx, there are two ways of getting started with a project, the `sphinx-quickstart` script and the `sphinx-apidoc` script. If you want to create and customize an entire Sphinx project then `sphinx-quickstart` may be best as it assists you in configuring a fully featured Sphinx project. If you simply want API documentation for an existing project then `sphinx-apidoc` might be better suited since it takes a single command and no further input to create a project.

In the end, both are valid options for creating Sphinx projects and personally I usually end up generating the initial configuration using `sphinx-quickstart` and call the `sphinx-apidoc` command every time I add a Python module to add the new module. Since `sphinx-apidoc` does not overwrite any files by default, it is a safe operation.

Using sphinx-quickstart

The `sphinx-quickstart` script interactively asks you about the most important decisions in your Sphinx project. No need to worry if you've accidently made a typo however. Most of the configuration is stored in the `conf.py` directory so it's easy enough to edit the configuration later in case you still want to enable a certain module.

Usage is easy enough, as a default I would recommend using the following settings. The output uses the following conventions:

- Inline comments start with #
- User input lines start with >

- Cropped output is indicated with . . . and all questions skipped in between use the default settings

```
# sphinx-quickstart
Welcome to the Sphinx 1.3.3 quickstart utility.


...


Enter the root path for documentation.
> Root path for the documentation [.]: docs


...


The project name will occur in several places in the built documentation.
> Project name: Mastering Python
> Author name(s): Rick van Hattem


# As version you might want to start below 1.0 or add an extra digit
# but I would recommend leaving the default and modify the
# configuration file instead. Just make it import from the Python
# package instead. An example can be found in the numpy-stl package:
# https://github.com/WoLpH/numpy-stl/blob/develop/docs/conf.py
...
> Project version: 1.0
> Project release [1.0]:


...


# Enabling the epub builder can be useful for people using e-readers to
# read the documentation.
Sphinx can also add configuration for epub output:
> Do you want to use the epub builder (y/n) [n]: y


...


# Autodoc is required to document the code, definitely recommended to
# enable
> autodoc: automatically insert docstrings from
```

```
modules (y/n) [n]: y


# With the doctest feature we can run tests embedded in the
# documentation. This is meant for doctests in the .rst files.
> doctest: automatically test code snippets in
  doctest blocks (y/n) [n]: y


# Intersphinx enables linking between Sphinx documentation sets
# allowing for links to external documentation. After enabling this
# you can make str link to the regular Python documentation about str
# for example.
> intersphinx: link between Sphinx documentation
  of different projects (y/n) [n]: y
...
# Mathjax enables LaTeX style mathematical rendering, not strictly
# needed but very useful for rendering equations.
> mathjax: include math, rendered in the browser
  by MathJax (y/n) [n]: y
...
> viewcode: include links to the source code of
  documented Python objects (y/n) [n]: y


...


Creating file docs/conf.py.
Creating file docs/index.rst.
Creating file docs/Makefile.
Creating file docs/make.bat.


Finished: An initial directory structure has been created.
```

You should now populate your master file `docs/index.rst` and create other documentation source files. Use the Makefile to build the docs, like so:

```
make builder
```

```
where "builder" is one of the supported builders, e.g. html, latex or
linkcheck.
```

After running this, we should have a docs directory containing the Sphinx project. Let's see what the command actually created for us:

```
# find docs
docs
docs/_build
docs/_static
docs/_templates
docs/conf.py
docs/index.rst
docs/make.bat
docs/Makefile
```

The _build, _static, and _templates directories are initially empty and can be ignored for now. The _build directory is used to output the generated documentation whereas the _static directory can be used to easily include custom CSS files and such. The _templates directory makes it possible to style the HTML output to your liking as well. Examples of these can be found in the Sphinx Git repository at https://github.com/sphinx-doc/sphinx/tree/master/sphinx/themes.

Makefile and make.bat can be used to generate the documentation output. Makefile can be used for any operating system that supports the make utility and make.bat is there to support Windows systems out of the box. Now let's look at the index.rst source:

```
Welcome to Mastering Python's documentation!
============================================

Contents:

.. toctree::
   :maxdepth: 2



Indices and tables
==================

* :ref:`genindex`
* :ref:`modindex`
* :ref:`search`
```

We see the document title as expected, followed by `toctree` (table of contents tree; more about that later in this chapter), and the links to the indices and search. `toctree` automatically generates a tree out of the headers of all available documentation pages. The indices and tables are automatically generated Sphinx pages, which are very useful but nothing we need to worry about in terms of settings.

Now it's time to generate the HTML output:

```
cd docs
make html
```

The `make` html command generates the documentation for you and the result is placed in `_build/html/`. Just open `index.html` in your browser to see the results. You should have something looking similar to the following now:

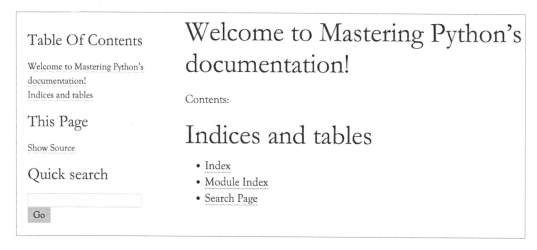

With just that single command and by answering a few questions, we now have a documentation project with an index, search, and table of contents on all the pages.

In addition to the HTML output, there are quite a few other formats supported by default, although some require external libraries to actually work:

```
# make
Please use `make <target>' where <target> is one of
  html       to make standalone HTML files
  dirhtml    to make HTML files named index.html in directories
  singlehtml to make a single large HTML file
  pickle     to make pickle files
  json       to make JSON files
```

```
htmlhelp    to make HTML files and a HTML help project
qthelp      to make HTML files and a qthelp project
applehelp   to make an Apple Help Book
devhelp     to make HTML files and a Devhelp project
epub        to make an epub
latex       to make LaTeX files, you can set PAPER=a4 or ...
latexpdf    to make LaTeX files and run them through pdflatex
latexpdfja  to make LaTeX files and run them through platex/...
text        to make text files
man         to make manual pages
texinfo     to make Texinfo files
info        to make Texinfo files and run them through makeinfo
gettext     to make PO message catalogs
changes     to make an overview of all changed/added/deprecate...
xml         to make Docutils-native XML files
pseudoxml   to make pseudoxml-XML files for display purposes
linkcheck   to check all external links for integrity
doctest     to run all doctests embedded in the documentation
coverage    to run coverage check of the documentation
```

Using sphinx-apidoc

The sphinx-apidoc command is generally used together with sphinx-quickstart. It is possible to generate an entire project with the --full parameter but it's generally a better idea to generate the entire project using sphinx-quickstart and simply add the API documentation using sphinx-apidoc. To properly demonstrate the sphinx-apidoc command, we need some Python files, so we'll create two files within a project called h09.

The first one is h09/spam.py containing a class called Spam with some methods:

```python
class Spam(object):
    def __init__(self, arg, *args, **kwargs):
        pass


    def regular_method(self, arg):
        pass


    @classmethod
```

```
def decorated_method(self, arg):
    pass


def _hidden_method(self):
    pass
```

Next we have h09/eggs.py containing a Eggs class that inherits Spam:

```
import spam



class Eggs(spam.Spam):
    def regular_method(self):
        '''This regular method overrides
        :meth:`spam.Spam.regular_method`
        '''
        pass
```

Now that we have our source files, it's time to generate the actual API documentation:

```
# sphinx-apidoc h09 -o docs
Creating file docs/eggs.rst.
Creating file docs/spam.rst.
Creating file docs/modules.rst.
```

This alone is not enough to include the API in the documentation. It needs to be added to toctree. Luckily, that's as simple as adding modules to toctree in the index.rst file to look something like this:

```
.. toctree::
   :maxdepth: 2


   modules
```

The toctree directive is discussed in further detail later in this chapter.

We also have to make sure that the modules can be imported, otherwise Sphinx won't be able to read the Python files. To do that, we simply add the h09 directory to sys.path; this can be put anywhere in the conf.py file:

```
import os
sys.path.insert(0, os.path.join(os.path.abspath('..'), 'h09'))
```

Now it's time to generate the documentation again:

```
cd docs
make html
```

Open the `docs/_build/index.html` file again. For the sake of brevity, the repeated parts of the document will be omitted from the screenshots. The cropped output is as follows:

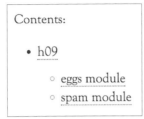

But it actually generated quite a bit more. When running the `sphinx-apidoc` command, it looks at all the Python modules in the specified directory recursively and generates a `rst` file for each of them. After generating all those separate files, it adds all those to a file called `modules.rst` which makes it easy to add them to your documentation.

The `modules.rst` file is really straight to the point; nothing more than a list of modules with the package name as the title really:

```
h09
===

.. toctree::
   :maxdepth: 4

   eggs
   spam
```

The output is as follows:

`spam.rst` and `eggs.rst` are equally simple, but more important in terms of customization. Within those files it adds the automodule directive which imports the Python module and lists the methods. The methods that are listed can be configured and by default we already get pretty useful output:

```
eggs module
===========


.. automodule:: eggs
    :members:
    :undoc-members:
    :show-inheritance:
```

Following is the output:

eggs module

class **eggs.Eggs**(*arg*, **args*, ***kwargs*)   [source]
    Bases: `spam.Spam`

    regular_method()   [source]
        This regular method overrides `spam.Spam.regular_method()`

Pretty, isn't it? And all that can be generated from most Python projects with virtually no effort whatsoever. The nice things about this is that the documentation we added to `Eggs.regular_method` is immediately added here, the inherited base (`spam.Spam`) is a clickable link to the `spam.Spam` documentation page, and the `:func:` role makes `spam.Spam.regular_method` immediately clickable as well.

The output for the spam module is similar:

spam module

class **spam.Spam**(*arg*, **args*, ***kwargs*)   [source]
    Bases: **object**

    classmethod **decorated_method**(*arg*)   [source]

    regular_method(*arg*)   [source]

New files won't be added to your docs automatically. It is safe to rerun the `sphinx-apidoc` command to add the new files but it won't update your existing files. Even though the `--force` option can be used to force overwriting the files, within existing files I recommend manually editing them instead. As we will see in the next sections, there are quite a few reasons to manually modify the generated files after.

Sphinx directives

Sphinx adds a few directives on top of the default ones in reStructuredText and an easy API to add new directives yourself. Most of them are generally not that relevant to modify but, as one would expect, Sphinx has pretty good documentation in case you need to know more about them. There are a few very commonly used ones which we will discus however.

The table of contents tree directive (toctree)

This is one of the most important directives in Sphinx; it generates `toctree` (table of contents tree). The `toctree` directive has a couple of options but the most important one is probably `maxdepth` which specifies how deep the tree needs to go. The top level of `toctree` has to be specified manually by specifying the files to be read, but beyond that every level within a document (section, chapter, paragraph, and so on) can be another level in `toctree`, depending on the depth of course. Even though the `maxdepth` option is optional, without it all the available levels will be shown, which is usually more than required. In most cases a `maxdepth` of 2 is a good default value which makes the basic example look like this:

```
.. toctree::
   :maxdepth: 2
```

The items in `toctree` are the `.rst` files in the same directory without the extension. This can include subdirectories, in which case the directories are separated with a `.` (period):

```
.. toctree::
   :maxdepth: 2


   module.a
   module.b
   module.c
```

Another very useful option is the `glob` option. It tells `toctree` to use the `glob` module in Python to automatically add all the documents matching a pattern. By simply adding a directory with a `glob` pattern, you can add all the files in that directory. This makes the `toctree` we had before as simple as:

```
.. toctree::

    :maxdepth: 2

    :glob:


    module.*
```

If for some reason the document title is not as you would have liked, you can easily change the title to something customized:

```
.. toctree::

    :maxdepth: 2


    The A module <module.a>
```

Autodoc, documenting Python modules, classes, and functions

The most powerful feature of Sphinx is the possibility of automatically documenting your modules, classes, and functions. The `sphinx-apidoc` command has already generated some of these for us, so let's use those files for the `Spam` and `Eggs` classes to extend the documentation a bit.

The original result from `sphinx-apidoc` was:

```
eggs module

===========


.. automodule:: eggs

    :members:

    :undoc-members:

    :show-inheritance:
```

This renders as:

> # eggs module
>
> *class* **eggs.Eggs**(*arg, *args, **kwargs*)   [source]
>
> > Bases: **spam.Spam**
>
> > **regular_method**()   [source]
> >
> > > This regular method overrides **spam.Spam.regular_method()**

The Eggs class has only a single function right now. We can of course click towards the parent class with ease, but in many cases it's useful to see all available functions in the class. So let's add all the functions that are inherited from Spam as well:

```
eggs module
===========
```

```
.. automodule:: eggs
    :members:
    :undoc-members:
    :show-inheritance:
    :inherited-members:
```

The output is as follows:

> # eggs module
>
> *class* **eggs.Eggs**(*arg, *args, **kwargs*)   [source]
> > Bases: **spam.Spam**
>
> > **decorated_method**(*arg*)
>
> > **regular_method**()   [source]
> >
> > > This regular method overrides **spam.Spam.regular_method()**

Much more useful already, but we are still missing the hidden method. Let's add the private members as well:

```
eggs module
===========
```

```
.. automodule:: eggs
    :members:
    :undoc-members:
    :show-inheritance:
    :inherited-members:
    :private-members:
```

Following is the output:

eggs module

class eggs.**Eggs**(*arg, *args, **kwargs*)   [source]

    Bases: **spam.Spam**

    _hidden_method()

    decorated_method(*arg*)

    regular_method()   [source]

        This regular method overrides **spam.Spam.regular_method()**

Now all the methods are shown, but what about the `members` option? Without the `members` option or the `*-members` options, no functions will be visible anymore.

`show-inheritance` is useful if you want to have the `Bases:` ... section so it is possible to click to the parent class.

Naturally, it is also possible to create classes manually. While this has little practical use, it does show the internal structure of Python classes within Sphinx.

There is a practical case however, if you are dynamically creating classes then `autodoc` will not always be able to document correctly and some additional help is required. There is more however, while it's generally not that useful as you're doing double work. In some cases, the `autodoc` extension won't be able to correctly identify the members of your class. This is true in case of dynamic class/function generation, for example. For such cases, it can be useful to add some manual documentation to the module/class/function:

```
eggs module
===========


.. automodule:: eggs
    :members:
    :undoc-members:
```

```
    :show-inheritance:


    .. class:: NonExistingClass
        This class doesn't actually exist, but it's in the documentation
now.


        .. method:: non_existing_function()


        And this function does not exist either.
```

Following is the output:

eggs module

class **eggs.Eggs**(*arg, *args, **kwargs*)   [source]
    Bases: **spam.Spam**

    regular_method()   [source]
        This regular method overrides **spam.Spam.regular_method()**

If at all possible, I would avoid this usage though. The biggest benefit of Sphinx is that it can automatically generate a large portion of your docs for you. By manually documenting, you may produce the one thing that's worse than no documentation, that is incorrect documentation. These statements are mainly useful for meta-documentation; documenting how a class might look instead of an actual example.

Sphinx roles

We have seen Sphinx directives, which are separate blocks. Now we will discuss Sphinx roles, which can be used in-line. A role allows you to tell Sphinx how to parse some input. Examples of these roles are links, math, code, and markup. But the most important ones are the roles within the Sphinx domains for referencing other classes, even for external projects. Within Sphinx, the default domain is the Python one so a role such as `:py:meth:` can be used as `:meth:` as well. These roles are really useful to link to different packages, modules, classes, methods, and other objects. The basic usage is simple enough. To link to a class, use the following:

```
Spam: :class:`spam.Spam`
```

The output is:

> Spam: **spam.Spam**

The same goes for just about any other object, functions, exceptions, attributes, and so on. The Sphinx documentation offers a list of supported objects: `http://sphinx-doc.org/domains.html#cross-referencing-python-objects`.

One of the nicer features of Sphinx is that this is actually possible across projects as well, adding a reference to the `int` object in the standard Python documentation is easily possible using `:obj:`int``. And adding references to your own projects on other sites is fairly trivial as well. Perhaps you remember the `intersphinx` question from the `sphinx-quickstart` script:

```
> intersphinx: link between Sphinx documentation
  of different projects (y/n) [n]: y
```

That's what makes cross-referencing between external Sphinx documentation and your local one possible. With `intersphinx` you can add links between projects with virtually no effort whatsoever. The standard `intersphinx_mapping` in `conf.py` is a bit limited:

```
intersphinx_mapping = {'https://docs.python.org/': None}
```

However, it can easily be extended to other documentation sites:

```
intersphinx_mapping = {
    'https://docs.python.org/': None,
    'sphinx': ('http://sphinx-doc.org/', None),
}
```

Now we can easily link to the documentation on the Sphinx homepage:

```
Link to the intersphinx module: :mod:`sphinx.ext.intersphinx`
```

Following is the output:

> Link to the intersphinx module: **sphinx.ext.intersphinx**

This links to `http://www.sphinx-doc.org/en/stable/ext/intersphinx.html`.

Documenting code

There are currently three different documentation styles supported by Sphinx: the original Sphinx style and the more recent NumPy and Google styles. The differences between them are mainly in style but it's actually slightly more than that.

The Sphinx style was developed using a bunch of reStructuredText roles, a very effective method but when used a lot it can be detrimental for readability. You can probably tell what the following does but it's not the nicest syntax:

```
:param amount: The amount of eggs to return

:type amount: int
```

The Google style was (as the name suggests) developed by Google. The goal was to have a simple/readable format which works both as in-code documentation and parse able for Sphinx. In my opinion, this comes closer to the original idea of reStructuredText, a format that's very close to how you would document instinctively. This example has the same meaning as the Sphinx style example shown earlier:

```
Args:
    amount (int): The amount of eggs to return
```

The NumPy style was created specifically for the NumPy project. The NumPy project has many functions with a huge amount of documentation and generally a lot of documentation per argument. It is slightly more verbose than the Google format but quite easy to read as well:

```
Parameters
----------
amount : int
    The amount of eggs to return
```

> In the future, with the Python 3.5 type hint annotations, at least the argument type part of these syntaxes might become useless. For the time being, Sphinx has no specific support for the annotations yet, so explicit type hinting through the docs must be used. But perhaps we can use the following soon:
> ```
> def eggs(amount: int):
>     pass
> ```

Documenting a class with the Sphinx style

First of all, let's look at the traditional style, the Sphinx style. While it's easy to understand what all the parameters mean, it's a bit verbose and not all that readable. Nonetheless, it's pretty clear and definitely not a bad style to use:

```
class Spam(object):
    '''
    The Spam object contains lots of spam

    :param arg: The arg is used for ...
    :type arg: str
    :param `*args`: The variable arguments are used for ...
    :param `**kwargs`: The keyword arguments are used for ...
    :ivar arg: This is where we store arg
    :vartype arg: str
    '''

    def __init__(self, arg, *args, **kwargs):
        self.arg = arg


    def eggs(self, amount, cooked):
        '''We can't have spam without eggs, so here's the eggs

        :param amount: The amount of eggs to return
        :type amount: int
        :param bool cooked: Should the eggs be cooked?
        :raises: :class:`RuntimeError`: Out of eggs

        :returns: A bunch of eggs
        :rtype: Eggs
        '''

        pass
```

Following is the output:

This is a very useful output indeed with documented functions, classes, and arguments. And more importantly, the types are documented as well, resulting in a clickable link towards the actual type. An added advantage of specifying the type is that many editors understand the documentation and will provide auto-completion based on the given types.

To explain what's actually happening here, Sphinx has a few roles within the docstrings that offer hints as to what we are documenting.

The `param` role paired with a name sets the documentation for the parameter with that name. The `type` role paired with a name tells Sphinx the data type of the parameter. Both the roles are optional and the parameter simply won't have any added documentation if they are omitted, but the `param` role is always required for any documentation to show. Simply adding the `type` role without the `param` role will result in no output whatsoever, so take note to always pair them.

The `returns` role is similar to the `param` role with regards to documenting. While the `param` role documents a parameter, the `returns` role documents the returned object. They are slightly different however. Opposed to the `param` role, the `returns` role is not dependent of the `rtype` role or vice versa. They both work independently of each other making it possible to use either or both of the roles.

The `rtype`, as you can expect, tells Sphinx (and several editors) what type of object is returned from the function.

Documenting a class with the Google style

The Google style is just a more legible version of the Sphinx style documentation. It doesn't actually support more or less but it's a lot more intuitive to use. The only thing to keep in mind is that it's a fairly recent feature of Sphinx. With the older versions, you were required to install the `sphinxcontrib-napoleon` package. These days it comes bundled with Sphinx but still needs to be enabled through the `conf.py` file. So, depending on the Sphinx version (Napoleon was added in Sphinx 1.3), you will need to add either `sphinx.ext.napoleon` or `sphinxcontrib.napoleon` to the extensions list in `conf.py`.

Once you have everything configured correctly, we can use both the Google and NumPy style. Here's the Google style version of the `Spam` class:

```
class Spam(object):
    '''
    The Spam object contains lots of spam

    Args:
        arg (str): The arg is used for ...
        *args: The variable arguments are used for ...
        **kwargs: The keyword arguments are used for ...

    Attributes:
        arg (str): This is where we store arg,
    '''
    def __init__(self, arg, *args, **kwargs):
        self.arg = arg

    def eggs(self, amount, cooked):
        '''We can't have spam without eggs, so here's the eggs

        Args:
            amount (int): The amount of eggs to return
            cooked (bool): Should the eggs be cooked?

        Raises:
            RuntimeError: Out of eggs
```

```
    Returns:

        Eggs: A bunch of eggs
    '''

    pass
```

This is easier on the eyes than the Sphinx style and has the same amount of possibilities. For longer argument documentation, it's less than convenient though. Just imagine how a multiline description of `amount` would look. That is why the NumPy style was developed, a lot of documentation for its arguments.

Documenting a class with the NumPy style

The NumPy style is meant for having a lot of documentation. Honestly, most people are too lazy for that, so for most projects it would not be a good fit. If you do plan to have extensive documentation of your functions and all their parameters, the NumPy style might be a good option for you. It's a bit more verbose than the Google style but it's very legible, especially with more detailed documentation. Just remember that, similar to the Google style, this requires the Napoleon extension for Sphinx, so make sure you have Sphinx 1.3 or above installed. Following is the NumPy version of the `Spam` class:

```
class Spam(object):
    '''
    The Spam object contains lots of spam

    Parameters
    ----------
    arg : str
        The arg is used for ...
    *args
        The variable arguments are used for ...
    **kwargs
        The keyword arguments are used for ...

    Attributes
    ----------
    arg : str
        This is where we store arg,
    '''
```

```python
    def __init__(self, arg, *args, **kwargs):
        self.arg = arg


    def eggs(self, amount, cooked):
        '''We can't have spam without eggs, so here's the eggs

        Parameters
        ----------
        amount : int
            The amount of eggs to return
        cooked : bool
            Should the eggs be cooked?

        Raises
        ------
        RuntimeError
            Out of eggs

        Returns
        -------
        Eggs
            A bunch of eggs
        '''

        pass
```

While the NumPy style definitely isn't bad, it's just very verbose. This example alone is about 1.5 times as long as the alternatives. So, for longer and more detailed documentation it's a very good choice, but if you're planning to have short documentation anyhow, just use the Google style instead.

Which style to choose

For most projects, the Google style is the best choice since it is readable but not too verbose. If you are planning to use large amounts of documentation per parameter then the NumPy style might be a good option as well.

The only reason to choose the Sphinx style is legacy. Even though the Google style might be more legible, consistency is more important.

Summary

Documentation can help greatly in a project's popularity and bad documentation can kill productivity. I think there are few aspects of a library that have more impact on the usage by third parties than documentation. Thus in many cases, documentation is a more important factor in deciding the usage of a project than the actual code quality. That's why it is very important to always try to have some documentation available.

With Sphinx it is actually easy to generate documentation. With just a few minutes of your time, you can have a fully functioning website with documentation available, or a PDF, or ePub, or one of the many other output formats. There really is no excuse for having no documentation anymore. And even if you don't use the documentation that much yourself, offering type hints to your editor can help a lot in productivity as well. Making your editor smarter should always help in productivity. I for one have added type hints to several projects simply to increase my productivity.

The next chapter will explain how code can be tested in Python and some part of the documentation will return there. Using `doctest`, it is possible to have example code, documentation, and tests in one.

10
Testing and Logging – Preparing for Bugs

When programming, most developers plan a bit and immediately continue writing code. After all, we all expect to write bug-free code! Unfortunately, we don't. At some point, an incorrect assumption, a misinterpretation, or just a silly mistake is bound to happen. Debugging (covered in *Chapter 11, Debugging – Solving the Bugs*) will always be required at some point, but there are several methods that you can use to prevent bugs or, at the very least, make it much easier to solve them when they do occur.

To prevent bugs from occurring in the first place, test-driven development or, at the very least, functional/regression/unit tests are very useful. The standard Python installation alone offers several options such as the `doctest`, `unittest`, and `test` modules. The `doctest` module allows you to combine tests with example documentation. The `unittest` module allows you to easily write regression tests. The `test` module is meant for internal usage only, so unless you are planning to modify the Python core, you probably won't need this one.

The test modules we will discuss in this chapter are:

- `doctest`
- `py.test` (and why it's more convenient than `unittest`)
- `unittest.mock`

The `py.test` module has roughly the same purpose as the `unittest` module, but it's much more convenient to use and has a few extra options.

After learning how to avoid the bugs, it's time to take a look at logging so that we can inspect what is happening in our program and why. The logging module in Python is highly configurable and can be adjusted for just about any use case. If you've ever written Java code, you should feel right at home with the `logging` module, as its design is largely based on the `log4j` module and is very similar in both implementation and naming. The latter makes it a bit of an odd module in Python as well, as it is one of the few modules that do not follow the `pep8` naming standards.

This chapter will explain the following topics:

- Combining documentation with tests using `doctest`
- Regression and unit tests using `py.test` and `unittest`
- Testing with fake objects using `unittest.mock`
- Using the `logging` module effectively
- Combining `logging` and `py.test`

Using examples as tests with doctest

The `doctest` module is one of the most useful modules within Python. It allows you to combine documenting your code with tests to make sure that it keeps working as it is supposed to.

A simple doctest example

Let's start with a quick example: a function that squares the input. The following example is a fully functional command-line application, containing not only code but also functioning tests. The first few tests cover how the function is supposed to behave when executing normally, followed by a few tests to demonstrate the expected errors:

```python
def square(n):
    '''
    Returns the input number, squared

    >>> square(0)
    0
    >>> square(1)
    1
    >>> square(2)
    4
```

```
>>> square(3)
9
>>> square()
Traceback (most recent call last):
...
TypeError: square() missing 1 required positional argument: 'n'
>>> square('x')
Traceback (most recent call last):
...
TypeError: can't multiply sequence by non-int of type 'str'

Args:
    n (int): The number to square

Returns:
    int: The squared result
'''
return n * n


if __name__ == '__main__':
    import doctest
    doctest.testmod()
```

It can be executed as any Python script, but the regular command won't give any output as all tests are successful. The `doctest.testmod` function takes verbosity parameters, luckily:

```
# python square.py -v
Trying:
    square(0)
Expecting:
    0
ok
Trying:
    square(1)
Expecting:
    1
```

```
ok
Trying:
    square(2)
Expecting:
    4
ok
Trying:
    square(3)
Expecting:
    9
ok
Trying:
    square()
Expecting:
    Traceback (most recent call last):
    ...
    TypeError: square() missing 1 required positional argument: 'n'
ok
Trying:
    square('x')
Expecting:
    Traceback (most recent call last):
    ...
    TypeError: can't multiply sequence by non-int of type 'str'
ok
1 items had no tests:
    __main__
1 items passed all tests:
   6 tests in __main__.square
6 tests in 2 items.
6 passed and 0 failed.
Test passed.
```

Additionally, since it uses the Google syntax (as discussed in *Chapter 9, Documentation – How to Use Sphinx and reStructuredText*, the documentation chapter), we can generate pretty documentation using Sphinx:

square module

square.**square**(*n*)   [source]

> Returns the input number, squared
>
> ```
> >>> square(0)
> 0
> >>> square(1)
> 1
> >>> square(2)
> 4
> >>> square(3)
> 9
> >>> square()
> Traceback (most recent call last):
> ...
> TypeError: square() missing 1 required positional argument: 'n'
> >>> square('x')
> Traceback (most recent call last):
> ...
> TypeError: can't multiply sequence by non-int of type 'str'
> ```
>
> | Parameters: | n (int) – The number to square |
> |---|---|
> | Returns: | The squared result |
> | Return type: | int |

However, the code is not always correct, of course. What would happen if we modify the code so that the tests do not pass anymore?

This time, instead of n * n, we use n ** 2. Both square a number right? So the results must be identical. Right? These are the types of assumptions that create bugs, and the types of assumptions that are trivial to catch using a few basic tests:

```
def square(n):
    '''

    Returns the input number, squared

    >>> square(0)
    0
    >>> square(1)
    1
    >>> square(2)
```

```
4
>>> square(3)
9
>>> square()
Traceback (most recent call last):
...
TypeError: square() missing 1 required positional argument: 'n'
>>> square('x')
Traceback (most recent call last):
...
TypeError: can't multiply sequence by non-int of type 'str'

Args:
    n (int): The number to square

Returns:
    int: The squared result
'''
return n ** 2


if __name__ == '__main__':
    import doctest
    doctest.testmod()
```

So let's execute the test again and see what happens this time. For brevity, we will skip the verbosity flag this time:

```
# python square.py
**********************************************************************
File "square.py", line 17, in __main__.square
Failed example:
    square('x')
Expected:
    Traceback (most recent call last):
    ...
    TypeError: can't multiply sequence by non-int of type 'str'
Got:
```

```
    Traceback (most recent call last):
      File "doctest.py", line 1320, in __run
        compileflags, 1), test.globs)
      File "<doctest __main__.square[5]>", line 1, in <module>
        square('x')
      File "square.py", line 28, in square
        return n ** 2
    TypeError: unsupported operand type(s) for ** or pow(): 'str' and
'int'
**********************************************************************
1 items had failures:
   1 of   6 in __main__.square
***Test Failed*** 1 failures.
```

The only modification we made to the code was replacing n * n with n ** 2, which translates to the power function. Since multiplication is not the same as taking the power of a number, the results are slightly different but similar enough in practice that most programmers wouldn't notice the difference.

The only difference caused by the code change was that we now have a different exception—an innocent mistake, only breaking the tests in this case. But it shows how useful these tests are. When rewriting code, an incorrect assumption is easily made, and that is where tests are most useful—knowing you are breaking code as soon as you break it instead of finding out months later.

Writing doctests

Perhaps, you have noticed from the preceding examples that the syntax is very similar to the regular Python console, and that is exactly the point. The doctest input is nothing more than the output of a regular Python shell session. This is what makes testing with this module so intuitive; simply write the code in the Python console and copy the output into a docstring to get tests. Here is an example:

```
# python
>>> from square import square
>>> square(5)
25
>>> square()
Traceback (most recent call last):
  File "<stdin>", line 1, in <module>
TypeError: square() missing 1 required positional argument: 'n'
```

That's why this is probably the easiest way to test code. With almost no effort, you can check whether your code is working as you would expect it, add tests, and add documentation at the same time. Simply copy the output from the interpreter to your function or class documentation and you have functioning doctests.

Testing with pure documentation

The docstrings in functions, classes, and modules are usually the most obvious way to add doctests to your code, but they are not the only way. The Sphinx documentation, as we discussed in the previous chapter, also supports the `doctest` module. You might remember that when creating the Sphinx project, we enabled the `doctest` module:

```
> doctest: automatically test code snippets in doctest blocks (y/n) [n]:y
```

This flag enables the `sphinx.ext.doctest` extension in Sphinx, which tells Sphinx to run those tests as well. Since not all the examples in the code are useful, let's see whether we can split them between the ones that are actually useful and the ones that are only relevant for documentation. Moreover, to see the results, we will add an error to the documentation:

square.py

```
def square(n):
    '''
    Returns the input number, squared

    >>> square(2)
    4

    Args:
        n (int): The number to square

    Returns:
        int: The squared result
    '''

    return n * n


if __name__ == '__main__':
    import doctest
    doctest.testmod()
```

square.rst

```
square module
=============

.. automodule:: square
   :members:
   :undoc-members:
   :show-inheritance:

Examples:

.. testsetup::

   from square import square

.. doctest::

   >>> square(100)

   >>> square(0)
   0
   >>> square(1)
   1
   >>> square(3)
   9
   >>> square()
   Traceback (most recent call last):
   ...
   TypeError: square() missing 1 required positional argument: 'n'
   >>> square('x')
   Traceback (most recent call last):
   ...
   TypeError: can't multiply sequence by non-int of type 'str'
```

Now, it's time to execute the tests. In the case of Sphinx, there is a specific command for this:

```
# make doctest
sphinx-build -b doctest -d _build/doctrees . _build/doctest
Running Sphinx v1.3.3
loading translations [en]... done
loading pickled environment... done
building [mo]: targets for 0 po files that are out of date
building [doctest]: targets for 3 source files that are out of date
updating environment: 0 added, 0 changed, 0 removed
looking for now-outdated files... none found
running tests...


Document: square
----------------
**********************************************************************
File "square.rst", line 16, in default
Failed example:
    square(100)
Expected nothing
Got:
    10000
**********************************************************************
1 items had failures:
   1 of   7 in default
7 tests in 1 items.
6 passed and 1 failed.
***Test Failed*** 1 failures.


Doctest summary
===============
    7 tests
    1 failure in tests
    0 failures in setup code
    0 failures in cleanup code
build finished with problems.
make: *** [doctest] Error 1
```

As expected, we are getting an error for the incomplete `doctest`, but beyond that, all tests executed correctly. To make sure that the tests know what `square` is, we had to add the `testsetup` directive, and this still generates a pretty output:

---

square module

square.**square**(*n*)   [source]

Returns the input number, squared

```
>>> square(2)
4
:param n: The number to square
:type n: int
```

Returns: The squared result

Return type: int

Examples:

```
>>> square(100)

>>> square(0)
0
>>> square(1)
1
>>> square(3)
9
>>> square()
Traceback (most recent call last):
...
TypeError: square() missing 1 required positional argument: 'n'
>>> square('x')
Traceback (most recent call last):
...
TypeError: can't multiply sequence by non-int of type 'str'
```

The doctest flags

The `doctest` module features several option flags. They affect how `doctest` processes the tests. These option flags can be passed globally using your test suite, through command-line parameters while running the tests, and through inline commands. For this book, I have globally enabled the following option flags through a `pytest.ini` file (we will cover more about `py.test` later in this chapter):

```
doctest_optionflags = ELLIPSIS NORMALIZE_WHITESPACE
```

Without these option flags, some of the examples in this book will not function properly. This is because they have to be reformatted to fit. The next few paragraphs will cover the following option flags:

- DONT_ACCEPT_TRUE_FOR_1
- NORMALIZE_WHITESPACE
- ELLIPSIS

There are several other option flags available with varying degrees of usefulness, but these are better left to the Python documentation:

```
https://docs.python.org/3/library/doctest.html#option-flags
```

True and False versus 1 and 0

Having `True` evaluating to `1` and `False` evaluating to `0` is useful in most cases, but it can give unexpected results. To demonstrate the difference, we have these lines:

```
'''
>>> False
0
>>> True
1
>>> False  # doctest: +DONT_ACCEPT_TRUE_FOR_1
0
>>> True   # doctest: +DONT_ACCEPT_TRUE_FOR_1
1
'''


if __name__ == '__main__':
    import doctest
    doctest.testmod()
```

Here are the results of the DONT_ACCEPT_TRUE_FOR_1 flag:

```
# python test.py
**********************************************************************
File "test.py", line 6, in __main__
Failed example:
    False  # doctest: +DONT_ACCEPT_TRUE_FOR_1
```

```
Expected:
    0
Got:
    False
******************************************************************
File "test.py", line 8, in __main__
Failed example:
    True   # doctest: +DONT_ACCEPT_TRUE_FOR_1
Expected:
    1
Got:
    True
******************************************************************
1 items had failures:
   2 of   4 in __main__
***Test Failed*** 2 failures.
```

As you can see, the DONT_ACCEPT_TRUE_FOR_1 flag makes doctest reject 1 as a valid response for True as well as 0 for False.

Normalizing whitespace

Since doctests are used for both documentation and test purposes, it is pretty much a requirement to keep them readable. Without normalizing whitespace, this can be tricky, however. Consider the following example:

```
>>> [list(range(5)) for i in range(5)]
[[0, 1, 2, 3, 4], [0, 1, 2, 3, 4], [0, 1, 2, 3, 4], [0, 1, 2, 3, 4], [0,
1, 2, 3, 4]]
```

While not all that bad, this output isn't the best for readability. With whitespace normalizing, here is what we can do instead:

```
>>> [list(range(5)) for i in range(5)]   # doctest: +NORMALIZE_WHITESPACE
[[0, 1, 2, 3, 4],
 [0, 1, 2, 3, 4],
 [0, 1, 2, 3, 4],
 [0, 1, 2, 3, 4],
 [0, 1, 2, 3, 4]]
```

Formatting the output in this manner is both more readable and convenient for keeping your line length less.

Ellipsis

The `ELLIPSIS` flag is very useful but also a bit dangerous, as it can easily lead to incorrect matches. It makes . . . match any substring, which is very useful for exceptions but dangerous in other cases:

```
>>> {10: 'a', 20: 'b'}  # doctest: +ELLIPSIS
{...}
>>> [True, 1, 'a']  # doctest: +ELLIPSIS
[...]
>>> True,  # doctest: +ELLIPSIS
(...)
>>> [1, 2, 3, 4]  # doctest: +ELLIPSIS
[1, ..., 4]
>>> [1, 0, 0, 0, 0, 0, 4]  # doctest: +ELLIPSIS
[1, ..., 4]
```

These cases are not too useful in real scenarios, but they demonstrate how the `ELLIPSIS` option flag functions. They also indicate the danger. Both `[1, 2, 3, 4]` and `[1, 0, ... , 4]` match the `[1, ..., 4]` test, which is probably unintentional, so be very careful while using `ELLIPSIS`.

A more useful case is when documenting class instances:

```
>>> class Spam(object):
...     pass
>>> Spam()  # doctest: +ELLIPSIS
<__main__.Spam object at 0x...>
```

Without the `ELLIPSIS` flag, the memory address (the `0x...` part) would never be what you expect. Let's demonstrate an actual run in a normal CPython instance:

```
Failed example:
    Spam()
Expected:
    <__main__.Spam object at 0x...>
Got:
    <__main__.Spam object at 0x10d9ad160>
```

Doctest quirks

The three option flags discussed earlier take care of quite a few quirks found in doctests, but there are several more cases that require care. In these cases, you just need to be a bit careful and work around the limitations of the doctest module. The doctest module effectively uses the representation string, and those are not always consistent.

The most important cases are floating-point inaccuracies, dictionaries, and random values, such as timers. The following example will fail most of the time because certain types in Python have no consistent ordering and depend on external variables:

```
>>> dict.fromkeys('spam')
{'s': None, 'p': None, 'a': None, 'm': None}
>>> 1./7.
0.14285714285714285

>>> import time
>>> time.time() - time.time()
-9.5367431640625e-07
```

All the problems have several possible solutions, which differ mostly in style and your personal preference.

Testing dictionaries

The problem with dictionaries is that they are internally implemented as hash tables, resulting in an effectively random representation order. Since the doctest system requires a representation string that is identical in meaning (save for certain doctest flags, of course) to the docstring, this does not work. Naturally, there are several workaround options available and all have some advantages and disadvantages.

The first is using the pprint library to format it in a pretty way:

```
>>> import pprint
>>> data = dict.fromkeys('spam')
>>> pprint.pprint(data)
{'a': None, 'm': None, 'p': None, 's': None}
```

Since the pprint library always sorts the items before outputting, this solves the problem with random representation orders. However, it does require an extra import and function call, which some people prefer to avoid.

Another option is manual sorting of the items:

```
>>> data = dict.fromkeys('spam')
>>> sorted(data.items())
[('a', None), ('m', None), ('p', None), ('s', None)]
```

The downside here is that it is not visible from the output that `data` is a dictionary, which makes the output less readable.

Lastly, comparing the `dict` with a different `dict` comprised of the same elements works as well:

```
>>> data = dict.fromkeys('spam')
>>> data == {'a': None, 'm': None, 'p': None, 's': None}
True
```

A perfectly okay solution, of course! But `True` is not really the clearest output, especially if the comparison doesn't work:

```
Failed example:
    data == {'a': None, 'm': None, 'p': None}
Expected:
    True
Got:
    False
```

On the other hand, the other options presented previously show both the expected value and the returned value correctly:

```
Failed example:
    sorted(data.items())
Expected:
    [('a', None), ('m', None), ('p', None)]
Got:
    [('a', None), ('m', None), ('p', None), ('s', None)]


Failed example:
    pprint.pprint(data)
Expected:
    {'a': None, 'm': None, 'p': None}
Got:
    {'a': None, 'm': None, 'p': None, 's': None}
```

Personally, out of the solutions presented, I would recommend using `pprint`, as I find it the most readable solution, but all the solutions have some merits to them.

Testing floating-point numbers

For the same reason as a floating-point comparison can be problematic (that is, `1/3 == 0.333`), a representation string comparison is also problematic. The easiest solution is to simply add some rounding/clipping to your code, but the `ELLIPSIS` flag is also an option here. Here is a list of several solutions:

```
>>> 1/3  # doctest: +ELLIPSIS
0.333...
>>> '%.3f' % (1/3)
'0.333'
>>> '{:.3f}'.format(1/3)
'0.333'
>>> round(1/3, 3)
0.333
>>> 0.333 < 1/3 < 0.334
True
```

When the `ELLIPSIS` option flag is enabled globally anyhow, that would be the most obvious solution. In other cases, I recommend one of the alternative solutions.

Times and durations

For timings, the problems that you will encounter are quite similar to the floating-point issues. When measuring the duration execution time of a code snippet, there will always be some variation present. That's why the most stable solution for tests, including time, is limiting the precision, although even that is no guarantee. Regardless, the simplest solution checks whether the delta between the two times is smaller than a certain number, as follows:

```
>>> import time
>>> a = time.time()
>>> b = time.time()
>>> (b - a) < 0.01
True
```

For the `timedelta` objects, however, it's slightly more complicated. Yet, this is where the `ELLIPSIS` flag definitely comes in handy again:

```
>>> import datetime
>>> a = datetime.datetime.now()
>>> b = datetime.datetime.now()
>>> str(b - a)  # doctest: +ELLIPSIS
'0:00:00.000...
```

The alternative to the `ELLIPSIS` option flag would be comparing the days, hours, minutes, and microseconds in `timedelta` separately.

In a later paragraph, we will see a completely stable solution for problems like these using mock objects. For doctests, however, that is generally overkill.

Testing with py.test

The `py.test` tool makes it very easy to write tests and run them. There are a few other options such as `nose` and the bundled `unittest` module available, but the `py.test` library offers a very good combination of usability and active development. In the past, I was an avid `nose` user but have since switched to `py.test` as it tends to be easier to use and has better community support, in my experience at least. Regardless, `nose` is still a good choice, and if you're already using it, there is little reason to switch and rewrite all of your tests. When writing tests for a new project, however, `py.test` can be much more convenient.

Now, we will run the doctests from the previously discussed `square.py` file using `py.test`.

First, start by installing `py.test`, of course:

```
pip install pytest
```

Now you can do a test run, so let's give the doctests we have in `square.py` a try:

```
# py.test --doctest-modules -v square.py

======================== test session starts ========================
platform darwin -- Python 3.5.1, pytest-2.8.2, py-1.4.30, pluggy-0.3.1 --
python3.5
cachedir: .cache
rootdir: code, inifile: pytest.ini
collected 1 items
```

```
square.py::square.square PASSED


==================== 1 passed in 0.02 seconds =====================
```

The difference between the unittest and py.test output

We have the doctests in `square.py`. Let's create a new class called `cube` and create a proper set of tests outside of the code.

First of all, we have the code of `cube.py`, similar to `square.py` but minus the doctests, since we don't need them anymore:

```
def cube(n):
    '''

    Returns the input number, cubed

    Args:
        n (int): The number to cube

    Returns:
        int: The cubed result
    '''
    return n ** 3
```

Now let's start with the `unittest` example, `test_cube.py`:

```
import cube
import unittest


class TestCube(unittest.TestCase):
    def test_0(self):
        self.assertEqual(cube.cube(0), 0)

    def test_1(self):
        self.assertEqual(cube.cube(1), 1)

    def test_2(self):
```

```
        self.assertEqual(cube.cube(2), 8)


    def test_3(self):
        self.assertEqual(cube.cube(3), 27)


    def test_no_arguments(self):
        with self.assertRaises(TypeError):
            cube.cube()


    def test_exception_str(self):
        with self.assertRaises(TypeError):
            cube.cube('x')


if __name__ == '__main__':
    unittest.main()
```

This can be executed by executing the file itself:

```
# python test_cube.py -v
test_0 (__main__.TestCube) ... ok
test_1 (__main__.TestCube) ... ok
test_2 (__main__.TestCube) ... ok
test_3 (__main__.TestCube) ... ok
test_exception_str (__main__.TestCube) ... ok
test_no_arguments (__main__.TestCube) ... ok


----------------------------------------------------------------------

Ran 6 tests in 0.001s


OK
```

Alternatively, it can be done through the module:

```
# python -m unittest -v test_cube.py
test_0 (test_cube.TestCube) ... ok
test_1 (test_cube.TestCube) ... ok
test_2 (test_cube.TestCube) ... ok
test_3 (test_cube.TestCube) ... ok
test_exception_str (test_cube.TestCube) ... ok
```

```
test_no_arguments (test_cube.TestCube) ... ok
```

```
----------------------------------------------------------------------
```

```
Ran 6 tests in 0.001s
```

```
OK
```

This one is through `py.test`:

```
# py.test -v test_cube.py
====================== test session starts ======================
platform darwin -- Python 3.5.1, pytest-2.8.5, py-1.4.31, pluggy-0.3.1 --
python3.5
cachedir: ../.cache
rootdir: code, inifile: pytest.ini
collected 6 items

test_cube.py::TestCube::test_0 PASSED
test_cube.py::TestCube::test_1 PASSED
test_cube.py::TestCube::test_2 PASSED
test_cube.py::TestCube::test_3 PASSED
test_cube.py::TestCube::test_exception_str PASSED
test_cube.py::TestCube::test_no_arguments PASSED

=================== 6 passed in 0.02 seconds ====================
```

We even have `nose`:

```
# nosetests -v test_cube.py
test_0 (test_cube.TestCube) ... ok
test_1 (test_cube.TestCube) ... ok
test_2 (test_cube.TestCube) ... ok
test_3 (test_cube.TestCube) ... ok
test_exception_str (test_cube.TestCube) ... ok
test_no_arguments (test_cube.TestCube) ... ok

----------------------------------------------------------------------
Ran 6 tests in 0.001s

OK
```

As long as all the results are successful, the differences between `unittest` and `py.test` are slim. In the case of `unittest` and `nose`, the results are identical. This time around, however, we are going to break the code to show the difference when it actually matters. Instead of the `cube` code, we will add the `square` code. So returning `n ** 2` instead of `n ** 3` from `square`.

First of all, we have the regular `unittest` output:

```
# python test_cube.py -v
test_0 (__main__.TestCube) ... ok
test_1 (__main__.TestCube) ... ok
test_2 (__main__.TestCube) ... FAIL
test_3 (__main__.TestCube) ... FAIL
test_exception_str (__main__.TestCube) ... ok
test_no_arguments (__main__.TestCube) ... ok


======================================================================
FAIL: test_2 (__main__.TestCube)
----------------------------------------------------------------------
Traceback (most recent call last):
  File "test_cube.py", line 13, in test_2
    self.assertEqual(cube.cube(2), 8)
AssertionError: 4 != 8


======================================================================
FAIL: test_3 (__main__.TestCube)
----------------------------------------------------------------------
Traceback (most recent call last):
  File "test_cube.py", line 16, in test_3
    self.assertEqual(cube.cube(3), 27)
AssertionError: 9 != 27


----------------------------------------------------------------------
Ran 6 tests in 0.001s


FAILED (failures=2)
```

Not all that bad, as per each test returns a nice stack trace that includes the values and everything. Yet, we can observe a small difference here when compared with the py.test run:

```
# py.test -v test_cube.py
======================= test session starts =======================
platform darwin -- Python 3.5.1, pytest-2.8.5, py-1.4.31, pluggy-0.3.1 --
python3.5
cachedir: ../.cache
rootdir: code, inifile: pytest.ini
collected 6 items

test_cube.py::TestCube::test_0 PASSED
test_cube.py::TestCube::test_1 PASSED
test_cube.py::TestCube::test_2 FAILED
test_cube.py::TestCube::test_3 FAILED
test_cube.py::TestCube::test_exception_str PASSED
test_cube.py::TestCube::test_no_arguments PASSED


============================= FAILURES =============================
_____ TestCube.test_2 _____


self = <test_cube.TestCube testMethod=test_2>

    def test_2(self):
>       self.assertEqual(cube.cube(2), 8)
E       AssertionError: 4 != 8

test_cube.py:13: AssertionError
_____ TestCube.test_3 _____


self = <test_cube.TestCube testMethod=test_3>

    def test_3(self):
>       self.assertEqual(cube.cube(3), 27)
E       AssertionError: 9 != 27

test_cube.py:16: AssertionError
================== 2 failed, 4 passed in 0.03 seconds ==================
```

In small cases such as these, the difference is not all that apparent, but when testing complicated code with large stack traces, it becomes even more useful. However, for me personally, seeing the surrounding test code is a big advantage. In the example that was just discussed, the `self.assertEqual(...)` line shows the entire test, but in many other cases, you will need more information. The difference between the regular `unittest` module and the `py.test` module is that you can see the entire function with all of the code and the output. Later in this chapter, we will see how powerful this can be when writing more advanced tests.

To truly appreciate the `py.test` output, we need to enable colors as well. The colors depend on your local color schemes, of course, but it's useful to see them side by side at least once, as shown here:

```
# py.test -v test_cube.py
============================ test session starts ============================
collected 7 items

test_cube.py PASSED
test_cube.py::TestCube::test_0 PASSED
test_cube.py::TestCube::test_1 PASSED
test_cube.py::TestCube::test_2 FAILED
test_cube.py::TestCube::test_3 FAILED
test_cube.py::TestCube::test_exception_str PASSED
test_cube.py::TestCube::test_no_arguments PASSED


============================ FAILURES ============================
_____ TestCube.test_2 _____

self = <test_cube.TestCube testMethod=test_2>

    def test_2(self):
>       self.assertEqual(cube.cube(2), 8)
E       AssertionError: 4 != 8

test_cube.py:14: AssertionError
_____ TestCube.test_3 _____

self = <test_cube.TestCube testMethod=test_3>

    def test_3(self):
>       self.assertEqual(cube.cube(3), 27)
E       AssertionError: 9 != 27

test_cube.py:17: AssertionError
============== 2 failed, 5 passed in 0.02 seconds ===============
>       self.assertEqual(cube.cube(3), 27)
E       AssertionError: 9 != 27

test_cube.py:17: AssertionError
============== 2 failed, 5 passed in 0.02 seconds ===============
```

```
# python test_cube.py -v
test_0 (__main__.TestCube) ... ok
test_1 (__main__.TestCube) ... ok
test_2 (__main__.TestCube) ... FAIL
test_3 (__main__.TestCube) ... FAIL
test_exception_str (__main__.TestCube) ... ok
test_no_arguments (__main__.TestCube) ... ok


======================================================================
FAIL: test_2 (__main__.TestCube)
----------------------------------------------------------------------
Traceback (most recent call last):
  File "test_cube.py", line 14, in test_2
    self.assertEqual(cube.cube(2), 8)
AssertionError: 4 != 8

======================================================================
FAIL: test_3 (__main__.TestCube)
----------------------------------------------------------------------
Traceback (most recent call last):
  File "test_cube.py", line 17, in test_3
    self.assertEqual(cube.cube(3), 27)
AssertionError: 9 != 27

----------------------------------------------------------------------
Ran 6 tests in 0.001s

FAILED (failures=2)
```

Perhaps you are wondering now, "Is that all?" The only difference between `py.test` and `unittest` is a bit of color and a slightly different output? Well, far from it, there are many other differences, but this alone is enough reason to give it a try.

The difference between unittest and py.test tests

The improved output does help a bit, but the combination of improved output and a much easier way to write tests is what makes `py.test` so useful. There are quite a few methods for making the tests simpler and more legible, and in many cases, you can choose which you prefer. As always, readability counts, so choose wisely and try not to over-engineer the solutions.

Simplifying assertions

Where the unittest library requires the usage of `self.assertEqual` to compare variables, `py.test` uses some magic to allow for simpler tests using regular `assert` statements.

The following test file contains both styles of tests, so they can be compared easily:

```
import cube
import pytest
import unittest


class TestCube(unittest.TestCase):
    def test_0(self):
        self.assertEqual(cube.cube(0), 0)

    def test_1(self):
        self.assertEqual(cube.cube(1), 1)

    def test_2(self):
        self.assertEqual(cube.cube(2), 8)

    def test_3(self):
        self.assertEqual(cube.cube(3), 27)

    def test_no_arguments(self):
        with self.assertRaises(TypeError):
            cube.cube()

    def test_exception_str(self):
        with self.assertRaises(TypeError):
            cube.cube('x')


class TestPyCube(object):
    def test_0(self):
        assert cube.cube(0) == 0

    def test_1(self):
        assert cube.cube(1) == 1

    def test_2(self):
        assert cube.cube(2) == 8
```

```
def test_3(self):
    assert cube.cube(3) == 27

def test_no_arguments(self):
    with pytest.raises(TypeError):
        cube.cube()

def test_exception_str(self):
    with pytest.raises(TypeError):
        cube.cube('x')
```

So what did we do? Well, we simply replaced `self.assertEqual` with `assert` `... == ...` and `with self.assertRaises` with `with pytest.raises`. A minor improvement indeed, but the actual benefit is seen in the failure output. The first two use the `unittest` style and the latter two use the `py.test` style:

```
============================= FAILURES =============================
_____ TestCube.test_2 _____


self = <test_cube.TestCube testMethod=test_2>


    def test_2(self):
>       self.assertEqual(cube.cube(2), 8)
E       AssertionError: 4 != 8


test_cube.py:14: AssertionError
_____ TestCube.test_3 _____


self = <test_cube.TestCube testMethod=test_3>


    def test_3(self):
>       self.assertEqual(cube.cube(3), 27)
E       AssertionError: 9 != 27


test_cube.py:17: AssertionError
_____ TestPyCube.test_2 _____


self = <test_cube.TestPyCube object at 0x107c7bef0>
```

```
    def test_2(self):
>       assert cube.cube(2) == 8
E       assert 4 == 8
E        +  where 4 = <function cube at 0x107bb7c80>(2)
E        +    where <function cube at 0x107bb7c80> = cube.cube


test_cube.py:36: AssertionError
_____ TestPyCube.test_3 _____


self = <test_cube.TestPyCube object at 0x107c56a90>


    def test_3(self):
>       assert cube.cube(3) == 27
E       assert 9 == 27
E        +  where 9 = <function cube at 0x107bb7c80>(3)
E        +    where <function cube at 0x107bb7c80> = cube.cube


test_cube.py:39: AssertionError
================ 4 failed, 8 passed in 0.05 seconds ================
```

Therefore, in addition to seeing the values that were compared, we can actually see the function that was called and which input parameters it received. With the static numbers that we have here, it may not be that useful, but it is invaluable when using variables, as we'll see in the next paragraphs.

> The preceding tests are all stored in a class. With py.test, that's completely optional, however. If readability or inheritance makes it useful to encapsulate the tests in a class, then feel free to do so, but as far as py.test is concerned, there is no advantage.

The standard py.test behavior works for most test cases, but it may not be enough for some custom types. For example, let's say that we have a Spam object with a count attribute that should be compared with the count attribute on another object. This part can easily be achieved by implementing the __eq__ method on Spam, but it does not improve clarity. Since count is the attribute that we compare, it would be useful if the tests show count when errors are displayed. First is the class with two tests, one working and one broken to demonstrate the regular output:

test_spam.py

```
    class Spam(object):
        def __init__(self, count):
```

```
            self.count = count

        def __eq__(self, other):
            return self.count == other.count


    def test_spam_equal_correct():
        a = Spam(5)
        b = Spam(5)

        assert a == b


    def test_spam_equal_broken():
        a = Spam(5)
        b = Spam(10)

        assert a == b
```

And here is the regular py.test output:

```
============================== FAILURES ==============================
_____ test_spam_equal_broken _____

    def test_spam_equal_broken():
        a = Spam(5)
        b = Spam(10)

>       assert a == b
E       assert <test_spam.Spam object at 0x105b484e0> == <test_spam.Spam
object at 0x105b48518>

test_spam.py:20: AssertionError
================= 1 failed, 1 passed in 0.01 seconds =================
```

The default test output is still usable since the function is fairly straightforward, and the value for count is visible due to it being available in the constructor. However, it would have been more useful if we could explicitly see the value of count. By adding a pytest_assertrepr_compare function to the conftest.py file, we can modify the behavior of the assert statements.

> That's a special file for py.test that can be used to override or extend py.test. Note that this file will automatically be loaded by every test run in that directory, so we need to test the types of both the left-hand side and the right-hand side of the operator. In this case, it's a and b.

conftest.py

```
import test_spam


def pytest_assertrepr_compare(config, op, left, right):
    left_spam = isinstance(left, test_spam.Spam)
    right_spam = isinstance(right, test_spam.Spam)
    if left_spam and right_spam and op == '==':
        return [
            'Comparing Spam instances:',
            '    counts: %s != %s' % (left.count, right.count),
        ]
```

The preceding function will be used as the output for our test. So when it fails, this time we get our own, slightly more useful, output:

```
============================== FAILURES ==============================
_____ test_spam_equal_broken _____

    def test_spam_equal_broken():
        a = Spam(5)
        b = Spam(10)

>       assert a == b
E       assert Comparing Spam instances:
E               counts: 5 != 10

test_spam.py:20: AssertionError
================= 1 failed, 1 passed in 0.01 seconds =================
```

In this case, we could have easily changed the __repr__ function of Spam as well, but there are many cases where modifying the py.test output can be useful. Similar to this, there is specific support for many types, such as sets, dictionaries, and texts.

Parameterizing tests

So far, we have specified every test separately, but we can simplify tests a lot by parameterizing them. Both the square and cube tests were very similar; a certain input gave a certain output. This is something that can easily be verified using a loop, of course, but using a loop in a test has a pretty big downside. It will be executed as a single test. This means that it will fail in its entirety if a single test iteration of the loop fails, and that is a problem. Instead of having an output for every version, you will get it only once, while they actually might be separate bugs. That's where parameters help. You can simply create a list of parameters and the expected data and make it run the test function for every parameter separately:

```python
import cube
import pytest


cubes = (
    (0, 0),
    (1, 1),
    (2, 8),
    (3, 27),
)


@pytest.mark.parametrize('n,expected', cubes)
def test_cube(n, expected):
    assert cube.cube(n) == expected
```

This outputs the following, as you might have already expected:

```
=============================== FAILURES ===============================
_____ test_cube[2-8] _____


n = 2, expected = 8

    @pytest.mark.parametrize('n,expected', cubes)
    def test_cube(n, expected):
>       assert cube.cube(n) == expected
E       assert 4 == 8
E        +  where 4 = <function cube at 0x106576268>(2)
E        +    where <function cube at 0x106576268> = cube.cube

test_cube.py:15: AssertionError
_____ test_cube[3-27] _____
```

```
n = 3, expected = 27

    @pytest.mark.parametrize('n,expected', cubes)
    def test_cube(n, expected):
>       assert cube.cube(n) == expected
E       assert 9 == 27
E        +  where 9 = <function cube at 0x106576268>(3)
E        +    where <function cube at 0x106576268> = cube.cube

test_cube.py:15: AssertionError
================ 2 failed, 2 passed in 0.02 seconds ================
```

With the parameterized tests, we can see the parameters clearly, which means we can see all inputs and outputs without any extra effort.

Generating the list of tests dynamically at runtime is also possible with a global function. Similar to the `pytest_assertrepr_compare` function that we added to `conftest.py` earlier, we can add a `pytest_generate_tests` function, which generates tests.

Creating the `pytest_generate_tests` function can be useful only to test a subset of options depending on the configuration options. If possible, however, I recommend trying to configure selective tests using fixtures instead, as they are somewhat more explicit. The problem with functions such as `pytest_generate_tests` is that they are global and don't discriminate between specific tests, resulting in strange behavior if you are not expecting that.

Automatic arguments using fixtures

The fixture system is one of the most magical features of `py.test`. It magically executes a fixture function with the same name as your arguments. Because of this, the naming of the arguments becomes very important, as they can easily collide with other fixtures. To prevent collisions, the scope is set to `function` by default. However, `class`, `module`, and `session` are also valid options for the scope. There are several fixtures available by default, some of which you will use often, and others most likely never. A complete list can always be generated with the following command:

```
# py.test --quiet --fixtures
cache
    Return a cache object that can persist state between testing
sessions.

    cache.get(key, default)
```

```
cache.set(key, value)
```

Keys must be a ``/`` separated value, where the first part is usually the

name of your plugin or application to avoid clashes with other cache users.

Values can be any object handled by the json stdlib module.

capsys

enables capturing of writes to sys.stdout/sys.stderr and makes

captured output available via ``capsys.readouterr()`` method calls

which return a ``(out, err)`` tuple.

capfd

enables capturing of writes to file descriptors 1 and 2 and makes

captured output available via ``capfd.readouterr()`` method calls

which return a ``(out, err)`` tuple.

record_xml_property

Fixture that adds extra xml properties to the tag for the calling test.

The fixture is callable with (name, value), with value being automatically

xml-encoded.

monkeypatch

The returned ``monkeypatch`` funcarg provides these

helper methods to modify objects, dictionaries or os.environ::

```
monkeypatch.setattr(obj, name, value, raising=True)

monkeypatch.delattr(obj, name, raising=True)

monkeypatch.setitem(mapping, name, value)

monkeypatch.delitem(obj, name, raising=True)

monkeypatch.setenv(name, value, prepend=False)

monkeypatch.delenv(name, value, raising=True)

monkeypatch.syspath_prepend(path)

monkeypatch.chdir(path)
```

All modifications will be undone after the requesting

test function has finished. The ``raising``

```
    parameter determines if a KeyError or AttributeError
    will be raised if the set/deletion operation has no target.
pytestconfig
    the pytest config object with access to command line opts.
recwarn
    Return a WarningsRecorder instance that provides these methods:


    * ``pop(category=None)``: return last warning matching the category.
    * ``clear()``: clear list of warnings


    See http://docs.python.org/library/warnings.html for information
    on warning categories.
tmpdir_factory
    Return a TempdirFactory instance for the test session.
tmpdir
    return a temporary directory path object
    which is unique to each test function invocation,
    created as a sub directory of the base temporary
    directory.  The returned object is a `py.path.local`_
    path object.
```

The standard fixtures are quite well documented, but a few examples never hurt. The next paragraphs demonstrate fixture usage.

Cache

The cache fixture is as simple as it is useful; there is a get function and a set function, and it remains between sessions. This test, for example, will allow five executions and raise an error every time after that. While it is not the most useful and elaborate example, it does show how the cache function works:

```
def test_cache(cache):
    counter = cache.get('counter', 0)
    assert counter < 5
    cache.set('counter', counter + 1)
```

 The default value (0 in this case) is required for the cache.get function.

The cache can be cleared through the --cache-clear command-line parameter, and all caches can be shown through --cache-show.

Custom fixtures

Bundled fixtures are quite useful, but within most projects, you will need to create your own fixtures to make things easier. Fixtures make it trivial to repeat code that is needed more often. You are most likely wondering how this is different from a regular function, context wrapper, or something else, but the special thing about fixtures is that they themselves can accept fixtures as well. So, if your function needs the `pytestconfig` variables, it can ask for it without needing to modify the calling functions.

The use cases for fixtures strongly depend on the projects, and because of that, it is difficult to generate a universally useful example, but a theoretical one is of course an option. The basic premise is simple enough, though: a function with the `pytest.fixture` decorator, which returns a value that will be passed along as an argument. Also, the function can take parameters and fixtures just as any test can. The only notable variation is `pytest.yield_fixture`. This fixture variation has one small difference; the actual test will be executed at the `yield` (more than one `yield` results in errors) and the code before/after functions as setup/teardown code. The most basic example of a `fixture` with `yield_fixture` looks like this:

```
import pytest


@pytest.yield_fixture
def some_yield_fixture():
    # Before the function
    yield 'some_value_to_pass_as_parameter'
    # After the function


@pytest.fixture
def some_regular_fixture():
    # Do something here
    return 'some_value_to_pass_as_parameter'
```

These fixtures take no parameters and simply pass a parameter to the `py.test` functions. A more useful example would be setting up a database connection and executing a query in a transaction:

```
import pytest
import sqlite3


@pytest.fixture(params=[':memory:'])
def connection(request):
    return sqlite3.connect(request.param)
```

```
@pytest.yield_fixture
def transaction(connection):
    with connection:
        yield connection


def test_insert(transaction):
    transaction.execute('create table test (id integer)')
    transaction.execute('insert into test values (1), (2), (3)')
```

Naturally, instead of using the `:memory:` database in `sqlite3`, we can use a different database name (or several) as well.

Print statements and logging

Even though print statements are generally not the most optimal way to debug code, I admit that it is still my default method of debugging. This means that when running and trying tests, I will include many print statements. However, let's see what happens when we try this with `py.test`. Here is the testing code:

```
import sys
import logging


def test_print():
    print('Printing to stdout')
    print('Printing to stderr', file=sys.stderr)
    logging.debug('Printing to debug')
    logging.info('Printing to info')
    logging.warning('Printing to warning')
    logging.error('Printing to error')
```

The following is the actual output:

```
# py.test test_print.py -v
======================= test session starts ========================
platform darwin -- Python 3.5.1, pytest-2.8.5, py-1.4.31, pluggy-0.3.1
cachedir: ../.cache
rootdir: code, inifile: pytest.ini
collected 1 items


test_print.py .


==================== 1 passed in 0.01 seconds =====================
```

So, all of our print statements and logging got trashed? Well, not really. In this case, py.test assumed that it wouldn't be relevant to you, so it ignored the output. But what about the same test with an error?

```
import sys
import logging


def test_print():
    print('Printing to stdout')
    print('Printing to stderr', file=sys.stderr)
    logging.debug('Printing to debug')
    logging.info('Printing to info')
    logging.warning('Printing to warning')
    logging.error('Printing to error')
    assert False, 'Dying because we can'
```

And the output with the error?

```
============================== FAILURES ===============================
_____ test_print _____


    def test_print():
        print('Printing to stdout')
        print('Printing to stderr', file=sys.stderr)
        logging.debug('Printing to debug')
        logging.info('Printing to info')
        logging.warning('Printing to warning')
        logging.error('Printing to error')
>       assert False, 'Dying because we can'
E       AssertionError: Dying because we can
E       assert False

test_print.py:12: AssertionError
---------------------- Captured stdout call ----------------------
Printing to stdout
---------------------- Captured stderr call ----------------------
Printing to stderr
WARNING:root:Printing to warning
ERROR:root:Printing to error
===================== 1 failed in 0.01 seconds =====================
```

Wow! Do you see that? The `stdout`, `stderr`, and logging with a level of `WARNING` or higher do get output now. `DEBUG` and `INFO` still won't be visible, but we'll see more about that later in this chapter, in the logging section.

Plugins

One of the most powerful features of `py.test` is the plugin system. Within `py.test`, nearly everything can be modified using the available hooks, the result of which is that writing plugins is almost simple. Actually, you already wrote a few plugins in the previous paragraphs without realizing it. By packaging `conftest.py` in a different package or directory, it becomes a `py.test` plugin. We will explain more about packaging in *Chapter 15, Packaging – Creating Your Own Libraries or Applications*. Generally, it won't be required to write your own plugin because the odds are that the plugins you seek are already available. A small list of plugins can be found on the `py.test` website at `https://pytest.org/latest/plugins.html`, and a longer list can be found through the Python package index at `https://pypi.python.org/pypi?%3Aaction=search&term=pytest-`.

By default, `py.test` does cover quite a bit of the desirable features, so you can easily do without plugins, but within the packages that I write myself, I generally default to the following list:

- `pytest-cov`
- `pytest-pep8`
- `pytest-flakes`

By using these plugins, it becomes much easier to maintain the code quality of your project. In order to understand why, we will take a closer look at these packages in the following paragraphs.

pytest-cov

Using the `pytest-cov` package, you can see whether your code is properly covered by tests or not. Internally, it uses the `coverage` package to detect how much of the code is being tested. To demonstrate the principle, we will check the coverage of a `cube_root` function.

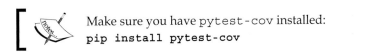
Make sure you have `pytest-cov` installed:
pip install pytest-cov

First of all, let's create a `.coveragerc` file with some useful defaults:

```
[report]
# The test coverage you require, keeping to 100% is not easily
# possible for all projects but it's a good default for new projects.
fail_under = 100

# These functions are generally only needed for debugging and/or
# extra safety so we want to ignore them from the coverage
# requirements
exclude_lines =
    # Make it possible to ignore blocks of code
    pragma: no cover

    # Generally only debug code uses this
    def __repr__

    # If a debug setting is set, skip testing
    if self\.debug:
    if settings.DEBUG

    # Don't worry about safety checks and expected errors
    raise AssertionError
    raise NotImplementedError

    # This code will probably never run so don't complain about that
    if 0:
    if __name__ == .__main__.:
    @abc.abstractmethod

[run]
# Make sure we require that all branches of the code is covered. So
# both the if and the else
branch = True

# No need to test the testing code
omit =
    test_*.py
```

Here is the `cube_root.py` code:

```
def cube_root(n):
    '''
    Returns the cube root of the input number
```

```
Args:
    n (int): The number to cube root

Returns:
    int: The cube root result
'''
if n >= 0:
    return n ** (1/3)
else:
    raise ValueError('A number larger than 0 was expected')
```

And the `test_cube_root.py` code:

```python
import pytest
import cube_root


cubes = (
    (0, 0),
    (1, 1),
    (8, 2),
    (27, 3),
)


@pytest.mark.parametrize('n,expected', cubes)
def test_cube_root(n, expected):
    assert cube_root.cube_root(n) == expected
```

Now let's see what happens when we run this with the `--cov-report=html` parameter:

```
# py.test test_cube_root.py --cov-report=html --cov-report=term-missing
--cov=cube_root.py

======================= test session starts ========================
platform darwin -- Python 3.5.1, pytest-2.8.5, py-1.4.31, pluggy-0.3.1
rootdir: code, inifile: pytest.ini
plugins: cov-2.2.0
collected 4 items


test_cube_root.py ....
--------- coverage: platform darwin, python 3.5.1-final-0 ----------
Name            Stmts   Miss Branch BrPart  Cover   Missing
```

```
----------------------------------------------------------
cube_root.py        4     1     2     1    67%    14, 11->14
Coverage HTML written to dir htmlcov
Traceback (most recent call last):

...

pytest_cov.plugin.CoverageError: Required test coverage of 100% not
reached. Total coverage: 66.67%
```

What happened here? It looks like we forgot to test some part of the code: line 14 and the branch that goes from line 11 to line 14. This output isn't all that readable, and that's why we specified the HTML output as well:

```
Coverage for cube_root.py : 67%

4 statements   3 run   1 missing   0 excluded   1 partial

 1 | def cube_root(n):
 2 |     '''
 3 |     Returns the cube root of the input number
 4 |
 5 |     Args:
 6 |         n (int): The number to cube root
 7 |     Returns:
 8 |         int: The cube root result
 9 |     '''
10 |
11 |     if n >= 0:                                            11↛14 [?]
12 |         return n ** (1 / 3)
13 |     else:
14 |         raise ValueError('A number larger than 0 was expected')
```

Perfect! So now we know. We forgot to test for values smaller than 0.

The yellow line indicates that only one part of the branch was executed ((n >= 0) == True) and not the other ((n >= 0) == False), this occurs with if statements, loops, and other things where at least one of the branches is not covered. For example, if a loop over an empty array is an impossible scenario, then the test can be partially skipped:

```
#   pragma: no branch
```

But since we know the problem, that is, the missing test for `ValueError`, let's add the test case:

```
import cube
import pytest


cubes = (
    (0, 0),
    (1, 1),
    (2, 8),
    (3, 27),
)


@pytest.mark.parametrize('n,expected', cubes)
def test_cube(n, expected):
    assert cube.cube(n) == expected


def test_cube_root_below_zero():
    with pytest.raises(ValueError):
        cube_root.cube_root(-1)
```

Then we run the test again:

```
# py.test test_cube_root.py --cov-report=html --cov-report=term-missing
--cov=cube_root.py
========================= test session starts =========================
platform darwin -- Python 3.5.1, pytest-2.8.5, py-1.4.31, pluggy-0.3.1
rootdir: code, inifile: pytest.ini
plugins: cov-2.2.0
collected 5 items


test_cube_root.py .....
---------- coverage: platform darwin, python 3.5.1-final-0 -----------
Name           Stmts   Miss Branch BrPart   Cover   Missing
------------------------------------------------------------
cube_root.py       4      0      2      0    100%
Coverage HTML written to dir htmlcov


===================== 5 passed in 0.03 seconds =====================
```

Perfect! 100% coverage without a problem, and the HTML output is also exactly what we expect:

```
Coverage for cube_root.py : 100%

4 statements    4 run    0 missing    0 excluded    0 partial


 1  def cube_root(n):
 2      '''
 3      Returns the cube root of the input number
 4
 5      Args:
 6          n (int): The number to cube root
 7
 8      Returns:
 9          int: The cube root result
10      '''
11      if n >= 0:
12          return n ** (1 / 3)
13      else:
14          raise ValueError('A number larger than 0 was expected')
15
```

But what if the code was slightly different? Instead of raising a `ValueError` for values below 0, what if we just raise a `NotImplementedError`?

```
def cube_root(n):
    '''
    Returns the cube root of the input number

    Args:
        n (int): The number to cube root

    Returns:
        int: The cube root result
    '''
    if n >= 0:
        return n ** (1 / 3)
    else:
        raise NotImplementedError(
            'A number larger than 0 was expected')
```

And remove the extra test as well:

```
import cube_root
import pytest


cubes = (
    (0, 0),
    (1, 1),
    (8, 2),
    (27, 3),
)


@pytest.mark.parametrize('n,expected', cubes)
def test_cube_root(n, expected):
    assert cube_root.cube_root(n) == expected
```

Run the test again:

```
# py.test test_cube_root.py --cov-report=html --cov-report=term-missing
--cov=cube_root.py
======================= test session starts ========================
platform darwin -- Python 3.5.1, pytest-2.8.5, py-1.4.31, pluggy-0.3.1
rootdir: code, inifile: pytest.ini
plugins: cov-2.2.0
collected 4 items


test_cube_root.py ....
---------- coverage: platform darwin, python 3.5.1-final-0 -----------
Name            Stmts   Miss Branch BrPart  Cover   Missing
--------------------------------------------------------------
cube_root.py        3      0      0      0   100%
Coverage HTML written to dir htmlcov


==================== 4 passed in 0.03 seconds ====================
```

You might wonder why we get 100% test coverage now though we actually didn't cover `NotImplementedError`. This is because we added `raise NotImplementedError` to the ignore list in the `.coveragerc` file. This also gives us a different result in the HTML output:

Coverage for **cube_root.py** : 100%

3 statements   3 run   0 missing   1 excluded   0 partial

```
1  def cube_root(n):
2      '''
3      Returns the cube root of the input number
4
5      Args:
6          n (int): The number to cube root
7      Returns:
8          int: The cube root result
9      '''
10
11      if n >= 0:
12          return n ** (1 / 3)
13      else:
14          raise NotImplementedError(
15              'A number larger than 0 was expected')
```

Even if we add the test for `NotImplementedError` in the test file, the coverage report will still ignore the line.

pytest-pep8 and pytest-flakes

Pyflakes and pep8 are code quality testing tools that are very useful for making your code readable and pep8 compliant. The `pytest-pep8` and `pytest-flakes` modules automatically execute these checks before running the actual tests. To install them, simply execute this line:

```
# pip install pytest-flakes pytest-pep8
```

After that, you'll be able to run both of them like this:

```
# py.test --flakes --pep8 cube_root.py
======================= test session starts =========================
platform darwin -- Python 3.5.1, pytest-2.8.5, py-1.4.31, pluggy-0.3.1
rootdir: code, inifile: pytest.ini
plugins: cov-2.2.0, flakes-1.0.1, pep8-1.0.6
```

```
collected 2 items


cube_root.py ..


===================== 2 passed in 0.01 seconds =====================
```

Configuring plugins

To make sure that all the plugins get executed and to configure them, simply add the settings to the pytest.ini file. The following example can be a reasonable default for development, but for production releases, you will probably want to care of the UnusedImport warnings.

pytest.ini:

```
[pytest]
python_files =
    your_project_source/*.py
    tests/*.py


addopts =
    --doctest-modules
    --cov your_project_source
    --cov-report term-missing
    --cov-report html
    --pep8
    --flakes


# W391 is the error about blank lines at the end of a file
pep8ignore =
    *.py W391


# Ignore unused imports
flakes-ignore =
    *.py UnusedImport
```

 When debugging to find out why a test is failing, it can be useful to simply look at the first test that fails. The py.test module offers both a -x flag to stop after the first failure and --maxfail=n to stop after *n* failures.

Mock objects

When writing tests, this regularly occurs: you are testing not only your own code but also the interaction with external resources, such as hardware, databases, web hosts, servers, and others. Some of these can be run safely, but certain tests are too slow, too dangerous, or even impossible to run. In those cases, mock objects are your friends; they can be used to fake anything, so you can be certain that your code still returns the expected results without having any variation from external factors.

Using unittest.mock

The `unittest.mock` library provides two base objects, `Mock` and `MagicMock`, to easily mock any external resources. The `Mock` object is just a general generic mock object and `MagicMock` is mostly the same, but it has all the magic methods such as `__contains__` and `__len__` defined. In addition to this, it can make your life even easier. This is because in addition to creating mock objects manually, it is possible to patch objects directly using the `patch` decorator/context manager.

The following function uses `random` to return `True` or `False` given governed by a certain probability distribution. Due to the random nature of a function like this, it is notoriously difficult to test, but not with `unittest.mock`. With the use of `unittest.mock`, it's easy to get repeatable results:

```
from unittest import mock
import random


def bernoulli(p):
    return random.random() > p


@mock.patch('random.random')
def test_bernoulli(mock_random):
    # Test for random value of 0.1
    mock_random.return_value = 0.1
    assert bernoulli(0.0)
    assert not bernoulli(0.1)
    assert mock_random.call_count == 2
```

Wonderful, isn't it? Without having to modify the original code, we can make sure that `random.random` now returns `0.1` instead of some random number. For completeness, the version that uses a context manager is given here:

```
from unittest import mock
import random


def bernoulli(p):
    return random.random() > p


def test_bernoulli():
    with mock.patch('random.random') as mock_random:
        mock_random.return_value = 0.1
        assert bernoulli(0.0)
        assert not bernoulli(0.1)
        assert mock_random.call_count == 2
```

The possibilities with mock objects are nearly endless. They vary from raising exceptions on access to faking entire APIs and returning different results on multiple calls. For example, let's fake deleting a file:

```
import os
from unittest import mock


def delete_file(filename):
    while os.path.exists(filename):
        os.unlink(filename)


@mock.patch('os.path.exists', side_effect=(True, False, False))
@mock.patch('os.unlink')
def test_delete_file(mock_exists, mock_unlink):
    # First try:
    delete_file('some non-existing file')

    # Second try:
    delete_file('some non-existing file')
```

Quite a bit of magic in this example! The `side_effect` parameter tells mock to return those values in that sequence, making sure that the first call to `os.path.exists` returns `True` and the other two return `False`. The `mock.patch` without arguments simply returns a callable that does nothing.

Using py.test monkeypatch

The `monkeypatch` object in `py.test` is a fixture that allows mocking as well. While it may seem useless after seeing the possibilities with `unittest.mock`, in summary, it's not. Some of the functionality does overlap, but while `unittest.mock` focuses on controlling and recording the actions of an object, the `monkeypatch` fixture focuses on simple and temporary environmental changes. Some examples of these are given in the following list:

- Setting and deleting attributes using `monkeypatch.setattr` and `monkeypatch.delattr`
- Setting and deleting dictionary items using `monkeypatch.setitem` and `monkeypatch.delitem`
- Setting and deleting environment variables using `monkeypatch.setenv` and `monkeypatch.delenv`
- Inserting an extra path to `sys.path` before all others using `monkeypatch.syspath_prepend`
- Changing the directory using `monkeypatch.chdir`

To undo all modifications, simply use `monkeypatch.undo`.

For example, let's say that for a certain test, we need to work from a different directory. With mock, your options would be to mock pretty much all file functions, including the `os.path` functions, and even in that case, you will probably forget about a few. So, it's definitely not useful in this case. Another option would be to put the entire test into a `try...finally` block and just do an `os.chdir` before and after the testing code. This is quite a good and safe solution, but it's a bit of extra work, so let's compare the two methods:

```
import os


def test_chdir_monkeypatch(monkeypatch):
    monkeypatch.chdir('/dev')
    assert os.getcwd() == '/dev'
    monkeypatch.chdir('/')
    assert os.getcwd() == '/'


def test_chdir():
    original_directory = os.getcwd()
    try:
        os.chdir('/dev')
```

```
        assert os.getcwd() == '/dev'
        os.chdir('/')
        assert os.getcwd() == '/'
    finally:
        os.chdir(original_directory)
```

They effectively do the same, but one needs four lines of code whereas the other needs eight. All of these can easily be worked around with a few extra lines of code, of course, but the simpler the code is, the fewer mistakes you can make and the more readable it is.

Logging

The Python logging module is one of those modules that are extremely useful, but it tends to be very difficult to use correctly. The result is often that people just disable logging completely and use print statements instead. This is insightful but a waste of the very extensive logging system in Python. If you've written Java code before, you might be familiar with the Log4j Java library. The Python logging module is largely and primarily based on that library.

The most important objects of the logging module are the following:

- **Logger**: the actual logging interface
- **Handler**: This processes the log statements and outputs them
- **Formatter**: This formats the input data into a string
- **Filter**: This allows filtering of certain messages

Within these objects, you can set the logging levels to one of the default levels:

- CRITICAL: 50
- ERROR: 40
- WARNING: 30
- INFO: 20
- DEBUG: 10
- NOTSET: 0

The numbers are the numeric values of these log levels. While you can generally ignore them, the order is obviously important while setting the minimum level. Also, when defining custom levels, you will have to overwrite existing levels if they have the same numeric value.

Configuration

There are several ways to configure the logging system, ranging from pure code to JSON files or even remote configuration. The examples will use parts of the logging module later discussed in this chapter, but the usage of the config system is all that matters here. If you are not interested in the internal workings of the logging module, you should be able to get by with just this paragraph of the logging section.

Basic logging configuration

The most basic logging configuration is, of course, no configuration, but that will not get you much useful output:

```
import logging

logging.debug('debug')
logging.info('info')
logging.warning('warning')
logging.error('error')
logging.critical('critical')
```

With the default log level, you will only see a warning and up:

```
# python log.py
WARNING:root:warning
ERROR:root:error
CRITICAL:root:critical
```

A quick and easy start for a configuration is `basicConfig`. I recommend using this if you just need some quick logging for a script you're writing, but not for a full-blown application. While you can configure pretty much anything you wish, once you get a more complicated setup, there are usually more convenient options. We will talk more about that in later paragraphs, but first, we have a `basicConfig` that configures our logger to display some more information, including the logger name:

```
import logging

log_format = (
    '[%(asctime)s] %(levelname)-8s %(name)-12s %(message)s')

logging.basicConfig(
    filename='debug.log',
    format=log_format,
    level=logging.DEBUG,
)
```

```
formatter = logging.Formatter(log_format)
handler = logging.StreamHandler()
handler.setLevel(logging.WARNING)
handler.setFormatter(formatter)
logging.getLogger().addHandler(handler)
```

We test the code:

```
logging.debug('debug')
logging.info('info')
some_logger = logging.getLogger('some')
some_logger.warning('warning')
some_logger.error('error')
other_logger = some_logger.getChild('other')
other_logger.critical('critical')
```

This will give us the following output on our screen:

```
# python log.py
[2015-12-02 15:56:19,449] WARNING   some          warning
[2015-12-02 15:56:19,449] ERROR     some          error
[2015-12-02 15:56:19,449] CRITICAL  some.other    critical
```

And here is the output in the `debug.log` file:

```
[2015-12-02 15:56:19,449] DEBUG     root          debug
[2015-12-02 15:56:19,449] INFO      root          info
[2015-12-02 15:56:19,449] WARNING   some          warning
[2015-12-02 15:56:19,449] ERROR     some          error
[2015-12-02 15:56:19,449] CRITICAL  some.other    critical
```

This configuration shows how log outputs can be configured with separate configurations, log levels, and, if you choose so, formatting. It tends to become unreadable though, which is why it's usually a better idea to use `basicConfig` only for simple configurations that don't involve multiple handlers.

Dictionary configuration

The `dictconfig` makes it possible to name all parts so that they can be reused easily, for example, a single formatter for multiple loggers and handlers. So let's rewrite our previous configuration using `dictconfig`:

```
from logging import config

config.dictConfig({
    'version': 1,
```

```
        'formatters': {
            'standard': {
                'format': '[%(asctime)s] %(levelname)-8s '
                '%(name)-12s %(message)s',
            },
        },
        'handlers': {
            'file': {
                'filename': 'debug.log',
                'level': 'DEBUG',
                'class': 'logging.FileHandler',
                'formatter': 'standard',
            },
            'stream': {
                'level': 'WARNING',
                'class': 'logging.StreamHandler',
                'formatter': 'standard',
            },
        },
        'loggers': {
            '': {
                'handlers': ['file', 'stream'],
                'level': 'DEBUG',
            },
        },
    })
```

The nice thing about the dictionary configuration is that it's very easy to extend and/or overwrite the logging configuration. For example, if you want to change the formatter for all of your logging, you can simply change the standard formatter or even loop through handlers.

JSON configuration

Since dictconfig takes any type of dictionary, it is actually quite simple to implement a different type of reader employing JSON or YAML files. This is especially useful as they tend to be a bit friendlier towards non-Python programmers. As opposed to Python files, they are easily readable and writable from outside of Python.

Let's assume that we have a log_config.json file such as the following:

```
{
    "version": 1,
    "formatters": {
        "standard": {
            "format": "[%(asctime)s] %(levelname)-8s %(name)-12s
%(message)s"
```

```
            }
        },
        "handlers": {
            "file": {
                "filename": "debug.log",
                "level": "DEBUG",
                "class": "logging.FileHandler",
                "formatter": "standard"
            },
            "stream": {
                "level": "WARNING",
                "class": "logging.StreamHandler",
                "formatter": "standard"
            }
        },
        "loggers": {
            "": {
                "handlers": ["file", "stream"],
                "level": "DEBUG"
            }
        }
    }
}
```

We can simply use this code to read the config:

```
import json
from logging import config

with open('log_config.json') as fh:
    config.dictConfig(json.load(fh))
```

Ini file configuration

The file configuration is probably the most readable format for non-programmers.
It uses the `ini-style` configuration format and uses the `configparser` module
internally. The downside is that it is perhaps a little verbose, but it is clear enough
and makes it easy to combine several configuration files without us having to worry
too much about overwriting other configurations. Having said that, if `dictConfig` is
an option, then it is most likely a better option. This is because `fileConfig` is slightly
limited and awkward at times. Just look at the handlers as an example:

```
[formatters]
keys=standard

[handlers]
```

```
keys=file,stream

[loggers]
keys=root

[formatter_standard]
format=[%(asctime)s] %(levelname)-8s %(name)-12s %(message)s

[handler_file]
level=DEBUG
class=FileHandler
formatter=standard
args=('debug.log',)

[handler_stream]
level=WARNING
class=StreamHandler
formatter=standard
args=(sys.stderr,)

[logger_root]
handlers=file,stream
level=DEBUG
```

Reading the files is extremely easy though:

```
from logging import config

config.fileConfig('log_config.ini')
```

One thing to make note of, however, is that if you look carefully, you will see that this config is slightly different from the other configs. With `fileConfig` you can't just use keyword arguments alone. The `args` is required for both `FileHandler` and `StreamHandler`.

The network configuration

The network configuration is both very convenient and a bit dangerous, because it allows you to configure your logger on the fly while your application/script is still running. The dangerous part is that the config is (partially) read by using the `eval` function, which allows people to potentially execute code within your application remotely. Even though `logging.config.listen` only listens to local connections, it can still be dangerous if you execute the code on a shared/unsafe host.

Luckily, since version Python 3.4, it is possible to add a `verify` parameter, which is a function that will be executed to convert the input into the output. The default is obviously something along the lines of `lambda config: config`, but it can be configured to return just about anything.

To prove this point through an example, we need two scripts. One script will continuously print a few messages to the loggers and the other will change the logging configuration. We will start with the same test code that we had before but keep it running in an endless loop with a `sleep` in between:

```python
import time
import logging
from logging import config

listener = config.listen()
listener.start()

try:
    while True:
        logging.debug('debug')
        logging.info('info')
        some_logger = logging.getLogger('some')
        some_logger.warning('warning')
        some_logger.error('error')
        other_logger = some_logger.getChild('other')
        other_logger.critical('critical')

        time.sleep(5)

except KeyboardInterrupt:
    # Stop listening and finish the listening thread
    logging.config.stopListening()
    listener.join()
```

Now comes the code that will send the configuration file:

```python
import struct
import socket
from logging import config

with open('log_config.ini') as fh:
    data = fh.read()

# Open the socket
sock = socket.socket(socket.AF_INET, socket.SOCK_STREAM)
```

```
# Connect to the server
sock.connect(('127.0.0.1', config.DEFAULT_LOGGING_CONFIG_PORT))
# Send the magic logging packet
sock.send(struct.pack('>L', len(data)))
# Send the config
sock.send(data)
# And close the connection again
sock.close()
```

Next, let's see the output. After the first execution of the loop, we will execute the second script to read the logging configuration:

 # python log_networkconfig.py

WARNING:some:warning

ERROR:some:error

CRITICAL:some.other:critical

You might be wondering where the rest of the output is. There is none. The debug.log file has been filled with messages like these, however:

```
[2015-12-03 12:32:38,894]  DEBUG     root          debug
[2015-12-03 12:32:38,894]  INFO      root          info
```

So what happened? This is where we see the pitfalls of custom loggers and configuration after using the loggers. The logging.config.listen function will modify the root logger as requested, but since the other loggers (some and some. other) weren't specified, they weren't modified. We modify the configuration to include them, as follows:

```
[formatters]
keys=standard

[handlers]
keys=file,stream

[loggers]
keys=root,some

[formatter_standard]
format=[%(asctime)s] %(levelname)-8s %(name)-12s %(message)s

[handler_file]
level=DEBUG
class=FileHandler
formatter=standard
```

```
args=('debug.log',)

[handler_stream]
level=WARNING
class=StreamHandler
formatter=standard
args=(sys.stderr,)

[logger_root]
handlers=file,stream
level=DEBUG

[logger_some]
level=DEBUG
qualname=some
handlers=
```

Now it works as expected:

```
# python log_networkconfig.py
WARNING:some:warning
ERROR:some:error
CRITICAL:some.other:critical
[2015-12-03 12:42:05,621] WARNING   some         warning
[2015-12-03 12:42:05,622] ERROR     some         error
[2015-12-03 12:42:05,622] CRITICAL  some.other   critical
```

You will probably notice that we didn't add any handlers to the some logger. That's because the handler is already present—at the root level. However, without manually telling the logging module that the logger is there, it won't send it to the handler anymore. This is not problematic generally, but it's a dangerous pitfall when modifying logging configurations at runtime.

An alternative way to configure it without having this propagation issue is by disabling propagation altogether, but that will create an entirely new logger and will forget any configuration added to the root. So, if you have a handler for the error level at the root that gets sent to your error reporting system, it won't arrive anymore. In this case, however, the config is slightly clearer:

```
[logger_some]
handlers=file,stream
level=DEBUG
qualname=some
propagate=0
```

Logger

The main object that you will be using all the time with the `logging` module is the `Logger` object. This object contains all the APIs that you will need to do the actual logging. Most are simple enough but some require attention.

First of all, loggers inherit the parent settings by default. As we have seen previously with the propagate setting, by default, all settings will propagate from the parent. This is really useful when incorporating loggers within your files. Assuming your modules are using sane names and import paths, I recommend the following style of naming your loggers:

```
import logging


logger = logging.getLogger(__name__)


class Spam(object):
    def __init__(self, count):
        self.logger = logger.getChild(self.__class__.__name__)
```

By using this style, your loggers will get names such as `main_module.sub_module.ClassName`. Not only does this make your logs easier to read, but also it is easily possible to enable or disable logging per module with the propagation of log settings. To create a new log file that logs everything from `main_module.sub_module`, we can simply do this:

```
import logging

logger = logging.getLogger('main_module.sub_module')
logger.addHandler(logging.FileHandler('sub_module.log'))
```

Alternatively, you can configure it using your chosen configuration option, of course. The relevant point is that with sub-loggers, you have very fine-grained control over your loggers.

This includes increasing the log level:

```
import logging

logger = logging.getLogger('main_module.sub_module')
logger.setLevel(logging.DEBUG)
```

Usage

The usage of the `Logger` object is mostly identical to that of the bare `logging` module, but `Logger` actually supports a bit more. This is because the bare `logging` module just calls the functions on the root logger. It has a few very useful properties, although most of these are undocumented in the library:

- `Propagate`: Whether to pass events to this logger or to the handlers of the parent loggers. Without this, a log message to `main_module.sub_module` won't be logged by `main_module`.

  The `handle` method will keep looking for parent handlers as long as those loggers have `propagate` set to `true`, which is the default.

- `Filters`: These are the filters attached to the logger. They can be added through `addFilter` and `removeFilter`, To see whether a message will be filtered, the `filter` method can be used.

- `Disabled`: By setting this property, it's possible to disable a certain logger. The regular API only allows disabling of all loggers below a certain level. This offers some fine-grained control.

- `Handlers`: These are the handlers attached to the logger. They can be added through `addHandler` and `removeHandler`. The existence of any (inherited) handlers can be checked through the `hasHandlers` function.

- `Level`: This is really an internal one as it simply has a numeric value and not a name. But beyond that, it doesn't take inheritance into account, so it's better to avoid the property and use the `getEffectiveLevel` function instead. To check whether the setting is enabled for a `DEBUG` for example, you can simply do `logger.isEnabledFor(logging.DEBUG)`. Setting the property is possible through the `setLevel` function, of course.

- `Name`: As this property's name says, it is very useful for your own reference, of course.

Now that you know about the properties, it is time to discuss the logging functions themselves. The functions you will use most often are the `log`, `debug`, `info`, `warning`, `error`, and `critical` log functions. They can be used quite simply, but they support string formatting as well, which is very useful:

```
import logging

logger = logging.getLogger()
exception = 'Oops...'
logger.error('Some horrible error: %r', exception)
```

You might wonder why we don't simply use the regular string formatting with %
or `string.format` instead. The reason is that when parameters are used instead of
preformatted strings, the handler gets them as parameters. The result is that you
can group log messages by the original string, which is what tools such as sentry
(`https://github.com/getsentry/sentry`) use.

There is more to it, however. In terms of parameters, `*args` are only for string
formatting, but it's possible to add extra parameters to a log object using the `extra`
keyword parameter:

```
import logging

logger = logging.getLogger()
logger.error('simple error', extra=dict(spam='some spam'))
```

These `extra` parameters can be used in the logging formatter to display extra
information just like the standard formatting options:

```
import logging

logging.basicConfig(format='%(spam)s: %(message)s')
logger = logging.getLogger()
logger.error('the message', extra=dict(spam='some spam'))
```

This results in the following:

```
# python test_spam.py
some spam: the message
```

However, one of the most useful features is the support for exceptions:

```
import logging

logger = logging.getLogger()

try:
    raise RuntimeError('Not enough spam')
except:
    logger.exception('Got an exception')

logger.error('And an error')
```

This results in a stack trace for the exception, but it will not kill the code:

```
# python test_spam.py
Got an exception
Traceback (most recent call last):
  File "test_spam.py", line 6, in <module>
    raise RuntimeError('Not enough spam')
RuntimeError: Not enough spam
And an error
```

Summary

This chapter showed us how to write `doctests`, make use of the shortcuts provided by `py.test`, and use the `logging` module. With testing, there is never a one-size-fits-all solution. While the `doctest` system is very useful in many cases for providing both documentation and tests at the same time, in many functions, there are edge cases that simply don't matter for documentation, but still need to be tested. This is where regular unit tests come in and where `py.test` helps a lot.

Because the `py.test` library is always evolving, this chapter cannot fully cover everything you will need, but it should provide you with enough of a basis to be able to use it effectively and extend it where needed.

The logging module is extremely useful but it's also a pain if configured incorrectly. Unfortunately, the right configuration can be a bit obscure when multiple modules are trying to configure logging simultaneously. The usage of the logging system should be clear enough for most of the common use cases now, and as long as you keep the `propagate` parameter in check, you should be fine when implementing a logging system.

Next up is debugging, where testing helps prevent bugs. We will see how to solve them effectively. In addition, the logging that we added in this chapter will help a lot in that area.

11
Debugging – Solving the Bugs

The previous chapter showed you how to add logging and tests to your code, but no matter how many tests you have, you will always have bugs. The biggest problem is always user input, as it is simply impossible to test all possible inputs, implying that at one point, we will need to debug the code.

There are many debugging techniques, and most certainly, you have already used a few of them. Within this chapter, we are going to focus on print/trace debugging and interactive debugging.

Debugging using print statements, stack traces, and logging is one of the most versatile methods to work with, and it is most likely the first type of debugging you've ever used. Even a `print 'Hello world'` can be considered this type, as the output will show you that your code is being executed correctly. There is obviously no point in explaining how and where to place print statements to debug your code, but there are quite a few nice tricks using decorators and other Python modules that render this type of debugging a lot more useful, such as `faulthandler`.

Interactive debugging is a more complicated debugging method. It allows you to debug a program while it's still running. Using this method, it's even possible to change variables while the application is running and pause the application at any point desired. The downside is that it requires some knowledge about the debugger commands to be really useful.

To summarize, we will cover the following topics:

- Debugging using `print`, `trace`, `logging`, and `faulthandler`
- Interactive debugging using `pdb`

Non-interactive debugging

The most basic form of debugging is adding a simple print statement into your code to see what is still working and what isn't. This is useful in a variety of cases and likely to help solve most of your issues. Later in this chapter, we will show some interactive debugging methods, but those are not always suitable. Interactive debugging tends to become difficult or even impossible in multithreaded environments, while on a closed-off remote server, you might need a different solution as well. Both methods have their merits, but I personally opt for non-interactive debugging 90% of the time since a simple print/log statement is usually enough to analyze the cause of a problem.

A basic example of this (I've been known to do similar) with a generator can be as follows:

```
>>> def spam_generator():
...     print('a')
...     yield 'spam'
...     print('b')
...     yield 'spam!'
...     print('c')
...     yield 'SPAM!'
...     print('d')

>>> generator = spam_generator()

>>> next(generator)
a
'spam'

>>> next(generator)
b
'spam!'
```

This shows exactly where the code does, and consequently, does not reach. Without this example, you might have expected the first print to come immediately after the `spam_generator()` call, since it's a generator. However, the execution completely stalls until we `yield` an item. Assuming you would have some setup code before the first `yield`, it won't run until `next` is actually called.

Although this is one of the simplest ways to debug functions using print statements, it's definitely not the best way. We can start by making an auto-print function that automatically increments the letter:

```
>>> import string


>>> def print_character():
...     i = 0
...     while True:
...         print('Letter: %r' % string.ascii_letters[i])
...         i = (i + 1) % len(string.ascii_letters)
...         yield
>>> # Always initialize
>>> print_character = print_character()


>>> next(print_character)
Letter: 'a'
>>> next(print_character)
Letter: 'b'
>>> next(print_character)
Letter: 'c'
```

While the print statement generator is slightly better than bare print statements, it doesn't help that much yet. It would be much more useful to see which lines were actually executed while running the code. We can do this manually using `inspect.currentframe`, but there is no need for hacking. Python has you covered with some dedicated tools.

Inspecting your script using trace

Simple print statements are useful in a lot of cases since you can easily incorporate print statements in nearly every application. It does not matter whether it's remote or local, threaded or using multiprocessing. It works almost everywhere, making it the most universal solution available, in addition to logging that is. The general solution is often not the best solution, however. There are better solutions available for the most common scenarios. One of them is the `trace` module. It offers you a way to trace every execution, relationships between functions, and a few others.

To demonstrate, we will use our previous code but without print statements:

```
def eggs_generator():
    yield 'eggs'
    yield 'EGGS!'


def spam_generator():
    yield 'spam'
    yield 'spam!'
    yield 'SPAM!'

generator = spam_generator()
print(next(generator))
print(next(generator))

generator = eggs_generator()
print(next(generator))
```

We will execute it with the trace module:

```
# python3 -m trace --trace --timing tracing.py
 --- modulename: tracing, funcname: <module>
0.00 tracing.py(1): def eggs_generator():
0.00 tracing.py(6): def spam_generator():
0.00 tracing.py(11): generator = spam_generator()
0.00 tracing.py(12): print(next(generator))
 --- modulename: tracing, funcname: spam_generator
0.00 tracing.py(7):     yield 'spam'
spam
0.00 tracing.py(13): print(next(generator))
 --- modulename: tracing, funcname: spam_generator
0.00 tracing.py(8):     yield 'spam!'
spam!
0.00 tracing.py(15): generator = eggs_generator()
 --- modulename: tracing, funcname: spam_generator
0.00 tracing.py(16): print(next(generator))
 --- modulename: tracing, funcname: eggs_generator
0.00 tracing.py(2):     yield 'eggs'
eggs
 --- modulename: trace, funcname: _unsettrace
0.00 trace.py(77):             sys.settrace(None)
```

Quite nice, isn't it? It shows you exactly which line is being executed with function names and, more importantly, which line was caused by which statement (or statements). Additionally, it shows you at what time it was executed relative to the start time of the program. This is due to the `--timing` flag.

As you might expect, this output is a bit too verbose to be universally useful. In spite of the fact that you can opt to ignore specific modules and directories by using command-line parameters, it is still too verbose in many cases. So let's go for the next solution—a context manager. The preceding output has already revealed some of the `trace` internals. The last line shows a `sys.settrace` call, which is exactly what we need for manual tracing:

```python
import- sys
import trace as trace_module
import contextlib


@contextlib.contextmanager
def trace(count=False, trace=True, timing=True):
    tracer = trace_module.Trace(
        count=count, trace=trace, timing=timing)
    sys.settrace(tracer.globaltrace)
    yield tracer
    sys.settrace(None)

    result = tracer.results()
    result.write_results(show_missing=False, summary=True)


def eggs_generator():
    yield 'eggs'
    yield 'EGGS!'


def spam_generator():
    yield 'spam'
    yield 'spam!'
    yield 'SPAM!'


with trace():
    generator = spam_generator()
    print(next(generator))
    print(next(generator))

generator = eggs_generator()
print(next(generator))
```

When executed as a regular Python file, this returns:

```
# python3 tracing.py
 --- modulename: tracing, funcname: spam_generator
0.00 tracing.py(24):      yield 'spam'
spam
 --- modulename: tracing, funcname: spam_generator
0.00 tracing.py(25):      yield 'spam!'
spam!
 --- modulename: contextlib, funcname: __exit__
0.00 contextlib.py(64):          if type is None:
0.00 contextlib.py(65):              try:
0.00 contextlib.py(66):                  next(self.gen)
 --- modulename: tracing, funcname: trace
0.00 tracing.py(12):      sys.settrace(None)
```

This code immediately reveals what the trace code does internally as well: it uses `sys.settrace` to tell the Python interpreter where to send every statement that is being executed. Given this, it's obviously trivial to write the function as a decorator, but I'll leave that as an exercise to you if you need it.

Another take-away from this is that you can easily add extra filters to your trace function by wrapping `tracer.globaltrace`. The function takes the following parameters (from the standard Python documentation):

Parameter	Description
Call	A function is called (or some other code block entered). The global trace function is called; `arg` is `None`. The return value specifies the local trace function.
Line	The interpreter is about to execute a new line of code or re-execute the condition of a loop. The local trace function is called; `arg` is `None`. The return value specifies the new local trace function. See `Objects/lnotab_notes.txt` for a detailed explanation of how this works.
return	A function (or another code block) is about to return. The local trace function is called; `arg` is the value that will be returned or `None` if the event is caused by an exception being raised. The trace function's return value is ignored.
exception	This means an exception has occurred. The local trace function is called; `arg` is a tuple (`exception`, `value`, `traceback`). The return value specifies the new local trace function.

Parameter	Description
c_call	A C function is about to be called. This may be an extension function or a built-in function. The `arg` is the C function object.
c_return	A C function has returned, and `arg` is the C function object.
c_exception	A C function has raised an exception, and `arg` is the C function object.

As you must have expected, with a simple filter function, you can easily make sure that only specific functions will be returned, instead of the long list you would normally get. You really shouldn't underestimate the amount of data generated by tracing code with a few imports. The preceding context manager code gives over 300 lines of output.

Debugging using logging

In *Chapter 10, Testing and Logging – Preparing for Bugs*, our chapter about testing and logging, we saw how to create custom loggers, set the levels for them, and add handlers to specific levels. We are going to use the `logging.DEBUG` level to log now, which is nothing special by itself, but with a few decorators, we can add some very useful debug-only code.

Whenever I'm debugging, I always find it very useful to know the input and output for a function. The basic version with a decorator is simple enough to write; just print the `args` and `kwargs` and you are done. The following example goes a little further. By using the `inspect` module, we can retrieve the default arguments as well, making it possible to show all arguments with the argument names and values in all cases, even if the argument was not specified:

```
import pprint
import inspect
import logging
import functools


logging.basicConfig(level=logging.DEBUG)


def debug(function):
    @functools.wraps(function)
    def _debug(*args, **kwargs):
        try:
            result = function(*args, **kwargs)
        finally:
            # Extract the signature from the function
            signature = inspect.signature(function)
```

```
            # Fill the arguments
            arguments = signature.bind(*args, **kwargs)
            # NOTE: This only works for Python 3.5 and up!
            arguments.apply_defaults()

            logging.debug('%s(%s): %s' % (
                function.__qualname__,
                ', '.join('%s=%r' % (k, v) for k, v in
                        arguments.arguments.items()),
                pprint.pformat(result),
            ))

        return _debug


    @debug
    def spam(a, b=123):
        return 'some spam'

    spam(1)
    spam(1, 456)
    spam(b=1, a=456)
```

The following output is returned:

```
# python3 logged.py
DEBUG:root:spam(a=1, b=123): 'some spam'
DEBUG:root:spam(a=1, b=456): 'some spam'
DEBUG:root:spam(a=456, b=1): 'some spam'
```

Very nice of course, as we have a clear sight of when the function is called, which parameters were used, and what is returned. However, this is something you will probably only execute when you are actively debugging your code. You can also make the regular logging.debug statements in your code quite a bit more useful by adding a debug-specific logger, which shows more information. Simply replace the logging config of the preceding example with this:

```
    import logging


    log_format = (
        '[%(relativeCreated)d %(levelname)s] '
        '%(pathname)s:%(lineno)d:%(funcName)s: %(message)s'
    )
    logging.basicConfig(level=logging.DEBUG, format=log_format)
```

Then your result will be something like this:

```
# time python3 logged.py
[0 DEBUG] logged.py:31:_debug: spam(a=1, b=123): 'some spam'
[0 DEBUG] logged.py:31:_debug: spam(a=1, b=456): 'some spam'
[0 DEBUG] logged.py:31:_debug: spam(a=456, b=1): 'some spam'
python3 logged.py  0.04s user 0.01s system 96% cpu 0.048 total
```

It shows the time relative to the start of the application in milliseconds and the log level. This is followed by an identification block that shows the filename, line number, and function name that originated the logs. Of course, there is a message at the end.

Showing call stack without exceptions

When looking at how and why a piece of code is being run, it's often useful to see the entire stack trace. Simply raising an exception is, of course, an option. However, that will kill the current code execution, which is generally not something we are looking for. This is where the `traceback` module comes in handy. With just a few simple lines, we get a full (or limited, if you prefer) stack list:

```python
import traceback


class Spam(object):

    def run(self):
        print('Before stack print')
        traceback.print_stack()
        print('After stack print')


class Eggs(Spam):
    pass


if __name__ == '__main__':
    eggs = Eggs()
    eggs.run()
```

This results in the following:

```
# python3 traceback_test.py
Before stack print
```

```
  File "traceback_test.py", line 18, in <module>
    eggs.run()
  File "traceback_test.py", line 8, in run
    traceback.print_stack()
After stack print
```

As you can see, the traceback simply prints without any exceptions. The `traceback` module actually has quite a few other methods for printing tracebacks based on exceptions and such, but you probably won't need them often. The most useful one is probably the `limit` parameter; this parameter allows you to limit the stack trace to the useful part. For example, if you've added this code using a decorator or helper function, you probably have no need to include those in the stack trace. That's where the `limit` parameter helps:

```python
import traceback


class Spam(object):

    def run(self):
        print('Before stack print')
        traceback.print_stack(limit=-1)
        print('After stack print')


class Eggs(Spam):
    pass


if __name__ == '__main__':
    eggs = Eggs()
    eggs.run()
```

This results in the following:

```
# python3 traceback_test.py
Before stack print
  File "traceback_test.py", line 18, in <module>
    eggs.run()
After stack print
```

As you can see, the `print_stack` function itself has now been hidden from the stack trace, which makes everything a bit cleaner.

 The negative limit support was added in Python 3.5. Before that, only positive limits were supported.

Debugging asyncio

The `asyncio` module has a few special provisions to make debugging somewhat easier. Given the asynchronous nature of functions within `asyncio`, this is a very welcome feat. While debugging of multithreaded/multiprocessing functions or classes can be difficult—since concurrent classes can easily change environment variables in parallel—with `asyncio`, it's just as difficult if not more.

 Within most Linux/Unix/Mac shell sessions, environment variables can be set using it as a prefix:

`SOME_ENVIRONMENT_VARIABLE=value python3 script.py`

Also, it can be configured for the current shell session using `export`:

`export SOME_ENVIRONMENT_VARIABLE=value`

The current value can be fetched using the following line:

`echo $SOME_ENVIRONMENT_VARIABLE`

On Windows, you can configure an environment variable for your local shell session using the `set` command:

`set SOME_ENVIRONMENT_VARIABLE=value`

The current value can be fetched using this line:

`set SOME_ENVIRONMENT_VARIABLE`

When enabling the debug mode using the `PYTHONASYNCIODEBUG` environment setting the `asyncio` module will check whether every defined coroutine is actually run:

```
import asyncio


@asyncio.coroutine
def printer():
    print('This is a coroutine')


printer()
```

This results in an error for the printer coroutine, which is never yielded here:

```
# PYTHONASYNCIODEBUG=1 python3 asyncio_test.py

<CoroWrapper printer() running, defined at asyncio_test.py:4, created at
asyncio_test.py:8> was never yielded from

Coroutine object created at (most recent call last):

  File "asyncio_test.py", line 8, in <module>

    printer()
```

Additionally, the event loop has some log messages by default:

```
import asyncio
import logging


logging.basicConfig(level=logging.DEBUG)
loop = asyncio.get_event_loop()
```

This results in debug messages such as the following:

```
# PYTHONASYNCIODEBUG=1 python3 asyncio_test.py

DEBUG:asyncio:Using selector: KqueueSelector

DEBUG:asyncio:Close <_UnixSelectorEventLoop running=False closed=False
debug=True>
```

You might wonder why we are using the PYTHONASYNCIODEBUG flag instead of loop.set_debug(True). The reason is that there are cases where this won't work because debugging is enabled too late. For example, when trying that with the preceding printer(), you will see that you won't get any errors when using loop.set_debug(True) alone.

When enabling debugging, the following will change:

- Coroutines that have not been yielded (as can be seen in the preceding lines) will raise an exception.
- Calling coroutines from the "wrong" thread raises an exception.
- The execution time of the selector will be logged.
- Slow callbacks (more than 100 ms) will be logged. This timeout can be modified through loop.slow_callback_duration.
- Warnings will be raised when resources are not closed properly.
- Tasks that were destroyed before execution will be logged.

Handling crashes using faulthandler

The `faulthandler` module helps when debugging really low-level crashes, that is, crashes that should only be possible when using low-level access to memory, such as C extensions.

For example, here's a bit of code that will cause your Python interpreter to crash:

```
import ctypes

# Get memory address 0, your kernel shouldn't allow this:
ctypes.string_at(0)
```

It results in something similar to the following:

```
# python faulthandler_test.py
zsh: segmentation fault  python faulthandler_test.py
```

That's quite an ugly response of course and gives you no possibility to handle the error. Just in case you are wondering, having a `try`/`except` structure won't help you in these cases either. The following code will crash exactly in the same way:

```
import ctypes

try:
    # Get memory address 0, your kernel shouldn't allow this:
    ctypes.string_at(0)
except Exception as e:
    print('Got exception:', e)
```

This is where the `faulthandler` module helps. It will still cause your interpreter to crash, but at least you will see a proper error message raised, so it's a good default if you (or any of the sublibraries) have any interaction with raw memory:

```
import ctypes
import faulthandler

faulthandler.enable()

# Get memory address 0, your kernel shouldn't allow this:
ctypes.string_at(0)
```

It results in something along these lines:

```
# python faulthandler_test.py
Fatal Python error: Segmentation fault
```

```
Current thread 0x00007fff79171300 (most recent call first):
  File "ctypes/__init__.py", line 491 in string_at
  File "faulthandler_test.py", line 7 in <module>
zsh: segmentation fault  python faulthandler_test.py
```

Obviously, it's not desirable to have a Python application exit in this manner as the code won't exit with a normal cleanup. Resources won't be closed cleanly and your exit handler won't be called. If you somehow need to catch this behavior, your best bet is to wrap the Python executable in a separate script.

Interactive debugging

Now that we have discussed basic debugging methods that will always work, we will look at interactive debugging for some more advanced debugging techniques. The previous debugging methods made variables and stacks visible through modifying the code and/or foresight. This time around, we will look at a slightly smarter method, which constitutes doing the same thing interactively, but once the need arises.

Console on demand

When testing some Python code, you may have used the interactive console a couple of times, since it's a simple yet effective tool for testing your Python code. What you might not have known is that it is actually simple to start your own shell from within your code. So, whenever you want to drop into a regular shell from a specific point in your code, that's easily possible:

```python
import code


def spam():
    eggs = 123
    print('The begin of spam')
    code.interact(banner='', local=locals())
    print('The end of spam')
    print('The value of eggs: %s' % eggs)


if __name__ == '__main__':
    spam()
```

When executing that, we will drop into an interactive console halfway:

```
# python3 test_code.py
The begin of spam
>>> eggs
123
>>> eggs = 456
>>>
The end of spam
The value of eggs: 123
```

To exit this console, we can use ^*d* (*Ctrl + d*) on Linux/Mac systems and ^*z* (*Ctrl + Z*) on Windows systems.

One important thing to note here is that the scope is not shared between the two. Even though we passed along `locals()` to share the local variables for convenience, this relation is not bidirectional. The result is that even though we set `eggs` to `456` in the interactive session, it does not carry over to the outside function. You can modify variables in the outside scope through direct manipulation (for example, setting the properties) if you wish, but all variables declared locally will remain local.

Debugging using pdb

When it comes to actually debugging code, the regular interactive console just isn't suited. With a bit of effort, you can make it work, but it's just not all that convenient for debugging since you can only see the current scope and can't jump around the stack easily. With `pdb` (Python debugger), this is easily possible. So let's look at a simple example of using `pdb`:

```python
import pdb


def spam():
    eggs = 123
    print('The begin of spam')
    pdb.set_trace()
    print('The end of spam')
    print('The value of eggs: %s' % eggs)


if __name__ == '__main__':
    spam()
```

This example is pretty much identical to the one in the previous paragraph, except that this time we end up in the pdb console instead of a regular interactive console. So let's give the interactive debugger a try:

```
# python3 test_pdb.py
The begin of spam
> test_pdb.py(8)spam()
-> print('The end of spam')
(Pdb) eggs
123
(Pdb) eggs = 456
(Pdb) continue
The end of spam
The value of eggs: 456
```

As you can see, we've actually modified the value of eggs now. In this case, we used the full continue command, but all the pdb commands have short versions as well. So, using c instead of continue gives the same result. Just typing eggs (or any other variable) will show the contents and setting the variable will simply set it, just as we would expect from an interactive session.

To get started with pdb, first of all, a list of the most useful (full) commands with shorthands is shown here:

Command	Explanation
h(elp)	This shows the list of commands (this list).
h(elp) command	This shows the help for the given command.
w(here)	Current stack trace with an arrow at the current frame.
d(own)	Move down/to a newer frame in the stack.
u(p)	Move up/to an older frame in the stack.
s(tep)	Execute the current line and stop as soon as possible.
n(ext)	Execute the current line and stop at the next line within the current function.
r(eturn)	Continue execution until the function returns.
c(ont(inue))	Continue execution up to the next breakpoint.
l(ist) [first[, last]]	List the lines of source code (by default, 11 lines) around the current line.
ll	longlist	List all of the source code for the current function or frame.
source expression	List the source code for the given object. This is similar to longlist.

Command	Explanation
a(rgs)	Print the arguments for the current function.
pp expression	Pretty-print the given expression.
b(reak)	Show the list of breakpoints.
b(reak) [filename:] lineno	Place a breakpoint at the given line number and, optionally, file.
b(reak) function[, condition]	Place a breakpoint at the given function. The condition is an expression that must evaluate to True for the breakpoint to work.
cl(ear) [filename:] lineno	Clear the breakpoint (or breakpoints) at this line.
cl(ear) breakpoint [breakpoint ...]	Clear the breakpoint (or breakpoints) with these numbers.
Command	List all defined commands.
command breakpoint	Specify a list of commands to execute whenever the given breakpoint is encountered. The list is ended using the end command.
Alias	List all aliases.
alias name command	Create an alias. The command can be any valid Python expression, so you can do the following to print all properties for an object: **alias pd pp %1.__dict__**
unalias name	Remove an alias.
! statement	Execute the statement at the current point in the stack. Normally the ! sign is not needed, but this can be useful if there are collisions with debugger commands. For example, try b = 123.
Interact	Open an interactive session similar to the previous paragraph. Note that variables set within that local scope will not be transferred.

Breakpoints

It's quite a long list, but you will probably use most of these quite regularly. To highlight one of the options shown in the preceding table, let's demonstrate the setting and use of breakpoints:

```
import pdb


def spam():
```

```
        print('The begin of spam')
        print('The end of spam')


    if __name__ == '__main__':
        pdb.set_trace()
        spam()
```

So far, nothing new has happened, but let's now open the interactive debugging session, as follows:

```
# python3 test_pdb.py
> test_pdb.py(11)<module>()
-> while True:
(Pdb) source spam  # View the source of spam
 4      def spam():
 5          print('The begin of spam')
 6          print('The end of spam')

(Pdb) b 5  # Add a breakpoint to line 5
Breakpoint 1 at test_pdb.py:5

(Pdb) w  # Where shows the current line
> test_pdb.py(11)<module>()
-> while True:

(Pdb) c  # Continue (until the next breakpoint or exception)
> test_pdb.py(5)spam()
-> print('The begin of spam')

(Pdb) w  # Where again
  test_pdb.py(12)<module>()
-> spam()
> test_pdb.py(5)spam()
-> print('The begin of spam')

(Pdb) ll  # List the lines of the current function
 4      def spam():
 5 B->      print('The begin of spam')
```

```
6           print('The end of spam')
```

```
(Pdb) b  # Show the breakpoints
Num Type         Disp Enb   Where
1    breakpoint   keep yes   at test_pdb.py:5
        breakpoint already hit 1 time
```

```
(Pdb) cl 1  # Clear breakpoint 1
Deleted breakpoint 1 at test_pdb.py:5
```

That was a lot of output, but it's actually not as complex as it seems:

1. First, we used the source spam command to see the source for the spam function.

2. After that, we knew the line number of the first print statement, which we used to place a breakpoint (b 5) at line 5.

3. To check whether we were still at the right position, we used the w command.

4. Since the breakpoint was set, we used c to continue up to the next breakpoint.

5. Having stopped at the breakpoint at line 5, we used w again to confirm that.

6. Listing the code of the current function using ll.

7. Listing the breakpoints using b.

8. Removing the breakpoint again using cl 1 with the breakpoint number from the previous command.

It all seems a bit complicated in the beginning, but you'll see that it's actually a very convenient way of debugging once you've tried a few times.

To make it even better, this time we will execute the breakpoint only when eggs = 3. The code is pretty much the same, although we need a variable in this case:

```
import pdb


def spam(eggs):
    print('eggs:', eggs)


if __name__ == '__main__':
    pdb.set_trace()
    for i in range(5):
        spam(i)
```

Now, let's execute the code and make sure that it only breaks at certain times:

```
# python3 test_breakpoint.py
> test_breakpoint.py(10)<module>()
-> for i in range(5):
(Pdb) source spam
  4       def spam(eggs):
  5           print('eggs:', eggs)
(Pdb) b 5, eggs == 3  # Add a breakpoint to line 5 whenever eggs=3
Breakpoint 1 at test_breakpoint.py:5
(Pdb) c  # Continue
eggs: 0
eggs: 1
eggs: 2
> test_breakpoint.py(5)spam()
-> print('eggs:', eggs)
(Pdb) a  # Show function arguments
eggs = 3
(Pdb) c  # Continue
eggs: 3
eggs: 4
```

To list what we have done:

1. First, using `source spam`, we looked for the line number.
2. After that, we placed a breakpoint with the `eggs == 3` condition.
3. Then we continued execution using `c`. As you can see, the values 0, 1, and 2 are printed as normal.
4. The breakpoint was reached at value 3. To verify this we used `a` to see the function arguments.
5. And we continued to execute the rest of the code.

Catching exceptions

All of these have been manual calls to the `pdb.set_trace()` function, but in general, you are just running your application and not really expecting issues. This is where exception catching can be very handy. In addition to importing `pdb` yourself, you can run scripts through `pdb` as a module as well. Let's examine this bit of code, which dies as soon as it reaches zero division:

```
print('This still works')
1/0
print('We shouldnt reach this code')
```

If we run it using the `pdb` parameter, we can end up in the Python Debugger whenever it crashes:

```
# python3 -m pdb test_zero.py
> test_zero.py(1)<module>()
-> print('This still works')
(Pdb) w  # Where
  bdb.py(431)run()
-> exec(cmd, globals, locals)
  <string>(1)<module>()
> test_zero.py(1)<module>()
-> print('This still works')
(Pdb) s  # Step into the next statement
This still works
> test_zero.py(2)<module>()
-> 1/0
(Pdb) c  # Continue
Traceback (most recent call last):
  File "pdb.py", line 1661, in main
    pdb._runscript(mainpyfile)
  File "pdb.py", line 1542, in _runscript
    self.run(statement)
  File "bdb.py", line 431, in run
    exec(cmd, globals, locals)
  File "<string>", line 1, in <module>
  File "test_zero.py", line 2, in <module>
    1/0
ZeroDivisionError: division by zero
Uncaught exception. Entering post mortem debugging
Running 'cont' or 'step' will restart the program
> test_zero.py(2)<module>()
-> 1/0
```

 A useful little trick within `pdb` is to use the *Enter* button, which, by default, will execute the previously executed command again. This is very useful when stepping through the program.

Commands

The `commands` command is a little complicated but very useful. It allows you to execute commands whenever a specific breakpoint is encountered. To illustrate this, let's start from a simple example again:

```python
import pdb


def spam(eggs):
    print('eggs:', eggs)


if __name__ == '__main__':
    pdb.set_trace()
    for i in range(5):
        spam(i)
```

The code is simple enough, so now we'll add the breakpoint and the commands, as follows:

```
# python3 test_breakpoint.py
> test_breakpoint.py(10)<module>()
-> for i in range(3):
(Pdb) b spam  # Add a breakpoint to function spam
Breakpoint 1 at test_breakpoint.py:4
(Pdb) commands 1  # Add a command to breakpoint 1
(com) print('The value of eggs: %s' % eggs)
(com) end  # End the entering of the commands
(Pdb) c  # Continue
The value of eggs: 0
> test_breakpoint.py(5)spam()
-> print('eggs:', eggs)
(Pdb) c  # Continue
eggs: 0
The value of eggs: 1
> test_breakpoint.py(5)spam()
-> print('eggs:', eggs)
(Pdb) cl 1  # Clear breakpoint 1
Deleted breakpoint 1 at test_breakpoint.py:4
(Pdb) c  # Continue
eggs: 1
eggs: 2
```

As you can see, we can easily add commands to the breakpoint. After removing the breakpoint, these commands obviously won't be executed anymore.

Debugging using ipdb

While the generic Python console is useful, it can be a little rough around the edges. The IPython console offers a whole new world of extra features, which make it a much nicer console to work with. One of those features is a more convenient debugger.

First, make sure you have `ipdb` installed:

pip install ipdb

Next, let's try the debugger again with our previous script. The only small change is that we now import `ipdb` instead of `pdb`:

```
import ipdb


def spam(eggs):
    print('eggs:', eggs)


if __name__ == '__main__':
    ipdb.set_trace()
    for i in range(3):
        spam(i)
```

Then we execute it:

```
# python3 test_ipdb.py
> test_ipdb.py(10)<module>()
      9       ipdb.set_trace()
---> 10       for i in range(3):
     11           spam(i)

ipdb> b spam   # Set a breakpoint
Breakpoint 1 at test_ipdb.py:4
ipdb> c   # Continue (until exception or breakpoint)
> test_ipdb.py(5)spam()
1    4 def spam(eggs):
----> 5       print('eggs:', eggs)
      6
```

```
ipdb> a  # Show the arguments
eggs = 0
ipdb> c  # Continue
eggs: 0
> test_ipdb.py(5)spam()
1    4 def spam(eggs):
----> 5        print('eggs:', eggs)
      6


ipdb>    # Repeat the previous command, so continue again
eggs: 1
> test_ipdb.py(5)spam()
1    4 def spam(eggs):
----> 5        print('eggs:', eggs)
      6


ipdb> cl 1  # Remove breakpoint 1
Deleted breakpoint 1 at test_ipdb.py:4
ipdb> c  # Continue
eggs: 2
```

The commands are all the same, but the output is just a tad more legible in my opinion. The actual version also includes syntax highlighting, which makes the output even easier to follow.

In short, you can just replace pdb with ipdb in most situations to simply get a more intuitive debugger. But I will give you the recommendation as well, to the ipdb context manager:

```
import ipdb


with ipdb.launch_ipdb_on_exception():
    main()
```

This is as convenient as it looks. It simply hooks ipdb into your exceptions so that you can easily debug whenever needed. Combine that with a debug flag to your application to easily allow debugging when needed.

Other debuggers

pdb and ipdb are just two of the large number of debuggers available for Python. Some of the currently noteworthy debuggers are as follows:

- pudb: This offers a a full-screen command-line debugger
- pdbpp: This hooks into the regular pdb
- rpdb2: This is a remote debugger that allows hooking into running (remote) applications
- Werkzeug: This is a web-based debugger that allows debugging of web applications while they are running

There are many others, of course, and there isn't a single one that's the absolute best. As is the case with all tools, they all have their advantages and their fallacies, and the one that is best for your current purpose can be properly decided only by you. Chances are that your current Python IDE already has an integrated debugger.

Debugging services

In addition to debugging when you encounter a problem, there are times when you simply need to keep track of errors for later debugging. Especially when working with remote servers, these can be invaluable to detect when and how a Python process is malfunctioning. Additionally, these services offer grouping of errors as well, making them far more useful than a simple e-mail-on-exception type of script, which can quickly spam your inbox.

A nice open source solution for keeping track of errors is sentry. If you need a full-fletched solution that offers performance tracking as well, then Opbeat and Newrelic are very nice solutions; they offer both free and paid versions. Note that all of these also support tracking of other languages, such as JavaScript.

Summary

This chapter explained a few different debugging techniques and gotchas. There is, of course, much more that can be said about debugging, but I hope you have acquired a nice vantage point for debugging your Python code now. Interactive debugging techniques are very useful for single-threaded applications and locations where interactive sessions are available. But since that's not always the case, we also discussed some non-interactive options.

Here's an overview of all the points discussed in this chapter:

- Non-interactive debugging using:
  - `print`
  - `logging`
  - `trace`
  - `traceback`
  - `asyncio`
  - `faulthandler`
- Interactive debugging using both `pdb` and `ipdb`

In the next chapter, we will see how to monitor and improve both CPU and memory performance, as well as finding and fixing memory leaks.

12
Performance – Tracking and Reducing Your Memory and CPU Usage

Before we talk about performance, there is a quote by *Donald Knuth* you need to consider first:

> *"The real problem is that programmers have spent far too much time worrying about efficiency in the wrong places and at the wrong times; premature optimization is the root of all evil (or at least most of it) in programming."*

 Donald Knuth is often called the father of algorithm analysis. His book series, *The Art of Computer Programming*, can be considered the Bible of all fundamental algorithms.

As long as you pick the correct data structures with the right algorithms, performance should not be something to worry about. That does not mean you should ignore performance entirely, but just make sure you pick the right battles and optimize only when it is actually needed. Micro/premature optimizations can definitely be fun, but only very rarely useful.

We have seen the performance characteristics of many data structures in *Chapter 2, Pythonic Syntax, Common Pitfalls, and Style Guide*, already, so we won't discuss that, but we will show you how performance can be measured and how problems can be detected. There are cases where micro optimizations make a difference, but you won't know until you measure the performance.

Within this chapter, we will cover:

- Profiling CPU usage
- Profiling memory usage
- Learning how to correctly compare performance metrics
- Optimizing performance
- Finding and fixing memory leaks

What is performance?

Performance is a very broad term. It has many different meanings and in many cases it is defined incorrectly. You have probably heard statements similar to "Language X is faster than Python". However, that statement is inherently wrong. Python is neither fast nor slow; Python is a programming language and a language has no performance metrics whatsoever. If one were to say that the CPython interpreter is faster or slower than interpreter Y for language X, that would be possible. The performance characteristics of code can vary greatly between different interpreters. Just take a look at this small test:

```
# python3 -m timeit '"".join(str(i) for i in range(10000))'
100 loops, best of 3: 2.91 msec per loop
# python2 -m timeit '"".join(str(i) for i in range(10000))'
100 loops, best of 3: 2.13 msec per loop
# pypy -m timeit '"".join(str(i) for i in range(10000))'
1000 loops, best of 3: 677 usec per loop
```

Three different interpreters with all vastly different performance! All are Python but the interpreters obviously vary. Looking at this benchmark, you might be tempted to drop the CPython interpreter completely and only use Pypy. The danger with benchmarks such as these is that they rarely offer any meaningful results. For this limited example, the Pypy interpreter was about four times faster than the CPython3 interpreter, but that has no relevance whatsoever for the general case. The only conclusion that can safely be drawn here is that this specific version of the Pypy interpreter is more than four times faster than this specific version of CPython3 for this exact test. For any other test and interpreter version the results could be vastly different.

Timeit – comparing code snippet performance

Before we can start improving performance, we need a reliable method to measure it. Python has a really nice module (`timeit`) with the specific purpose of measuring execution times of bits of code. It executes a bit of code many times to make sure there is as little variation as possible and to make the measurement fairly clean. It's very useful if you want to compare a few code snippets. Following are example executions:

```
# python3 -m timeit 'x=[]; [x.insert(0, i) for i in range(10000)]'
10 loops, best of 3: 30.2 msec per loop
# python3 -m timeit 'x=[]; [x.append(i) for i in range(10000)]'
1000 loops, best of 3: 1.01 msec per loop
# python3 -m timeit 'x=[i for i in range(10000)]'
1000 loops, best of 3: 381 usec per loop
# python3 -m timeit 'x=list(range(10000))'
10000 loops, best of 3: 212 usec per loop
```

These few examples demonstrate the performance difference between `list.insert`, `list.append`, a list comprehension, and the `list` function. But more importantly, it demonstrates how to use the `timeit` command. Naturally, the command can be used with regular scripts as well, but the `timeit` module only accepts statements as strings to execute which is a bit of an annoyance. Luckily, you can easily work around that by wrapping your code in a function and just timing that function:

```python
import timeit


def test_list():
    return list(range(10000))


def test_list_comprehension():
    return [i for i in range(10000)]


def test_append():
    x = []
    for i in range(10000):
        x.append(i)

    return x
```

```
def test_insert():
    x = []
    for i in range(10000):
        x.insert(0, i)

    return x


def benchmark(function, number=100, repeat=10):
    # Measure the execution times
    times = timeit.repeat(function, number=number, globals=globals())
    # The repeat function gives `repeat` results so we take the min()
    # and divide it by the number of runs
    time = min(times) / number
    print('%d loops, best of %d: %9.6fs :: %s' % (
        number, repeat, time, function))


if __name__ == '__main__':
    benchmark('test_list()')
    benchmark('test_list_comprehension()')
    benchmark('test_append()')
    benchmark('test_insert()')
```

When executing this, you will get something along the following lines:

```
# python3 test_timeit.py
100 loops, best of 10:  0.000238s :: test_list()
100 loops, best of 10:  0.000407s :: test_list_comprehension()
100 loops, best of 10:  0.000838s :: test_append()
100 loops, best of 10:  0.031795s :: test_insert()
```

As you may have noticed, this script is still a bit basic. While the regular version keeps trying until it reaches 0.2 seconds or more, this script just has a fixed number of executions. Unfortunately, the timeit module wasn't entirely written with re-use in mind, so besides calling timeit.main() from your script there is not much you can do to re-use that logic.

Personally, I recommend using IPython instead, as it makes measurements much easier:

```
# ipython3
In [1]: import test_timeit
In [2]: %timeit test_timeit.test_list()
1000 loops, best of 3: 255 µs per loop
```

```
In [3]: %timeit test_timeit.test_list_comprehension()
1000 loops, best of 3: 430 µs per loop
In [4]: %timeit test_timeit.test_append()
1000 loops, best of 3: 934 µs per loop
In [5]: %timeit test_timeit.test_insert()
10 loops, best of 3: 31.6 ms per loop
```

In this case, IPython automatically takes care of the string wrapping and passing of `globals()`. Still, this is all very limited and useful only for comparing multiple methods of doing the same thing. When it comes to full Python applications, there are more methods available.

 To view the source of both IPython functions and regular modules, entering `object??` in the IPython shell returns the source. In this case just enter `timeit??` to view the `timeit` IPython function definition.

The easiest way you can implement the `%timeit` function yourself is to simply call `timeit.main`:

```
import timeit

timeit.main(args=['[x for x in range(1000000)]'])
```

The internals of the `timeit` module are nothing special. A basic version can be implemented with just an `eval` and a `time.perf_counter` (the highest resolution timer available in Python) combination:

```
import time
import functools


TIMEIT_TEMPLATE = '''
import time

def run(number):
    %(setup)s
    start = time.perf_counter()
    for i in range(number):
        %(statement)s
    return time.perf_counter() - start
'''
```

```
def timeit(statement='pass', setup='pass', repeat=1, number=1000000,
           globals_=None):
    # Get or create globals
    globals_ = globals() if globals_ is None else globals_

    # Create the test code so we can separate the namespace
    src = TIMEIT_TEMPLATE % dict(
        statement=statement,
        setup=setup,
        number=number,
    )
    # Compile the source
    code = compile(src, '<source>', 'exec')

    # Define locals for the benchmarked code
    locals_ = {}

    # Execute the code so we can get the benchmark fuction
    exec(code, globals_, locals_)

    # Get the run function
    run = functools.partial(locals_['run'], number=number)
    for i in range(repeat):
        yield run()
```

The actual `timeit` code is a bit more advanced in terms of checking the input but this example roughly shows how the `timeit.repeat` function can be implemented.

To register your own function in IPython, you need to use some IPython magic. Note that the magic is not a pun. The IPython module that takes care of commands such as these is actually called `magic`. To demonstrate:

```
from IPython.core import magic
```

```
@magic.register_line_magic(line):
    import timeit
    timeit.main(args[line])
```

To learn more about custom magic in IPython, take a look at the IPython documentation at `https://ipython.org/ipython-doc/3/config/custommagics.html`.

cProfile – finding the slowest components

The `profile` module makes it easily possible to analyze the relative CPU cycles used in a script/application. Be very careful not to compare these with the results from the `timeit` module. While the `timeit` module tries as best as possible to give an accurate benchmark of the absolute amount of time it takes to execute a code snippet, the `profile` module is only useful for relative results. The reason is that the profiling code itself incurs such a slowdown that the results are not comparable with non-profiled code. There is a way to make it a bit more accurate however, but more about that later.

 Within this section we will be talking about the `profile` module but in the examples we will actually use the `cProfile` module. The `cProfile` module is a high-performance emulation of the pure Python `profile` module.

First profiling run

Let's profile our Fibonacci function from *Chapter 5, Decorators– Enabling Code Reuse by Decorating*, both with and without the cache function. First, the code:

```
import sys
import functools


@functools.lru_cache()
def fibonacci_cached(n):
    if n < 2:
        return n
    else:
        return fibonacci_cached(n - 1) + fibonacci_cached(n - 2)


def fibonacci(n):
    if n < 2:
        return n
    else:
        return fibonacci(n - 1) + fibonacci(n - 2)


if __name__ == '__main__':
    n = 30
```

```
        if sys.argv[-1] == 'cache':
            fibonacci_cached(n)
        else:
            fibonacci(n)
```

 For readabilities sake, all `cProfile` statistics will be stripped of the `percall` and `cumtime` columns in all `cProfile` outputs. These columns are irrelevant for the purposes of these examples.

First we'll execute the function without cache:

```
# python3 -m cProfile -s calls test_fibonacci.py no_cache
        2692557 function calls (21 primitive calls) in 0.815
        seconds


    Ordered by: call count


    ncalls tottime percall filename:lineno(function)
2692537/1   0.815    0.815 test_fibonacci.py:13(fibonacci)
         7   0.000    0.000 {built-in method builtins.getattr}
         5   0.000    0.000 {built-in method builtins.setattr}
         1   0.000    0.000 {method 'update' of 'dict' objects}
         1   0.000    0.000 {built-in method builtins.isinstance}
         1   0.000    0.000 functools.py:422(decorating_function)
         1   0.000    0.815 test_fibonacci.py:1(<module>)
         1   0.000    0.000 {method 'disable' of '_lsprof.Profiler'}
         1   0.000    0.815 {built-in method builtins.exec}
         1   0.000    0.000 functools.py:43(update_wrapper)
         1   0.000    0.000 functools.py:391(lru_cache)
```

That's quite a lot of calls, isn't it? Apparently, we called the `test_fibonacci` function nearly 3 million times. That is where the profiling modules provide a lot of insight. Let's analyze the metrics a bit further:

- **Ncalls**: The number of calls that were made to the function
- **Tottime**: The total time spent in seconds within this function with all sub-functions excluded

  Percall, `tottime / ncalls`

- **Cumtime**: The total time spent within this function, including sub-functions

  Percall, `cumtime / ncalls`

Which is the most useful depends on your use case. It's quite simple to change the sort order using the -s parameter within the default output. But now let's see what the result is with the cached version. Once again, with stripped output:

```
# python3 -m cProfile -s calls test_fibonacci.py cache
        51 function calls (21 primitive calls) in 0.000 seconds


   Ordered by: call count


   ncalls tottime percall filename:lineno(function)
     31/1   0.000   0.000 test_fibonacci.py:5(fibonacci_cached)
        7   0.000   0.000 {built-in method builtins.getattr}
        5   0.000   0.000 {built-in method builtins.setattr}
        1   0.000   0.000 test_fibonacci.py:1(<module>)
        1   0.000   0.000 {built-in method builtins.isinstance}
        1   0.000   0.000 {built-in method builtins.exec}
        1   0.000   0.000 functools.py:422(decorating_function)
        1   0.000   0.000 {method 'disable' of '_lsprof.Profiler'}
        1   0.000   0.000 {method 'update' of 'dict' objects}
        1   0.000   0.000 functools.py:391(lru_cache)
        1   0.000   0.000 functools.py:43(update_wrapper)
```

This time we see a tottime of 0.000 because it's just too fast to measure. But also, while the fibonacci_cached function is still the most executed function, it's only being executed 31 times instead of 3 million.

Calibrating your profiler

To illustrate the difference between profile and cProfile, let's try the uncached run again with the profile module instead. Just a heads up, this is much slower so don't be surprised if it stalls a little:

```
# python3 -m profile -s calls test_fibonacci.py no_cache
        2692558 function calls (22 primitive calls) in 7.696 seconds

   Ordered by: call count

   ncalls tottime percall filename:lineno(function)
2692537/1   7.695   7.695 test_fibonacci.py:13(fibonacci)
        7   0.000   0.000 :0(getattr)
        5   0.000   0.000 :0(setattr)
```

```
1    0.000    0.000  :0(isinstance)
1    0.001    0.001  :0(setprofile)
1    0.000    0.000  :0(update)
1    0.000    0.000  functools.py:43(update_wrapper)
1    0.000    7.696  profile:0(<code object <module> ...>)
1    0.000    7.695  test_fibonacci.py:1(<module>)
1    0.000    0.000  functools.py:391(lru_cache)
1    0.000    7.695  :0(exec)
1    0.000    0.000  functools.py:422(decorating_function)
0    0.000           profile:0(profiler)
```

Huge difference, isn't it? Now the code is nearly 10 times slower and the only difference is using the pure Python `profile` module instead of the `cProfile` module. This does indicate a big problem with the `profile` module. The overhead from the module itself is great enough to skew the results, which means we should account for that offset. That's what the `Profile.calibrate()` function takes care of, as it calculates the bias incurred by the profile module. To calculate the bias, we can use the following script:

```python
import profile


if __name__ == '__main__':
    profiler = profile.Profile()
    for i in range(10):
        print(profiler.calibrate(100000))
```

The numbers will vary slightly but you should be able to get a fair estimate of the bias using this code. If the numbers still vary a lot, you can increase the trials from `100000` to something even larger. This type of calibration only works for the profile module, but if you are looking for more accurate results and the `cProfile` module does not work for you due to inheritance or not being supported on your platform, you can use this code to set your bias globally and get more accurate results:

```python
import profile


# The number here is bias calculated earlier
profile.Profile.bias = 2.0939406059394783e-06
```

For a specific `Profile` instance:

```python
import profile


profiler = profile.Profile(bias=2.0939406059394783e-06)
```

Note that in general a smaller bias is better to use than a large one, because a large bias could cause very strange results. In some cases you will even get negative timings. Let's give it a try for our Fibonacci code:

```python
import sys
import pstats
import profile
import functools


@functools.lru_cache()
def fibonacci_cached(n):
    if n < 2:
        return n
    else:
        return fibonacci_cached(n - 1) + fibonacci_cached(n - 2)


def fibonacci(n):
    if n < 2:
        return n
    else:
        return fibonacci(n - 1) + fibonacci(n - 2)


if __name__ == '__main__':
    profiler = profile.Profile(bias=2.0939406059394783e-06)
    n = 30

    if sys.argv[-1] == 'cache':
        profiler.runcall(fibonacci_cached, n)
    else:
        profiler.runcall(fibonacci, n)

    stats = pstats.Stats(profiler).sort_stats('calls')
    stats.print_stats()
```

While running it, it indeed appears that I've used a bias that's too large:

```
# python3 test_fibonacci.py no_cache
        2692539 function calls (3 primitive calls) in -0.778
        seconds


Ordered by: call count
```

```
ncalls tottime percall filename:lineno(function)
2692537/1  -0.778  -0.778 test_fibonacci.py:15(fibonacci)
         1   0.000   0.000 :0(setprofile)
         1   0.000  -0.778 profile:0(<function fibonacci at 0x...>)
         0   0.000          profile:0(profiler)
```

Still, it shows how the code can be used properly. You can even incorporate the bias calculation within the script using a snippet like this:

```
import profile


if __name__ == '__main__':
    profiler = profile.Profile()
    profiler.bias = profiler.calibrate(100000)
```

Selective profiling using decorators

Calculating simple timings is easy enough using decorators, but profiling is also important. Both are useful but serve different goals. Let's look at both the options:

```
import cProfile
import datetime
import functools


def timer(function):
    @functools.wraps(function)
    def _timer(*args, **kwargs):
        start = datetime.datetime.now()
        try:
            return function(*args, **kwargs)
        finally:
            end = datetime.datetime.now()
            print('%s: %s' % (function.__name__, end - start))
    return _timer


def profiler(function):
    @functools.wraps(function)
    def _profiler(*args, **kwargs):
        profiler = cProfile.Profile()
        try:
            profiler.enable()
            return function(*args, **kwargs)
```

```
        finally:
            profiler.disable()
            profiler.print_stats()
    return _profiler


@profiler
def profiled_fibonacci(n):
    return fibonacci(n)


@timer
def timed_fibonacci(n):
    return fibonacci(n)


def fibonacci(n):
    if n < 2:
        return n
    else:
        return fibonacci(n - 1) + fibonacci(n - 2)


if __name__ == '__main__':
    timed_fibonacci(32)
    profiled_fibonacci(32)
```

The code is simple enough, just a basic timer and profiler printing some default statistics. Which functions best for you depends on your use-case of course, but they definitely both have their uses. The added advantage of this selective profiling is that the output is more limited which helps with readability:

```
# python3 test_fibonacci.py
 timed_fibonacci: 0:00:01.050200
         7049157 function calls (3 primitive calls) in 2.024
         seconds


   Ordered by: standard name


   ncalls tottime percall filename:lineno(function)
        1    0.000    2.024 test_fibonacci.py:31(profiled_fibonacci)
 7049155/1  2.024    2.024 test_fibonacci.py:41(fibonacci)
        1    0.000    0.000 {method 'disable' of '_lsprof.Profiler'}
```

As you can see, the profiler still makes the code about twice as slow, but it's definitely usable.

Using profile statistics

To get some more intricate profiling results, we will profile the `pystone` script. The `pystone` script is an internal Python performance test which benchmarks the Python interpreter fairly thoroughly. First, let's create the statistics using this script:

```
from test import pystone
import cProfile


if __name__ == '__main__':
    profiler = cProfile.Profile()
    profiler.runcall(pystone.main)
    profiler.dump_stats('pystone.profile')
```

When executing the script, you should get something like this:

```
# python3 test_pystone.py
Pystone(1.2) time for 50000 passes = 0.725432
This machine benchmarks at 68924.4 pystones/second
```

After running the script, you should have a `pystone.profile` file containing the profiling results. These results can be And the `pystone.profile` file which contains all of the profiling statistics. These statistics can be viewed through the `pstats` module which is bundled with Python:

```
import pstats


stats = pstats.Stats('pystone.profile')
stats.strip_dirs()
stats.sort_stats('calls', 'cumtime')
stats.print_stats(10)
```

In some cases, it can be interesting to combine the results from multiple measurements. That is possible by specifying multiple files or by using `stats.add(*filenames)`. But first, let's look at the regular output:

```
# python3 parse_statistics.py


        1050012 function calls in 0.776 seconds
```

```
Ordered by: call count, cumulative time

List reduced from 21 to 10 due to restriction <10>


   ncalls   tottime   percall   cumtime   percall  filename:lineno(function)
   150000     0.032     0.000     0.032     0.000  pystone.py:214(Proc7)
   150000     0.027     0.000     0.027     0.000  pystone.py:232(Func1)
   100000     0.016     0.000     0.016     0.000  {built-in method builtins.
chr}
   100000     0.010     0.000     0.010     0.000  {built-in method builtins.
ord}
    50002     0.029     0.000     0.029     0.000  pystone.py:52(__init__)
    50000     0.127     0.000     0.294     0.000  pystone.py:144(Proc1)
    50000     0.094     0.000     0.094     0.000  pystone.py:219(Proc8)
    50000     0.048     0.000     0.077     0.000  pystone.py:60(copy)
    50000     0.051     0.000     0.061     0.000  pystone.py:240(Func2)
    50000     0.031     0.000     0.043     0.000  pystone.py:171(Proc3)
```

Obviously, the parameters can easily be modified to change the sort order and the number of output lines. But that is not the only possibility of the statistics. There are quite a few packages around which can parse these results and visualize them. One option is RunSnakeRun, which although useful does not run on Python 3 currently. Also, we have QCacheGrind, a very nice visualizer for profile statistics but which requires some manual compiling to get running or some searching for binaries of course.

Let's look at the output from QCacheGrind. In the case of Windows, the QCacheGrindWin package provides a binary, whereas within Linux it is most likely available through your package manager, and with OS X you can try `brew install qcachegrind --with-graphviz`. But there is one more package you will require: the `pyprof2calltree` package. It transforms the `profile` output into a format that QCacheGrind understands. So, after a simple `pip install pyprof2calltree`, we can now convert the `profile` file into a `callgrind` file:

```
# pyprof2calltree -i pystone.profile -o pystone.callgrind
writing converted data to: pystone.callgrind
# qcachegrind pystone.callgrind
```

This results in running of the `QCacheGrind` application. After switching to the appropriate tabs, you should see something like the following image:

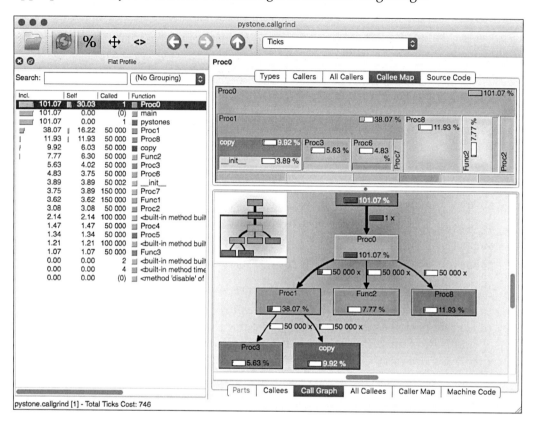

For a simple script such as this, pretty much all output works. However, with full applications, a tool such as QCacheGrind is invaluable. Looking at the output generated by QCacheGrind, it is immediately obvious which process took the most time. The structure at the top right shows bigger rectangles if the amount of time taken was greater, which is a very useful visualization of the chunks of CPU time that were used. The list at the left is very similar to `cProfile` and therefore nothing new. The tree at the bottom right can be very valuable or very useless as it is in this case. It shows you the percentage of CPU time taken in a function and more importantly, the relationship of that function with the other functions.

Because these tools scale depending on the input the results are useful for just about any application. Whether a function takes 100 milliseconds or 100 minutes makes no difference, the output will show a clear overview of the slow parts, which is what we will try to fix.

Line profiler

`line_profiler` is actually not a package that's bundled with Python, but it's far too useful to ignore. While the regular `profile` module profiles all (sub)functions within a certain block, `line_profiler` allows for profiling line per line within a function. The Fibonacci function is not best suited here, but we can use a prime number generator instead. But first, install `line_profiler`:

```
pip install line_profiler
```

Now that we have installed the `line_profiler` module (and with that the `kernprof` command), let's test `line_profiler`:

```python
import itertools


@profile
def primes():
    n = 2
    primes = set()
    while True:
        for p in primes:
            if n % p == 0:
                break
        else:
            primes.add(n)
            yield n
        n += 1


if __name__ == '__main__':
    total = 0
    n = 2000
    for prime in itertools.islice(primes(), n):
        total += prime

    print('The sum of the first %d primes is %d' % (n, total))
```

You might be wondering where the `profile` decorator is coming from. It originates from the `line_profiler` module, which is why we have to run the script with the `kernprof` command:

```
# kernprof -l test_primes.py
The sum of the first 2000 primes is 16274627
Wrote profile results to test_primes.py.lprof
```

As the command says, the results have been written to the `test_primes.py.lprof` file. So let's look at the output of that with the `Time` column skipped for readability:

```
# python3 -m line_profiler test_primes.py.lprof
Timer unit: 1e-06 s


Total time: 2.33179 s
File: test_primes.py
Function: primes at line 4


Line #      Hits     Per Hit    % Time   Line Contents
==============================================================
     4                                   @profile
     5                                   def primes():
     6         1         3.0       0.0       n = 2
     7         1         1.0       0.0       primes = set()
     8         1         0.0       0.0       while True:
     9   2058163         0.5      43.1           for p in primes:
    10   2056163         0.6      56.0               if n % p == 0:
    11     15388         0.5       0.3                   break
    12                                               else:
    13      2000         1.2       0.1                   primes.add(n)
    14      2000         0.5       0.0                   yield n
    15     17387         0.6       0.4           n += 1
```

Wonderful output, isn't it? It makes it trivial to find the slow part within a bit of code. Within this code, the slowness is obviously originating from the loop, but within other code it might not be that clear.

 This module can be added as an IPython extension as well, which enables the `%lprun` command within IPython. To load the extension, the `load_ext` command can be used from the IPython shell `%load_ext line_profiler`.

Improving performance

Much can be said about performance optimization, but truthfully, if you have read the entire book up to this point, you know most of the Python-specific techniques to write fast code. The most important factor in application performance will always be the choice of algorithms, and by extension, the data structures. Searching for an item within `list` is almost always a worse idea than searching for an item in `dict` or `set`.

Using the right algorithm

Within any application, the right choice of algorithm is by far the most important performance characteristic, which is why I am repeating it to illustrate the results of a bad choice:

```
In [1]: a = list(range(1000000))

In [2]: b = dict.fromkeys(range(1000000))

In [3]: %timeit 'x' in a
10 loops, best of 3: 20.5 ms per loop

In [4]: %timeit 'x' in b
10000000 loops, best of 3: 41.6 ns per loop
```

Checking whether an item is within a `list` is an $O(n)$ operation and checking whether an item is within a `dict` is an $O(1)$ operation. A huge difference when `n=1000000` obviously, in this simple test we can see that for 1 million items it's 500 times faster.

All other performance tips combined together might make your code twice as fast, but using the right algorithm for the job can cause a much greater improvement. Using an algorithm that takes $O(n)$ time instead of $O(n^2)$ time will make your code `1000` times faster for `n=1000`, and with a larger n the difference only grows further.

Global interpreter lock

One of the most obscure components of the CPython interpreter is the **global interpreter lock (GIL)**, a **mutual exclusion lock (mutex)** required to prevent memory corruption. The Python memory manager is not thread-safe and that is why the GIL is needed. Without the GIL, multiple threads might alter memory at the same time, causing all sorts of unexpected and potentially dangerous results.

So what is the impact of the GIL in a real-life application? Within single-threaded applications it makes no difference whatsoever and is actually an extremely fast method for memory consistency. Within multithreaded applications however, it can slow your application down a bit, because only a single thread can access the GIL at a time. So if your code has to access the GIL a lot, it might benefit from some restructuring.

Luckily, Python offers a few other options for parallel processing: the `asyncio` module that we saw earlier and the `multiprocessing` library that we will see in *Chapter 13, Multiprocessing – When a Single CPU Core Is Not Enough*.

Try versus if

In many languages a `try/except` type of block incurs quite a performance hit, but within Python this is not the case. It's not that an `if` statement is heavy, but if you expect your `try/except` to succeed most of the time and only fail in rare cases, it's definitely a valid alternative. As always though, focus on readability and conveying the purpose of the code. If the intention of the code is clearer using an `if` statement, use the `if` statement. If `try/except` conveys the intention in a better way, use that.

Lists versus generators

Evaluating code lazily using generators is almost always a better idea than calculating the entire dataset. The most important rule of performance optimization is probably that you shouldn't calculate anything you're not going to use. If you're not sure that you are going to need it, don't calculate it.

Don't forget that you can easily chain multiple generators, so everything is calculated only when it's actually needed. Do be careful that this won't result in recalculation though; `itertools.tee` is generally a better idea than recalculating your results completely.

String concatenation

You might have seen benchmarks saying that using `+=` is much slower than joining strings. At one point this made quite a lot of difference indeed. With Python 3 however, most of the differences have vanished.

```
In [1]: %%timeit
   ...: s = ''
   ...: for i in range(1000000):
   ...:     s += str(i)
```

```
    ...:
1 loops, best of 3: 362 ms per loop


In [2]: %%timeit
    ...: ss = []
    ...: for i in range(1000000):
    ...:     ss.append(str(i))
    ...: s = ''.join(ss)
    ...:
1 loops, best of 3: 332 ms per loop


In [3]: %timeit ''.join(str(i) for i in range(1000000))
1 loops, best of 3: 324 ms per loop


In [4]: %timeit ''.join([str(i) for i in range(1000000)])
1 loops, best of 3: 294 ms per loop
```

There are still some differences of course, but they are so small that I recommend to simply ignore them and choose the most readable option instead.

Addition versus generators

As is the case with string concatenation, once a significant difference now too small to mention.

```
    In [1]: %%timeit
       ...: x = 0
       ...: for i in range(1000000):
       ...:     x += i
       ...:
    10 loops, best of 3: 73.2 ms per loop


    In [2]: %timeit x = sum(i for i in range(1000000))
    10 loops, best of 3: 75.3 ms per loop


    In [3]: %timeit x = sum([i for i in range(1000000)])
    10 loops, best of 3: 71.2 ms per loop


    In [4]: %timeit x = sum(range(1000000))
    10 loops, best of 3: 25.6 ms per loop
```

What does help though is letting Python handle everything internally using native functions, as can be seen in the last example.

Map versus generators and list comprehensions

Once again, readability counts more than performance. There are a few cases where map is faster than list comprehensions and generators, but only if the map function can use a predefined function. As soon as you need to whip out lambda, it's actually slower. Not that it matters much, since readability should be key anyhow, use generators or list comprehensions instead of map:

```
In [1]: %timeit list(map(lambda x: x/2, range(1000000)))
10 loops, best of 3: 182 ms per loop

In [2]: %timeit list(x/2 for x in range(1000000))
10 loops, best of 3: 122 ms per loop

In [3]: %timeit [x/2 for x in range(1000000)]
10 loops, best of 3: 84.7 ms per loop
```

As you can see, the list comprehension is obviously quite a bit faster than the generator. In many cases I would still recommend the generator over the list comprehension though, if only because of the memory usage and the potential laziness. If for some reason you are only going to use the first 10 items, you're still wasting a lot of resources by calculating the full list of items.

Caching

We have already covered the functools.lru_cache decorator in *Chapter 5, Decorators – Enabling Code Reuse by Decorating* but the importance should not be underestimated. Regardless of how fast and smart your code is, not having to calculate results is always better and that's what caching does. Depending on your use case, there are many options available. Within a simple script, functools.lru_cache is a very good contender, but between multiple executions of an application, the cPickle module can be a life saver as well.

If multiple servers are involved, I recommend taking a look at **Redis**. The Redis server is a single threaded in-memory server which is extremely fast and has many useful data structures available. If you see articles or tutorials about improving performance using Memcached, simply replace Memcached with Redis everywhere. Redis is superior to Memcached in every way and in its most basic form the API is compatible.

Lazy imports

A common problem in application load times is that everything is loaded immediately at the start of the program, while with many applications this is actually not needed and certain parts of the application only require loading when they are actually used. To facilitate this, one can occasionally move the imports inside of functions so they can be loaded on demand.

While it's a valid strategy in some cases, I don't generally recommend it for two reasons:

1. It makes your code less clear; having all imports in the same style at the top of the file improves readability.

2. It doesn't make the code faster as it just moves the load time to a different part.

Using optimized libraries

This is actually a very broad tip, but useful nonetheless. If there's a highly optimized library which suits your purpose, you most likely won't be able to beat its performance without a significant amount of effort. Libraries such as numpy, pandas, scipy, and sklearn are highly optimized for performance and their native operations can be incredibly fast. If they suit your purpose, be sure to give them a try. Just to illustrate how fast numpy can be compared to plain Python, refer to the following:

```
In [1]: import numpy

In [2]: a = list(range(1000000))

In [3]: b = numpy.arange(1000000)

In [4]: %timeit c = [x for x in a if x > 500000]
10 loops, best of 3: 44 ms per loop

In [5]: %timeit d = b[b > 500000]
1000 loops, best of 3: 1.61 ms per loop
```

The numpy code does exactly the same as the Python code, except that it uses numpy arrays instead of Python lists. This little difference has made the code more than 25 times faster.

Just-in-time compiling

Just-in-time (JIT) compiling is a method of dynamically compiling (parts) an application during runtime. Because there is much more information available at runtime, this can have a huge effect and make your application much faster.

The `numba` package provides selective JIT compiling for you, allowing you to mark the functions that are JIT compiler compatible. Essentially, if your functions follow the functional programming paradigm of basing the calculations only on the input, then it will most likely work with the JIT compiler.

Basic example of how the `numba` JIT compiler can be used:

```
import numba


@numba.jit
def sum(array):
    total = 0.0
    for value in array:
        total += value
    return value
```

The use cases for these are limited, but if you are using `numpy` or pandas you will most likely benefit from `numba`.

Another very interesting fact to note is that `numba` supports not only CPU optimized execution but GPU as well. This means that for certain operations you can use the fast processor in your video card to process the results.

Converting parts of your code to C

We will see more about this in *Chapter 14*, *Extensions in C/C++, System Calls, and C/C++ Libraries*, but if high performance is really required, then a native C function can help quite a lot. This doesn't even have to be that difficult. The Cython module makes it trivial to write parts of your code with performance very close to native C code.

Following is an example from the Cython manual to approximate the value of pi:

```
cdef inline double recip_square(int i):
    return 1./(i*i)

def approx_pi(int n=10000000):
    cdef double val = 0.
    cdef int k
```

```
    for k in xrange(1,n+1):
        val += recip_square(k)
    return (6 * val)**.5
```

While there are some small differences such as `cdef` instead of `def` and type definitions for the values and parameters, the code is largely the same as regular Python would be, but certainly much faster.

Memory usage

So far we have simply looked at the execution times and ignored the memory usage of the scripts. In many cases, the execution times are the most important, but memory usage should not be ignored. In almost all cases, CPU and memory are traded; a code either uses a lot of CPU or a lot of memory, which means that both do matter a lot.

Tracemalloc

Monitoring memory usage used to be something that was only possible through external Python modules such as **Dowser** or **Heapy**. While those modules still work, they are largely obsolete now because of the `tracemalloc` module. Let's give the `tracemalloc` module a try to see how easy memory usage monitoring is nowadays:

```
import tracemalloc


if __name__ == '__main__':
    tracemalloc.start()

    # Reserve some memory
    x = list(range(1000000))

    # Import some modules
    import os
    import sys
    import asyncio

    # Take a snapshot to calculate the memory usage
    snapshot = tracemalloc.take_snapshot()
    for statistic in snapshot.statistics('lineno')[:10]:
        print(statistic)
```

This results in:

```
# python3 test_tracemalloc.py
test_tracemalloc.py:8: size=35.3 MiB, count=999745, average=37 B
<frozen importlib._bootstrap_external>:473: size=1909 KiB, count=20212,
average=97 B
<frozen importlib._bootstrap>:222: size=895 KiB, count=3798, average=241
B
collections/__init__.py:412: size=103 KiB, count=1451, average=72 B
<string>:5: size=36.6 KiB, count=133, average=282 B
collections/__init__.py:406: size=29.9 KiB, count=15, average=2039 B
abc.py:133: size=26.1 KiB, count=102, average=262 B
ipaddress.py:608: size=21.3 KiB, count=182, average=120 B
<frozen importlib._bootstrap_external>:53: size=21.2 KiB, count=140,
average=155 B
types.py:234: size=15.3 KiB, count=124, average=127 B
```

You can easily see how every part of the code allocated memory and where it might
be wasted. While it might still be unclear which part was actually causing the memory
usage, there are options for that as well, as we will see in the following sections.

Memory profiler

The `memory_profiler` module is very similar to `line_profiler` discussed earlier,
but for memory usage instead. Installing it is as easy as `pip install memory_profiler`, but the optional `pip install psutil` is also highly recommended (and
required in the case of Windows) as it increases your performance by a large amount.
To test `line_profiler`, we will use the following script:

```
import memory_profiler


@memory_profiler.profile
def main():
    n = 100000
    a = [i for i in range(n)]
    b = [i for i in range(n)]
    c = list(range(n))
    d = list(range(n))
    e = dict.fromkeys(a, b)
    f = dict.fromkeys(c, d)


if __name__ == '__main__':
    main()
```

Note that we actually import the `memory_profiler` here although that is not strictly required. It can also be executed through `python3 -m memory_profiler your_scripts.py`:

```
# python3 test_memory_profiler.py
Filename: test_memory_profiler.py
```

Line #	Mem usage	Increment	Line Contents
4	11.0 MiB	0.0 MiB	@memory_profiler.profile
5			def main():
6	11.0 MiB	0.0 MiB	n = 100000
7	14.6 MiB	3.5 MiB	a = [i for i in range(n)]
8	17.8 MiB	3.2 MiB	b = [i for i in range(n)]
9	21.7 MiB	3.9 MiB	c = list(range(n))
10	25.5 MiB	3.9 MiB	d = list(range(n))
11	38.0 MiB	12.5 MiB	e = dict.fromkeys(a, b)
12	44.1 MiB	6.1 MiB	f = dict.fromkeys(c, d)

Even though everything runs as expected, you might be wondering about the varying amounts of memory used by the lines of code here. Why does a take `3.5 MiB` and b only `3.2 MiB`? This is caused by the Python memory allocation code; it reserves memory in larger blocks, which is subdivided and reused internally. Another problem is that `memory_profiler` takes snapshots internally, which results in memory being attributed to the wrong variables in some cases. The variations should be small enough to not make a large difference in the end, but some changes are to be expected.

 This module can be added as an IPython extension as well, which enables the `%mprun` command within IPython. To load the extension, the `load_ext` command can be used from the IPython shell `%load_ext memory_profiler`. Another very useful command is `%memit` which is the memory equivalent of the `%timeit` command.

Memory leaks

The usage of these modules will generally be limited to the search for memory leaks. Especially the `tracemalloc` module has a few features to make that fairly easy. The Python memory management system is fairly simple; it just has a simple reference counter to see if an object is used. While this works great in most cases, it can easily introduce memory leaks when circular references are involved. The basic premise of a memory leak with leak detection code looks like this:

```
1 import tracemalloc
2
3
4 class Spam(object):
5     index = 0
6     cache = {}
7
8     def __init__(self):
9         Spam.index += 1
10        self.cache[Spam.index] = self
11
12
13 class Eggs(object):
14     eggs = []
15
16     def __init__(self):
17         self.eggs.append(self)
18
19
20 if __name__ == '__main__':
21     # Initialize some variables to ignore them from the leak
22     # detection
23     n = 200000
24     spam = Spam()
25
26     tracemalloc.start()
27     # Your application should initialize here
28
29     snapshot_a = tracemalloc.take_snapshot()
30     # This code should be the memory leaking part
31     for i in range(n):
32         Spam()
33
34     Spam.cache = {}
35     snapshot_b = tracemalloc.take_snapshot()
```

```
36          # And optionally more leaking code here
37          for i in range(n):
38              a = Eggs()
39              b = Eggs()
40              a.b = b
41              b.a = a
42
43          Eggs.eggs = []
44          snapshot_c = tracemalloc.take_snapshot()
45
46          print('The first leak:')
47          statistics = snapshot_b.compare_to(snapshot_a, 'lineno')
48          for statistic in statistics[:10]:
49              print(statistic)
50
51          print('\nThe second leak:')
52          statistics = snapshot_c.compare_to(snapshot_b, 'lineno')
53          for statistic in statistics[:10]:
54              print(statistic)
```

Let's see how bad this code is actually leaking:

```
# python3 test_leak.py
The first leak:
tracemalloc.py:349: size=528 B (+528 B), count=3 (+3), average=176 B
test_leak.py:34: size=288 B (+288 B), count=2 (+2), average=144 B
test_leak.py:32: size=120 B (+120 B), count=2 (+2), average=60 B
tracemalloc.py:485: size=64 B (+64 B), count=1 (+1), average=64 B
tracemalloc.py:487: size=56 B (+56 B), count=1 (+1), average=56 B
tracemalloc.py:277: size=32 B (+32 B), count=1 (+1), average=32 B
test_leak.py:31: size=28 B (+28 B), count=1 (+1), average=28 B
test_leak.py:9: size=28 B (+28 B), count=1 (+1), average=28 B


The second leak:
test_leak.py:41: size=18.3 MiB (+18.3 MiB), count=400000 (+400000),
average=48 B
test_leak.py:40: size=18.3 MiB (+18.3 MiB), count=400000 (+400000),
average=48 B
test_leak.py:38: size=10.7 MiB (+10.7 MiB), count=200001 (+200001),
average=56 B
test_leak.py:39: size=10.7 MiB (+10.7 MiB), count=200002 (+200002),
average=56 B
```

```
tracemalloc.py:349: size=680 B (+152 B), count=6 (+3), average=113 B
test_leak.py:17: size=72 B (+72 B), count=1 (+1), average=72 B
test_leak.py:43: size=64 B (+64 B), count=1 (+1), average=64 B
test_leak.py:32: size=56 B (-64 B), count=1 (-1), average=56 B
tracemalloc.py:487: size=112 B (+56 B), count=2 (+1), average=56 B
tracemalloc.py:277: size=64 B (+32 B), count=2 (+1), average=32 B
```

In absolute memory usage the increase is not even that great, but it is definitely leaking a little. The first leak is negligible; at the last iteration we see an increase of 28 bytes which is next to nothing. The second leak however leaks a lot and peaks at a 18.3 megabyte increase. Those are memory leaks, the Python garbage collector (gc) is smart enough to clean circular references eventually but it won't clean them until a certain limit is reached. More about that soon.

Whenever you want to have a circular reference that does not cause memory leaks, the weakref module is available. It creates reference which don't count towards the object reference count. Before we look at the weakref module, let's take a look at the object references themselves through the eyes of the Python garbage collector (gc):

```python
import gc


class Eggs(object):

    def __init__(self, name):
        self.name = name

    def __repr__(self):
        return '<%s: %s>' % (self.__class__.__name__, self.name)


# Create the objects
a = Eggs('a')
b = Eggs('b')

# Add some circular references
a.b = a
b.a = b

# Remove the objects
del a
del b

# See if the objects are still there
```

```
print('Before manual collection:')
for object_ in gc.get_objects():
    if isinstance(object_, Eggs):
        print('\t', object_, gc.get_referents(object_))

print('After manual collection:')
gc.collect()
for object_ in gc.get_objects():
    if isinstance(object_, Eggs):
        print('\t', object_, gc.get_referents(object_))

print('Thresholds:', gc.get_threshold())
```

So let's have a look at the output:

```
# python3 test_refcount.py
Before manual collection:
        <Eggs: a> [{'b': <Eggs: a>, 'name': 'a'}, <class '__main__.
Eggs'>]
        <Eggs: b> [{'name': 'b', 'a': <Eggs: b>}, <class '__main__.
Eggs'>]
After manual collection:
Thresholds: (700, 10, 10)
```

As we can see here, until we manually call the garbage collector, the Eggs objects will stay in the memory. Even after explicitly deleting the objects. So does this mean you are always required to manually call gc.collect() to remove these references? Luckily that's not needed, as the Python garbage collector will automatically collect once the thresholds have been reached. By default, the thresholds for the Python garbage collector are set to 700, 10, 10 for the three generations of collected objects. The collector keeps track of all the memory allocations and deallocations in Python, and as soon as the number of allocations minus the number of deallocations reaches 700, the object is either removed if it's not referenced anymore or it is moved to the next generation if it still has a reference. The same is repeated for generation 2 and 3, albeit with the lower thresholds of 10.

This begs the question: where and when is it useful to manually call the garbage collector? Since the Python memory allocator reuses blocks of memory and only rarely releases it, for long running scripts the garbage collector can be very useful. That's exactly where I recommend its usage: long running scripts in memory-strapped environments and specifically, right before you allocate a large amount of memory.

More to the point however, the gc module can help you a lot when looking for memory leaks as well. The tracemalloc module can show you the parts that take the most memory in bytes but the gc module can help you find the most defined objects. Just be careful with setting the garbage collector debug settings such as gc.set_debug(gc.DEBUG_LEAK); it returns a large amount of output even if you don't reserve any memory yourself. Revisiting our Spam and Eggs script from earlier, let's see where and how the memory is being used using the garbage collection module:

```python
import gc
import collections


class Spam(object):
    index = 0
    cache = {}

    def __init__(self):
        Spam.index += 1
        self.cache[Spam.index] = self


class Eggs(object):
    eggs = []

    def __init__(self):
        self.eggs.append(self)


if __name__ == '__main__':
    n = 200000
    for i in range(n):
        Spam()

    for i in range(n):
        a = Eggs()
        b = Eggs()
        a.b = b
        b.a = a

    Spam.cache = {}
    Eggs.eggs = []
    objects = collections.Counter()
    for object_ in gc.get_objects():
        objects[type(object_)] += 1

    for object_, count in objects.most_common(5):
        print('%d: %s' % (count, object_))
```

The output is probably close to what you were already expecting:

```
# python3 test_leak.py
400617: <class 'dict'>
400000: <class '__main__.Eggs'>
962: <class 'wrapper_descriptor'>
920: <class 'function'>
625: <class 'method_descriptor'>
```

The large amount of `dict` objects is because of the internal state of the classes, but beyond that we simply see the `Eggs` objects just as we would expect. The `Spam` objects were properly removed by the garbage collector because they and all of the references were just removed. The `Eggs` objects couldn't be removed because of the circular references. Now we will repeat the same example using the `weakref` module to see if it makes a difference:

```python
import gc
import weakref
import collections


class Eggs(object):
    eggs = []

    def __init__(self):
        self.eggs.append(self)


if __name__ == '__main__':
    n = 200000
    for i in range(n):
        a = Eggs()
        b = Eggs()
        a.b = weakref.ref(b)
        b.a = weakref.ref(a)

    Eggs.eggs = []
    objects = collections.Counter()
    for object_ in gc.get_objects():
        objects[type(object_)] += 1

    for object_, count in objects.most_common(5):
        print('%d: %s' % (count, object_))
```

Now let's see what remained this time:

```
# python3 test_leak.py
962: <class 'wrapper_descriptor'>
919: <class 'function'>
625: <class 'method_descriptor'>
618: <class 'dict'>
535: <class 'builtin_function_or_method'>
```

Nothing besides some standard built-in Python objects, which is exactly what we had hoped for. Be careful with weak references though, as they can easily blow up in your face if the referenced object has disappeared:

```
import weakref


class Eggs(object):
    pass


if __name__ == '__main__':
    a = Eggs()
    b = Eggs()
    a.b = weakref.ref(b)

    print(a.b())
    del b
    print(a.b())
```

This results in one working reference and a dead one:

```
# python3 test_weakref.py
<__main__.Eggs object at 0x104891a20>
None
```

Reducing memory usage

In general, memory usage probably won't be your biggest problem in Python, but it can still be useful to know what you can do to reduce memory usage. When trying to reduce memory usage, it's important to understand how Python allocates memory.

There are four concepts which you need to know about within the Python memory manager:

- First we have the heap. The heap is the collection of all Python managed memory. Note that this is separate from the regular heap and mixing the two could result in corrupt memory and crashes.

- Second are the arenas. These are the chunks that Python requests from the system. These chunks have a fixed size of 256 KiB each and they are the objects that make up the heap.

- Third we have the pools. These are the chunks of memory that make up the arenas. These chunks are 4 KiB each. Since the pools and arenas have fixed sizes, they are simple arrays.

- Fourth and last, we have the blocks. The Python objects get stored within these and every block has a specific format depending on the data type. Since an integer takes up more space than a character, for efficiency a different block size is used.

Now that we know how the memory is allocated, we can also understand how it can be returned to the operating system. Whenever an arena is completely empty, it can and will be freed. To increase the likelihood of this happening, some heuristics are used to maximize the usage of fuller arenas.

 It is important to note that the regular heap and Python heap are maintained separately as mixing them can result in corruption and/or crashing of applications. Unless you write your own extensions, you will probably never have to worry about manual memory allocation though.

Generators versus lists

The most important tip is to use generators whenever possible. Python 3 has come a long way in replacing lists with generators already, but it really pays off to keep that in mind as it saves not only memory, but CPU as well when not all of that memory needs to be kept at the same time.

To illustrate the difference:

```
Line #    Mem usage    Increment   Line Contents
================================================
     4    11.0 MiB      0.0 MiB     @memory_profiler.profile
     5                              def main():
     6    11.0 MiB      0.0 MiB       a = range(1000000)
     7    49.7 MiB     38.6 MiB       b = list(range(1000000))
```

The `range()` generator takes such little memory that it doesn't even register, whereas the list of numbers takes `38.6 MiB`.

Recreating collections versus removing items

One very important detail about collections in Python is that many of them can only grow; they won't just shrink by themselves. To illustrate:

```
Line #    Mem usage    Increment   Line Contents
================================================
     4    11.5 MiB      0.0 MiB    @memory_profiler.profile
     5                             def main():
     6                             # Generate a huge dict
     7    26.3 MiB     14.8 MiB    a = dict.fromkeys(range(100000))
     8
     9                             # Remove all items
    10    26.3 MiB      0.0 MiB    for k in list(a.keys()):
    11    26.3 MiB      0.0 MiB    del a[k]
    12
    13                             # Recreate the dict
    14    23.6 MiB     -2.8 MiB    a = dict((k, v) for k, v in a.items())
```

This is one of the most common memory usage mistakes made with lists and dictionaries. Besides recreating the objects, there is, of course, also the option of using generators instead so the memory is never allocated at all.

Using slots

If you've used Python for a long time you may have seen the __slots__ feature of classes. It allows you to specify which fields you want to store in a class and it skips all the others by not implementing `instance.__dict__`. While this method does save a little bit of memory in your class definitions, I recommend against its usage as there are several downsides to using it. The most important one is that they make inheritance non-obvious (adding __slots__ to a subclassed class that doesn't have __slots__ has no effect). It also makes it impossible to modify class attributes on the fly and breaks `weakref` by default. And lastly, classes with slots cannot be pickled without defining a __getstate__ function.

For completeness however, here's a demonstration of the slots feature and the difference in memory usage:

```python
import memory_profiler


class Slots(object):
    __slots__ = 'index', 'name', 'description'

    def __init__(self, index):
        self.index = index
        self.name = 'slot %d' % index
        self.description = 'some slot with index %d' % index


class NoSlots(object):

    def __init__(self, index):
        self.index = index
        self.name = 'slot %d' % index
        self.description = 'some slot with index %d' % index


@memory_profiler.profile
def main():
    slots = [Slots(i) for i in range(25000)]
    no_slots = [NoSlots(i) for i in range(25000)]
    return slots, no_slots


if __name__ == '__main__':
    main()
```

And the memory usage:

```
# python3 test_slots.py
Filename: test_slots.py


Line #    Mem usage    Increment   Line Contents
================================================
    21     11.1 MiB      0.0 MiB   @memory_profiler.profile
    22                             def main():
```

```
    23      17.0 MiB      5.9 MiB    slots = [Slots(i) for i in
range(25000)]
    24      25.0 MiB      8.0 MiB    no_slots = [NoSlots(i) for i in
range(25000)]
    25      25.0 MiB      0.0 MiB    return slots, no_slots
```

You might argue that this is not a fair comparison, since they both store a lot of data which skews the results. And you would indeed be right, because the "bare" comparison storing only `index` and nothing else gives 2 MiB versus 4.5 MiB. But let's be honest, if you're not going to store data, then what's the point in creating class instances? That's why I recommend against the usage of __slots__ and instead recommend the usage of tuples or `collections.namedtuple` if memory is that important. There is one more structure that's even more memory efficient, the `array` module. It stores the data in pretty much a bare memory array. Note that this is generally slower than lists and much less convenient to use.

Performance monitoring

So far we have seen how to measure and improve both CPU and memory performance, but there is one part we have completely skipped over. Performance changes due to external factors such as growing amounts of data are very hard to predict. In real life applications, bottlenecks aren't constant. They change all the time and code that was once extremely fast might bog down as soon as more load is applied.

Because of that I recommend implementing a monitoring solution that tracks the performance of anything and everything over time. The big problem with performance monitoring is that you can't know what will slow down in the future and what the cause is going to be. I've even had websites slow down because of Memcached and Redis calls. These are memory only caching servers that respond well within a millisecond which makes slowdowns highly unlikely, until you do over a 100 cache calls and the latency towards the cache server increases from 0.1 milliseconds to 2 milliseconds, and all of a sudden those 100 calls take 200 milliseconds instead of 10 milliseconds. Even though 200 milliseconds still sounds like very little, if your total page load time is generally below 100 milliseconds, that is all of a sudden an enormous increase and definitely noticeable.

To monitor performance and to be able to track changes over time and find the responsible components, I am personally a big fan of the Statsd statistic collection server together with the Graphite interface. Even though usability is a bit lacking, the result is a graphing interface which you can dynamically query to analyze when, where, and how your performance changed. To be able to use these you will have to send the metrics from your application towards the Statsd server. To do just that, I have written the Python-Statsd (`https://pypi.python.org/pypi/python-statsd`) and Django-Statsd (`https://pypi.python.org/pypi/django-statsd`) packages. These packages allow you to monitor your application from beginning to end, and in the case of Django you will be able to monitor your performance per application or view and within those see all of the components, such as the database, template, and caching layers. This way, you know exactly what is causing the slowdowns in your website (or application).

Summary

When it comes to performance, there is no holy grail, no single thing you can do to ensure peak performance in all cases. This shouldn't worry you however, as in most cases you will never need to tune the performance and if you do, a single tweak could probably fix your problem. You should be able to find performance problems and memory leaks in your code now which is what matters most, so just try to contain yourself and only tweak when it's actually needed.

The most important outtakes from this chapter are:

- Test before you invest any effort. Making some functions faster seems like a great achievement but it is only rarely needed.
- Choosing the correct data structure/algorithm is much more effective than any other performance optimization.
- Circular references drain the memory until the garbage collector starts cleaning.
- Slots are not worth the effort.

The next chapter will discuss multiprocessing, a library which makes it trivial to employ multiple processors for your scripts. If you can't squeeze any more performance out of your script, multiprocessing might be your answer, as every (remote?) CPU core can make your script faster.

13
Multiprocessing – When a Single CPU Core Is Not Enough

In the previous chapter, we discussed factors that influence performance and some methods to increase performance. This chapter can actually be seen as an extension to the list of performance tips. In this chapter, we will discuss the multiprocessing module, a module that makes it very easy to make your code run on multiple CPU cores and even on multiple machines. This is an easy way to work around the **Global Interpreter Lock** (**GIL**) that was discussed in the previous chapter.

To summarize, this chapter will cover:

- Local multiprocessing
- Remote multiprocessing
- Data sharing and synchronization between processes

Multithreading versus multiprocessing

Within this book we haven't really covered multithreading yet, but you have probably seen multithreaded code in the past. The big difference between multithreading and multiprocessing is that with multithreading everything is still executed within a single process. That effectively limits your performance to a single CPU core. It actually limits you even further because the code has to deal with the GIL limitations of CPython.

The GIL is the global lock that Python uses for safe memory access. It is discussed in more detail in *Chapter 12, Performance – Tracking and Reducing Your Memory and CPU Usage*, about performance.

To illustrate that multithreading code doesn't help performance in all cases and can actually be slightly slower than single threaded code, look at this example:

```python
import datetime
import threading


def busy_wait(n):
    while n > 0:
        n -= 1


if __name__ == '__main__':
    n = 10000000
    start = datetime.datetime.now()
    for _ in range(4):
        busy_wait(n)
    end = datetime.datetime.now()
    print('The single threaded loops took: %s' % (end - start))

    start = datetime.datetime.now()
    threads = []
    for _ in range(4):
        thread = threading.Thread(target=busy_wait, args=(n,))
        thread.start()
        threads.append(thread)

    for thread in threads:
        thread.join()

    end = datetime.datetime.now()
    print('The multithreaded loops took: %s' % (end - start))
```

With Python 3.5, which has the new and improved GIL implementation (introduced in Python 3.2), the performance is quite comparable but there is no improvement:

```
# python3 test_multithreading.py
The single threaded loops took: 0:00:02.623443
The multithreaded loops took: 0:00:02.597900
```

With Python 2.7, which still has the old GIL, the performance is a lot better in the single threaded variant:

```
# python2 test_multithreading.py
The single threaded loops took: 0:00:02.010967
The multithreaded loops took: 0:00:03.924950
```

From this test we can conclude that Python 2 is faster in some cases while Python 3 is faster in other cases. What you should take from this is that there is no performance reason to choose between Python 2 or Python 3 specifically. Just note that Python 3 is at least as fast as Python 2 in most cases and if that is not the case, it will be fixed soon.

Regardless, for CPU-bound operations, threading does not offer any performance benefit since it executes on a single processor core. For I/O bound operations however, the threading library does offer a clear benefit, but in that case I would recommend trying asyncio instead. The biggest problem with threading is that if one of the threads blocks, the main process blocks.

The multiprocessing library offers an API that is very similar to the threading library but utilizes multiple processes instead of multiple threads. The advantages are that the GIL is no longer an issue and that multiple processor cores and even multiple machines can be used for processing.

To illustrate the performance difference, let's repeat the test while using the multiprocessing module instead of threading:

```python
import datetime
import multiprocessing


def busy_wait(n):
    while n > 0:
        n -= 1


if __name__ == '__main__':
    n = 10000000
    start = datetime.datetime.now()

    processes = []
    for _ in range(4):
        process = multiprocessing.Process(
            target=busy_wait, args=(n,))
        process.start()
```

```
        processes.append(process)

    for process in processes:
        process.join()

    end = datetime.datetime.now()
    print('The multiprocessed loops took: %s' % (end - start))
```

When running it, we see a huge improvement:

```
# python3 test_multiprocessing.py
The multiprocessed loops took: 0:00:00.671249
```

Note that this was run on a quad core processor, which is why I chose four processes. The `multiprocessing` library defaults to `multiprocessing.cpu_count()` which counts the available CPU cores, but that method fails to take CPU hyper-threading into account. Which means it would return 8 in my case and that is why I hardcoded it to 4 instead.

> It's important to note that because the `multiprocessing` library uses multiple processes, the code needs to be imported from the sub processes. The result is that the `multiprocessing` library does not work within the Python or IPython shells. As we will see later in this chapter, IPython has its own provisions for multiprocessing.

Hyper-threading versus physical CPU cores

In most cases, hyper-threading is very useful and improves performance, but when you truly maximize CPU usage it is generally better to only use the physical processor count. To demonstrate how this affects the performance, we will run the tests from the previous section again. This time with 1, 2, 4, 8, and 16 processes to demonstrate how it affects the performance. Luckily, the `multiprocessing` library has a nice `Pool` class to manage the processes for us:

```
import sys
import datetime
import multiprocessing


def busy_wait(n):
    while n > 0:
```

```
        n -= 1


if __name__ == '__main__':
    n = 10000000
    start = datetime.datetime.now()
    if sys.argv[-1].isdigit():
        processes = int(sys.argv[-1])
    else:
        print('Please specify the number of processes')
        print('Example: %s 4' % ' '.join(sys.argv))
        sys.exit(1)

    with multiprocessing.Pool(processes=processes) as pool:
        # Execute the busy_wait function 8 times with parameter n
        pool.map(busy_wait, [n for _ in range(8)])

    end = datetime.datetime.now()
    print('The multithreaded loops took: %s' % (end - start))
```

The pool code makes starting a pool of workers and processing a queue a bit simpler as well. In this case we used map but there are several other options such as imap, map_async, imap_unordered, apply, apply_async, starmap, and starmap_async. Since these are very similar to how the similarly named itertools methods work, there won't be specific examples for all of them.

But now, the tests with varying amounts of processes:

```
# python3 test_multiprocessing.py 1
The multithreaded loops took: 0:00:05.297707
# python3 test_multiprocessing.py 2
The multithreaded loops took: 0:00:02.701344
# python3 test_multiprocessing.py 4
The multithreaded loops took: 0:00:01.477845
# python3 test_multiprocessing.py 8
The multithreaded loops took: 0:00:01.579218
# python3 test_multiprocessing.py 16
The multithreaded loops took: 0:00:01.595239
```

You probably weren't expecting these results, but this is exactly the problem with hyper-threading. As soon as the single processes actually use 100 percent of a CPU core, the task switching between the processes actually reduces performance. Since there are only 4 physical cores, the other 4 have to fight to get something done on the processor cores. This fight takes time which is why the 4 process version is slightly faster than the 8 process version. Additionally, the scheduling effect can be seen in the runs using 1 and 2 cores as well. If we look at the single core version, we see that it took 5.3 seconds, which means that 4 cores should do it in 5.3 / 4 = 1.325 seconds instead of the 1.48 seconds it actually took. The 2 core version has a similar effect, 2.7 / 2 = 1.35 seconds which is still faster than 4 core version.

If you are truly pressed for performance with a CPU-bound problem then matching the physical CPU cores is the best solution. If you do not expect to maximize all cores all the time, then I recommend leaving it to the default as hyper-threading definitely has some performance benefits in other scenarios.

It all depends on your use-case however and the only way to know for certain is to test for your specific scenario:

- Disk I/O bound? A single process is most likely your best bet.
- CPU bound? The amount of physical CPU cores is your best bet.
- Network I/O bound? Start with the defaults and tune if needed.
- No obvious bound but many parallel processes are needed? Perhaps you should try `asyncio` instead of `multiprocessing`.

Note that the creation of multiple processes is not free in terms of memory and open files, whereas you could have a nearly unlimited amount of coroutines this is not the case for processes. Depending on your operating system configuration, it could max out long before you even reach a hundred, and even if you reach those numbers, CPU scheduling will be your bottleneck instead.

Creating a pool of workers

Creating a processing pool of worker processes is generally a difficult task. You need to take care of scheduling jobs, processing the queue, handling the processes, and the most difficult part, handling synchronization between the processes without too much overhead.

With `multiprocessing` however, these problems have been solved already. You can simply create a process pool with a given number of processes and just add tasks to it whenever you need to. The following is an example of a multiprocessing version of the map operator and demonstrates that processing will not stall the application:

```
import time
import multiprocessing


def busy_wait(n):
    while n > 0:
        n -= 1


if __name__ == '__main__':
    n = 10000000
    items = [n for _ in range(8)]
    with multiprocessing.Pool() as pool:
        results = []
        start = time.time()
        print('Start processing...')
        for _ in range(5):
            results.append(pool.map_async(busy_wait, items))
        print('Still processing %.3f' % (time.time() - start))
        for result in results:
            result.wait()
            print('Result done %.3f' % (time.time() - start))
        print('Done processing: %.3f' % (time.time() - start))
```

The processing itself is pretty straightforward. The point is that the pool stays available and you are not required to wait for it. Just add jobs whenever you need to and use the asynchronous results as soon as they are available:

```
# python3 test_pool.py
Start processing...
Still processing 0.000
Result done 1.513
Result done 2.984
Result done 4.463
Result done 5.978
Result done 7.388
Done processing: 7.388
```

Sharing data between processes

This is really the most difficult part about multiprocessing, multithreading, and distributed programming - which data to pass along and which data to skip. The theory is really simple, however: whenever possible don't transfer any data, don't share anything, and keep everything local. Essentially the functional programming paradigm, which is why functional programming mixes really well with multiprocessing. In practice, regrettably, this is simply not always possible. The `multiprocessing` library has several options to share data: `Pipe`, `Namespace`, `Queue`, and a few others. All these options might tempt you to share your data between the processes all the time. This is indeed possible, but the performance impact is, in many cases, more than what the distributed calculation will offer as extra power. All data sharing options come at the price of synchronization between all processing kernels, which takes a lot of time. Especially with distributed options, these synchronizations can take several milliseconds or, if executed globally, cause hundreds of milliseconds of latency.

The multiprocessing namespace behaves just as a regular object would work, with one small difference that all the actions are safe for multiprocessing. With all this power, namespaces are still very easy to use:

```
import multiprocessing
manager = multiprocessing.Manager()
namespace = manager.Namespace()
namespace.spam = 123
namespace.eggs = 456
```

A pipe is not that much more interesting either. It's just a bidirectional communication endpoint which allows both reading and writing. In this regard, it simply offers you a reader and a writer, and because of that, you can combine multiple processes/endpoints. The only thing you must always keep in mind when synchronizing data is that locking takes time. For a proper lock to be set, all the parties need to agree that the data is locked, which is a process that takes time. And that simple fact slows down execution much more than most people would expect.

On a regular hard disk setup, the database servers aren't able to handle more than about 10 transactions per second on the same row due to locking and disk latency. Using lazy file syncing, SSDs, and battery backed RAID cache, that performance can be increased to handle, perhaps, a 100 transactions per second on the same row. Those are simple hardware limitations, because you have multiple processes trying to write to a single target you need to synchronize the actions between the processes and that takes a lot of time.

The "database servers" statistic is a common statistic for all database servers that offer safe and consistent data storage.

Even with the fastest hardware available, synchronization can lock all the processes and produce enormous slowdowns, so if at all possible, try to avoid sharing data between multiple processes. Put simply, if all the processes are reading and writing from/to the same object, it is generally faster to use a single process instead.

Remote processes

So far, we have only executed our scripts on multiple local processors, but we can actually expand this further. Using the `multiprocessing` library, it's actually very easy to execute jobs on remote servers, but the documentation is currently still a bit cryptic. There are actually a few ways of executing processes in a distributed way, but the most obvious one isn't the easiest one. The `multiprocessing.connection` module has both the `Client` and `Listener` classes, which facilitate secure communication between the clients and servers in a simple way. Communication is not the same as process management and queue management however, those features requires some extra effort. The multiprocessing library is still a bit bare in this regard, but it's most certainly possible given a few different processes.

Distributed processing using multiprocessing

First of all, we will start with a module with containing a few constants which should be shared between all clients and the server, so the secret password and the hostname of the server are available to all. In addition to that, we will add our prime calculation functions, which we will be using later. The imports in the following modules will expect this file to be stored as `constants.py`, but feel free to call it anything you like as long as you modify the imports and references:

```
host = 'localhost'
port = 12345
password = b'some secret password'


def primes(n):
    for i, prime in enumerate(prime_generator()):
        if i == n:
            return prime


def prime_generator():
```

```
n = 2
primes = set()
while True:
    for p in primes:
        if n % p == 0:
            break
    else:
        primes.add(n)
        yield n
    n += 1
```

Now it's time to create the actual server which links the functions and the job queue:

```
import constants
import multiprocessing
from multiprocessing import managers


queue = multiprocessing.Queue()
manager = managers.BaseManager(address=('', constants.port),
                               authkey=constants.password)

manager.register('queue', callable=lambda: queue)
manager.register('primes', callable=constants.primes)

server = manager.get_server()
server.serve_forever()
```

After creating the server, we need to have a script that sends the jobs, which will actually be a regular client. It's simple enough really and a regular client can also function as a processor, but to keep things sensible we will use them as separate scripts. The following script will add 0 to 999 to the queue for processing:

```
from multiprocessing import managers
import functions


manager = managers.BaseManager(
    address=(functions.host, functions.port),
    authkey=functions.password)
manager.register('queue')
manager.connect()

queue = manager.queue()
for i in range(1000):
    queue.put(i)
```

Lastly, we need to create a client to actually process the queue:

```
from multiprocessing import managers
import functions


manager = managers.BaseManager(
    address=(functions.host, functions.port),
    authkey=functions.password)
manager.register('queue')
manager.register('primes')
manager.connect()

queue = manager.queue()
while not queue.empty():
    print(manager.primes(queue.get()))
```

From the preceding code you can see how we pass along functions; the manager allows registering of functions and classes which can be called from the clients as well. With that we pass along a queue from the multiprocessing class which is safe for both multithreading and multiprocessing. Now we need to start the processes themselves. First the server which keeps on running:

 # python3 multiprocessing_server.py

After that, run the producer to generate the prime generation requests:

 # python3 multiprocessing_producer.py

And now we can run multiple clients on multiple machines to get the first 1000 primes. Since these clients now print the first 1000 primes, the output is a bit too lengthy to show here, but you can simply run this in parallel on multiple machines to generate your output:

 # python3 multiprocessing_client.py

Instead of printing, you can obviously use queues or pipes to send the output to a different process if you'd like. As you can see verify though, it's still a bit of work to process things in parallel and it requires some code synchronization to work. There are a few alternatives available, such as **ØMQ**, **Celery**, and **IPyparallel**. Which of these is the best and most suitable depends on your use case. If you are simply looking for processing tasks on multiple CPUs, then multiprocessing and IPyparallel are probably your best choices. If you are looking for background processing and/or easy offloading to multiple machines, then ØMQ and Celery are better choices.

Distributed processing using IPyparallel

The IPyparallel module (previously, IPython Parallel) is a module that makes it really easy to process code on multiple computers at the same time. The library supports more features than you are likely to need, but the basic usage is important to know just in case you need to do heavy calculations which can benefit from multiple computers. First let's start with installing the latest IPyparallel package and all the IPython components:

```
pip install -U ipython[all] ipyparallel
```

 Especially on Windows, it might be easier to install IPython using Anaconda instead, as it includes binaries for many science, math, engineering, and data analysis packages. To get a consistent installation, the Anaconda installer is also available for OS X and Linux systems.

Secondly, we need a cluster configuration. Technically this is optional, but since we are going to create a distributed IPython cluster, it is much more convenient to configure everything using a specific profile:

```
# ipython profile create --parallel --profile=mastering_python

[ProfileCreate] Generating default config file: '~/.ipython/profile_
mastering_python/ipython_config.py'

[ProfileCreate] Generating default config file: '~/.ipython/profile_
mastering_python/ipython_kernel_config.py'

[ProfileCreate] Generating default config file: '~/.ipython/profile_
mastering_python/ipcontroller_config.py'

[ProfileCreate] Generating default config file: '~/.ipython/profile_
mastering_python/ipengine_config.py'

[ProfileCreate] Generating default config file: '~/.ipython/profile_
mastering_python/ipcluster_config.py'
```

These configuration files contain a huge amount of options so I recommend searching for a specific section instead of walking through them. A quick listing gave me about 2500 lines of configuration in total for these five files. The filenames already provide hint about the purpose of the configuration files, but we'll explain them in a little more detail since they are still a tad confusing.

ipython_config.py

This is the generic IPython configuration file; you can customize pretty much everything about your IPython shell here. It defines how your shell should look, which modules should be loaded by default, whether or not to load a GUI, and quite a bit more. For the purpose of this chapter not all that important but it's definitely worth a look if you're going to use IPython more often. One of the things you can configure here is the automatic loading of extensions, such as `line_profiler` and `memory_profiler` discussed in the previous chapter. For example:

```
c.InteractiveShellApp.extensions = [
    'line_profiler',
    'memory_profiler',
]
```

ipython_kernel_config.py

This file configures your IPython kernel and allows you to overwrite/extend `ipython_config.py`. To understand its purpose, it's important to know what an IPython kernel is. The kernel, in this context, is the program that runs and introspects the code. By default this is `IPyKernel`, which is a regular Python interpreter, but there are also other options such as `IRuby` or `IJavascript` to run Ruby or JavaScript respectively.

One of the more useful options is the possibility to configure the listening port(s) and IP addresses for the kernel. By default the ports are all set to use a random number, but it is important to note that if someone else has access to the same machine while you are running your kernel, they will be able to connect to your IPython kernel which can be dangerous on shared machines.

ipcontroller_config.py

`ipcontroller` is the master process of your IPython cluster. It controls the engines and the distribution of tasks, and takes care of tasks such as logging.

The most important parameter in terms of performance is the `TaskScheduler` setting. By default, the `c.TaskScheduler.scheme_name` setting is set to use the Python LRU scheduler, but depending on your workload, others such as `leastload` and `weighted` might be better. And if you have to process so many tasks on such a large cluster that the scheduler becomes the bottleneck, there is also the `plainrandom` scheduler that works surprisingly well if all your machines have similar specs and the tasks have similar durations.

For the purpose of our test we will set the IP of the controller to *, which means that **all** IP addresses will be accepted and that every network connection will be accepted. If you are in an unsafe environment/network and/or don't have any firewalls which allow you to selectively enable certain IP addresses, then this method is **not** recommended! In such cases, I recommend launching through more secure options, such as `SSHEngineSetLauncher` or `WindowsHPCEngineSetLauncher` instead.

But, assuming your network is indeed safe, set the factory IP to all the local addresses:

```
c.HubFactory.client_ip = '*'
c.RegistrationFactory.ip = '*'
```

Now start the controller:

```
# ipcontroller --profile=mastering_python
[IPControllerApp] Hub listening on tcp://*:58412 for registration.
[IPControllerApp] Hub listening on tcp://127.0.0.1:58412 for
registration.
[IPControllerApp] Hub using DB backend: 'NoDB'
[IPControllerApp] hub::created hub
[IPControllerApp] writing connection info to ~/.ipython/profile_
mastering_python/security/ipcontroller-client.json
[IPControllerApp] writing connection info to ~/.ipython/profile_
mastering_python/security/ipcontroller-engine.json
[IPControllerApp] task::using Python leastload Task scheduler
[IPControllerApp] Heartmonitor started
[IPControllerApp] Creating pid file: .ipython/profile_mastering_python/
pid/ipcontroller.pid
[scheduler] Scheduler started [leastload]
[IPControllerApp] client::client b'\x00\x80\x00A\xa7' requested
'connection_request'
[IPControllerApp] client::client [b'\x00\x80\x00A\xa7'] connected
```

Pay attention to the files that were written to the security directory of the profile directory. They have the authentication information which is used by `ipengine` to find `ipcontroller`. It contains the ports, encryption keys, and IP address.

ipengine_config.py

`ipengine` is the actual worker process. These processes run the actual calculations, so to speed up the processing you will need these on as many machines as you have available. You probably won't need to change this file, but it can be useful if you want to configure centralized logging or need to change the working directory. Generally, you don't want to start the `ipengine` process manually since you will most likely want to launch multiple processes per computer. That's where our next command comes in, the `ipcluster` command.

ipcluster_config.py

The `ipcluster` command is actually just an easy shorthand to start a combination of `ipcontroller` and `ipengine` at the same time. For a simple local processing cluster, I recommend using this, but when starting a distributed cluster, it can be useful to have the control that the separate use of `ipcontroller` and `ipengine` offers. In most cases the command offers enough options, so you might have no need for the separate commands.

The most important configuration option is `c.IPClusterEngines.engine_launcher_class`, as this controls the communication method between the engines and the controller. Along with that, it is also the most important component for secure communication between the processes. By default it's set to `ipyparallel.apps.launcher.LocalControllerLauncher` which is designed for local processes but `ipyparallel.apps.launcher.SSHEngineSetLauncher` is also an option if you want to use SSH to communicate with the clients. Or `ipyparallel.apps.launcher.WindowsHPCEngineSetLauncher` for Windows HPC.

Before we can create the cluster on all machines, we need to transfer the configuration files. Your options are to transfer all the files or to simply transfer the files in your IPython profile's `security` directory.

Now it's time to start the cluster, since we already started the `ipcontroller` separately, we only need to start the engines. On the local machine we simply need to start it, but the other machines don't have the configuration yet. One option is copying the entire IPython profile directory, but the only file that really needs copying is `security/ipcontroller-engine.json`. After creating the profile using the profile creation command that is. So unless you are going to copy the entire IPython profile directory, you need to execute the profile creation command again:

```
# ipython profile create --parallel --profile=mastering_python
```

After that, simply copy the `ipcontroller-engine.json` file and you're done. Now we can start the actual engines:

```
# ipcluster engines --profile=mastering_python -n 4
[IPClusterEngines] IPython cluster: started
[IPClusterEngines] Starting engines with [daemon=False]
[IPClusterEngines] Starting 4 Engines with LocalEngineSetLauncher
```

Note that the 4 here was chosen for a quad-core processor, but any number would do. The default will use the amount of logical processor cores, but depending on the workload it might be better to match the amount of physical processor cores instead.

Now we can run some parallel code from our IPython shell. To demonstrate the performance difference, we will use a simple sum of all the numbers from 0 to 10,000,000. Not an extremely heavy task, but when performed 10 times in succession, a regular Python interpreter takes a while:

```
In [1]: %timeit for _ in range(10): sum(range(10000000))
1 loops, best of 3: 2.27 s per loop
```

This time however, to illustrate the difference, we will run it a 100 times to demonstrate how fast a distributed cluster is. Note that this is with only three machines cluster, but it's still quite a bit faster:

```
In [1]: import ipyparallel

In [2]: client = ipyparallel.Client(profile='mastering_python')

In [3]: view = client.load_balanced_view()

In [4]: %timeit view.map(lambda _: sum(range(10000000)), range(100)).
wait()
1 loop, best of 3: 909 ms per loop
```

More fun however is the definition of parallel functions in IPyParallel. With just a simple decorator, a function is marked as parallel:

```
In [1]: import ipyparallel

In [2]: client = ipyparallel.Client(profile='mastering_python')

In [3]: view = client.load_balanced_view()

In [4]: @view.parallel()
   ...: def loop():
```

```
    ...:        return sum(range(10000000))
    ...:

In [5]: loop.map(range(10))
Out[5]: <AsyncMapResult: loop>
```

The IPyParallel library offers many more useful features, but that is outside the scope of this book. Even though IPyParallel is a separate entity from the rest of Jupyter/ IPython, it does integrate well, which makes combining them easy enough.

One of the most convenient ways of using IPyParallel is through the Jupyter/ IPython Notebooks. To demonstrate, we first have to make sure to enable the parallel processing in the Jupyter Notebook since IPython notebooks execute single threaded by default:

```
ipcluster nbextension enable
```

After that we can start the `notebook` and see what it's all about:

```
# jupyter notebook

Unrecognized JSON config file version, assuming version 1

Loading IPython parallel extension

Serving notebooks from local directory: ./

0 active kernels

The Jupyter Notebook is running at: http://localhost:8888/

Use Control-C to stop this server and shut down all kernels (twice to
skip confirmation).
```

With the Jupyter Notebook you can create scripts in your web browser which can easily be shared with others later. It is really very useful for sharing scripts and debugging your code, especially since web pages (as opposed to command line environments) can display images easily. This helps a lot with graphing data. Here's a screenshot of our Notebook:

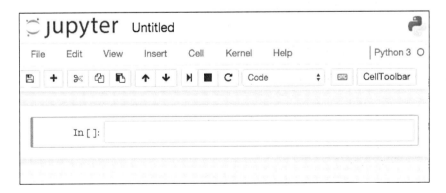

Summary

This chapter has shown us how multiprocessing works, how we can pool a lot of jobs, and how we should share data between multiple processes. But more interestingly, it has also shown how we can distribute processing across multiple machines which helps a lot in speeding up heavy calculations.

The most important lesson you can learn from this chapter is that you should always try to avoid data sharing and synchronisation between multiple processes or servers, as it is slow and will thus slow down your applications a lot. Whenever possible, keep your calculations and data local.

In the next chapter we will learn about creating extensions in C/C++ to increase performance and allow low-level access to memory and other hardware resources. While Python will generally protect you from silly mistakes, C and C++ most certainly won't.

> *"C makes it easy to shoot yourself in the foot; C++ makes it harder, but when you do, it blows away your whole leg."*
>
> *- Bjarne Stroustrup (the creator of C++)*

Extensions in C/C++, System Calls, and C/C++ Libraries

Now that we know a bit more about performance and multiprocessing, we will explain another subject that is at least somewhat performance-related—the usage of C and/or C++ extensions.

There are multiple reasons to consider C/C++ extensions. Having existing libraries available is an important one, but truthfully, the most important reason is performance. In *Chapter 12, Performance – Tracking and Reducing Your Memory and CPU Usage*, we saw that the cProfile module is about 10 times faster than the profile module, which indicates that at least some C extensions are faster than their pure Python equivalents. This chapter will not focus on performance that much, however. The goal here is interaction with non-Python libraries. Any performance improvement will just be a completely unintentional side effect.

We will discuss the following options in this chapter:

- Ctypes for handling foreign (C/C++) functions and data from Python
- **CFFI** (short for **C Foreign Function Interface**), similar to ctypes but with a slightly different approach
- Writing native C/C++ to extend Python

Introduction

Before you start with this chapter, it is important to note that this chapter will require a working compiler that plays nicely with your Python interpreter. Unfortunately, these vary from platform to platform. While generally easy enough for most Linux distributions, this can be a big challenge on Windows. With OS X, it's generally easy enough provided you install the correct tools.

The generic building instructions are always available in the Python manual:

```
https://docs.python.org/3.5/extending/building.html
```

Do you need C/C++ modules?

In almost all cases, I'm inclined to say that you don't need C/C++ modules. If you are really strapped for best performance, then there are almost always highly optimized libraries available that fit your purpose. There are some cases where native C/C++ (or just "not Python") is a requirement. If you need to communicate directly with hardware that has specific timings, then Python might just not do the trick for you. Generally, however, that kind of communication should be left to a driver that takes care of the specific timings. Regardless, even if you will never write one of these modules yourself, you might still need to know how they work when you are debugging a project.

Windows

For Windows, the general recommendation is Visual Studio. The specific version depends on your Python version:

- Python 3.2 and lower: Microsoft Visual Studio 2008
- Python 3.3 and 3.4: Microsoft Visual Studio 2010
- Python 3.5 and 3.6: Microsoft Visual Studio 2015

The specifics of installing Visual Studio and compiling Python modules fall a bit outside of the scope of this book. Luckily, the Python documentation has some documentation available to get you started:

```
https://docs.python.org/3.5/extending/windows.html
```

OS X

For a Mac, the process is mostly straightforward, but there are a few tips specific to OS X.

First, install Xcode through the Mac App Store. Once you have done that, you should be able to run the following command:

```
xcode-select --install
```

Next up is the fun part. Because OS X comes with a bundled Python version (which is generally out of date), I would recommend installing a new Python version through Homebrew instead. The most up-to-date instructions for installing Homebrew can be found on the Homebrew homepage (`http://brew.sh/`), but the gist of installing Homebrew is this command:

```
# /usr/bin/ruby -e "$(curl -fsSL \

https://raw.githubusercontent.com/Homebrew/install/master/install)"
```

After that, make sure you check whether everything is set up correctly using the `doctor` command:

```
# brew doctor
```

When all of this is done, simply install Python through Homebrew and make sure you use that Python release when executing your scripts:

```
# brew install python3
# python3 -version
Python 3.5.1
which python3
/usr/local/bin/python3
```

Also ensure that the Python process is in `/usr/local/bin`, that is, the homebrewed version. The regular OS X version would be in `/usr/bin/` instead.

Linux/Unix

The installation for Linux/Unix systems greatly depends on the distribution, but it is generally simple to do.

For Fedora, Red Hat, Centos, and other systems that use `yum` as the package manager, use these lines:

```
# sudo yum install yum-utils
# sudo yum-builddep python3
```

For Debian, Ubuntu, and other systems that use `apt` as the package manager, use the following line:

```
# sudo apt-get build-dep python3.5
```

Note that Python 3.5 is not available everywhere yet, so you might need Python 3.4 instead.

 For most systems, to get help with the installation, a web search along the lines of <operating system> python.h should do the trick.

Calling C/C++ with ctypes

The ctypes library makes it easily possible to call functions from C libraries, but you do need to be careful with memory access and data types. Python is generally very lenient in memory allocation and type casting; C is, most definitely, not that forgiving.

Platform-specific libraries

Even though all platforms will have a standard C library available somewhere, the location and the method of calling it differs per platform. For the purpose of having a simple environment that is easily accessible to most people, I will assume the use of an Ubuntu (virtual) machine. If you don't have a native Ubuntu available, you can easily run it through VirtualBox on Windows, Linux, and OS X.

Since you will often want to run examples on your native system instead, we will first show the basics of loading printf from the standard C library.

Windows

One problem of calling C functions from Python is that the default libraries are platform-specific. While the following example will work just fine on Windows systems, it won't run on other platforms:

```
>>> import ctypes
>>> ctypes.cdll
<ctypes.LibraryLoader object at 0x...>
>>> libc = ctypes.cdll.msvcrt
>>> libc
<CDLL 'msvcrt', handle ... at ...>
>>> libc.printf
<_FuncPtr object at 0x...>
```

Because of these limitations, not all examples can work for every Python version and distribution without requiring manual compilation. The basic premise of calling functions from external libraries functions is to simply access their names as properties of the `ctypes` import. There is a difference, however; on Windows, the modules will generally be auto-loaded, while on Linux/Unix systems, you will need to load them manually.

Linux/Unix

Calling standard system libraries from Linux/Unix does require manual loading, but it's nothing too involved luckily. Fetching the `printf` function from the standard C library is quite simple:

```
>>> import ctypes
>>> ctypes.cdll
<ctypes.LibraryLoader object at 0x...>
>>> libc = ctypes.cdll.LoadLibrary('libc.so.6')
>>> libc
<CDLL 'libc.so.6', handle ... at ...>
>>> libc.printf
<_FuncPtr object at 0x...>
```

OS X

For OS X, explicit loading is also required, but beyond that, it is quite similar to how everything works on regular Linux/Unix systems:

```
>>> import ctypes
>>> libc = ctypes.cdll.LoadLibrary('libc.dylib')
>>> libc
<CDLL 'libc.dylib', handle ... at 0x...>
>>> libc.printf
<_FuncPtr object at 0x...>
```

Making it easy

Besides the way libraries are loaded, there are more differences — unfortunately — but these examples at least give you the standard C library. It allows you to call functions such as `printf` straight from your C implementation. If, for some reason, you have trouble loading the right library, there is always the `ctypes.util.find_library` function. As always, I recommend explicit over implicit declarations, but things can be made easier using this function. Let's illustrate a run on an OS X system:

```
>>> from ctypes import util
>>> from ctypes import cdll
>>> libc = cdll.LoadLibrary(util.find_library('libc'))
>>> libc
<CDLL '/usr/lib/libc.dylib', handle ... at 0x...>
```

Calling functions and native types

Calling a function through `ctypes` is nearly as simple as calling native Python functions. The notable difference is the arguments and return statements. These should be converted to native C variables:

 These examples will assume that you have `libc` in your scope from one of the examples in the previous paragraphs.

```
>>> spam = ctypes.create_string_buffer(b'spam')
>>> ctypes.sizeof(spam)
5
>>> spam.raw
b'spam\x00'
>>> spam.value
b'spam'
>>> libc.printf(spam)
4
spam>>>
```

As you can see, to call the `printf` function you *must* — and I cannot stress this enough — convert your values from Python to C explicitly. While it might appear to work without this initially, it really doesn't:

```
>>> libc.printf(123)
segmentation fault (core dumped)  python3
```

Remember to use the `faulthandler` module from *Chapter 11,*
Debugging – Solving the Bugs to debug segfaults.

Another thing to note from the example is that `ctypes.sizeof(spam)` returns 5
instead of 4. This is caused by the trailing null character, which C strings require.
This is visible in the raw property of the C string. Without it, the `printf` function
won't know where the string will end.

To pass along other types (such as integers) towards `libc` functions, we have to use
some conversion as well. In some cases, it is optional:

```
>>> format_string = ctypes.create_string_buffer(b'Number: %d\n')
>>> libc.printf(format_string, 123)
Number: 123
12
>>> x = ctypes.c_int(123)
>>> libc.printf(format_string, x)
Number: 123
12
```

But not in all cases, so it's definitely recommended that you convert your values
explicitly in all cases:

```
>>> format_string = ctypes.create_string_buffer(b'Number: %.3f\n')
>>> libc.printf(format_string, 123.45)
Traceback (most recent call last):
  File "<stdin>", line 1, in <module>
ctypes.ArgumentError: argument 2: <class 'TypeError'>: Don't know how to
convert parameter 2
>>> x = ctypes.c_double(123.45)
>>> libc.printf(format_string, x)
Number: 123.450
16
```

It's important to note that even though these values are usable as native C types, they
are still mutable through the `value` attribute:

```
>>> x = ctypes.c_double(123.45)
>>> x.value
123.45
>>> x.value = 456
>>> x
c_double(456.0)
```

However, this is not the case if the original object was immutable, which is a very important distinction to make. The `create_string_buffer` object creates a mutable string object, whereas `c_wchar_p`, `c_char_p`, and `c_void_p` create references to the actual Python string. Since strings are immutable in Python, these values are also immutable. You can still change the `value` property, but it will only assign a new string. Actually, passing one of these to a C function that mutates the internal value will cause problems.

The only values that should convert to C without any issues are integers, strings, and bytes, but I personally recommend that you always convert all of your values so that you are certain of which type you will get and how to treat it.

Complex data structures

We have already seen that we can't just pass along Python values to C, but what if we need more complex objects? That is, not just bare values that are directly translatable to C but complex objects containing multiple values. Luckily, we can easily create (and access) C structures using `ctypes`:

```
>>> class Spam(ctypes.Structure):
...     _fields_ = [
...         ('spam', ctypes.c_int),
...         ('eggs', ctypes.c_double),
...     ]
...>>> spam = Spam(123, 456.789)
>>> spam.spam
123
>>> spam.eggs
456.789
```

Arrays

Within Python, we generally use a list to represent a collection of objects. These are very convenient in that you can easily add and remove values. Within C, the default collection object is the array, which is just a block of memory with a fixed size.

The size of the block in bytes is decided by multiplying the number of items with the size of the type. In the case of a `char`, this is 8 bits, so if you wish to store `100` chars, you would have `100 * 8 bits = 800 bits = 100 bytes`.

This is literally all it is—a block of memory—and the only reference you receive from C is a pointer to the memory address where the block of memory begins. Since the pointer does have a type, `char*` in this case, C will know how many bytes to jump ahead when trying to access a different item. Effectively, when trying to access item 25 in a `char` array, you simply need to do `array_pointer + 25 * sizeof(char)`. This has a convenient shortcut: `array_pointer[25]`.

Note that C does not store the number of items in the array, so even though our array has only 100 items, it won't block us from doing `array_pointer[1000]` and reading other (random) memory.

If you take all of that into account, it is definitely usable, but mistakes are quickly made and C is unforgiving. No warnings, just crashes and strangely behaving code. Beyond that, let's see how easily we can declare an array with `ctypes`:

```
>>> TenNumbers = 10 * ctypes.c_double
>>> numbers = TenNumbers()
>>> numbers[0]
0.0
```

As you can see, because of the fixed sizes and the requirement of declaring the type before using it, its usage is slightly awkward. However, it does function as you would expect, and the values are initialized to zero by default. Obviously, this can be combined with the previously discussed structures as well:

```
>>> Spams = 5 * Spam
>>> spams = Spams()
>>> spams[0].eggs = 123.456
>>> spams
<__main__.Spam_Array_5 object at 0x...>
>>> spams[0]
<__main__.Spam object at 0x...>
>>> spams[0].eggs
123.456
>>> spams[0].spam
0
```

Even though you cannot simply append to these arrays to resize them, they are actually resizable with a few constraints. Firstly, the new array needs to be larger than the original array. Secondly, the size needs to be specified in bytes, not items. To illustrate, we have this example:

```
>>> TenNumbers = 10 * ctypes.c_double
>>> numbers = TenNumbers()
>>> ctypes.resize(numbers, 11 * ctypes.sizeof(ctypes.c_double))
>>> ctypes.resize(numbers, 10 * ctypes.sizeof(ctypes.c_double))
>>> ctypes.resize(numbers, 9 * ctypes.sizeof(ctypes.c_double))
Traceback (most recent call last):
  File "<stdin>", line 1, in <module>
ValueError: minimum size is 80
>>> numbers[:5] = range(5)
>>> numbers[:]
[0.0, 1.0, 2.0, 3.0, 4.0, 0.0, 0.0, 0.0, 0.0, 0.0]
```

Gotchas with memory management

Besides the obvious memory allocation issues and mixing mutable and immutable objects, there is one more strange memory mutability issue:

```
>>> class Point(ctypes.Structure):
...     _fields_ = ('x', ctypes.c_int), ('y', ctypes.c_int)
...
>>> class Vertex(ctypes.Structure):
...     _fields_ = ('a', Point), ('b', Point), ('c', Point)
...
>>> v = Vertex()
>>> v.a = Point(0, 1)
>>> v.b = Point(2, 3)
>>> v.c = Point(4, 5)
>>> v.a.x, v.a.y, v.b.x, v.b.y, v.c.x, v.c.y
(0, 1, 2, 3, 4, 5)
>>> v.a, v.b, v.c = v.b, v.c, v.a
>>> v.a.x, v.a.y, v.b.x, v.b.y, v.c.x, v.c.y
(2, 3, 4, 5, 2, 3)
>>> v.a.x = 123
>>> v.a.x, v.a.y, v.b.x, v.b.y, v.c.x, v.c.y
(123, 3, 4, 5, 2, 3)
```

Why didn't we get 2, 3, 4, 5, 0, 1? The problem is that these objects are copied to a temporary buffer variable. In the meantime, the values of that object are being changed because it contains separate objects internally. After that, the object is transferred back, but the values have already changed, giving the incorrect results.

CFFI

The CFFI library offers options very similar to ctypes, but it's a bit more direct. Unlike the ctypes library, a C compiler is really a necessity for CFFI. With it comes the opportunity to directly call your C compiler in a very easy way:

```
>>> import cffi
>>> ffi = cffi.FFI()
>>> ffi.cdef('int printf(const char* format, ...);')
>>> libc = ffi.dlopen(None)
>>> arg = ffi.new('char[]', b'spam')
>>> libc.printf(arg)
4
spam>>>
```

Okay... so that looks a bit weird right? We had to define how the printf function looks and specify the arguments to printf with a valid C type declaration. Getting back to the declarations, however, instead of None to ffi.dlopen, you can also specify the library you wish to load. If you remember the ctypes.util.find_library function, you can use that again in this case:

```
>>> from ctypes import util
>>> import cffi
>>> libc = ffi.dlopen(util.find_library('libc'))
>>> ffi.printf
Traceback (most recent call last):
  File "<stdin>", line 1, in <module>
AttributeError: 'FFI' object has no attribute 'printf'
```

But it still won't make its definitions readily available for you. The function definitions are still required to make sure that everything works as you would like it to.

Complex data structures

The CFFI definitions are somewhat similar to the ctypes definitions, but instead of having Python emulating C, it's just plain C that is accessible from Python. In reality, it's just a small syntactical difference. Whereas ctypes is a library for accessing C from Python while remaining as close to the Python syntax as possible, CFFI uses plain C syntax to access C systems, which actually removes some confusion for people experienced with C. I personally find CFFI easier to use because I know what is actually happening, whereas I am not always a 100% certain with ctypes. Let's repeat the Vertex and Point example with CFFI:

```
>>> import cffi
>>> ffi = cffi.FFI()
>>> ffi.cdef('''
... typedef struct {
...         int x;
...         int y;
... } point;
...
... typedef struct {
...         point a;
...         point b;
...         point c;
... } vertex;
... ''')
>>> vertices = ffi.new('vertex[]', 5)
>>> v = vertices[0]
>>> v.a.x = 1
>>> v.a.y = 2
>>> v.b.x = 3
>>> v.b.y = 4
>>> v.c.x = 5
>>> v.c.y = 6
>>> v.a.x, v.a.y, v.b.x, v.b.y, v.c.x, v.c.y
(1, 2, 3, 4, 5, 6)
v.a, v.b, v.c = v.b, v.c, v.a
v.a.x, v.a.y, v.b.x, v.b.y, v.c.x, v.c.y
>>> v.a, v.b, v.c = v.b, v.c, v.a
>>> v.a.x, v.a.y, v.b.x, v.b.y, v.c.x, v.c.y
(3, 4, 5, 6, 3, 4)
```

As you can see, the mutable variable issues remain but the code is just as usable.

Arrays

Allocation memory for new variables is almost trivial with CFFI. The previous paragraph showed you an example of array allocation; let's see the possibilities of array definitions now:

```
>>> import cffi
>>> ffi = cffi.FFI()
>>> x = ffi.new('int[10]')
>>> y = ffi.new('int[]', 10)
>>> x[0:10] = range(10)
>>> y[0:10] = range(10, 0, -1)
>>> list(x)
[0, 1, 2, 3, 4, 5, 6, 7, 8, 9]
>>> list(y)
[10, 9, 8, 7, 6, 5, 4, 3, 2, 1]
```

In this case, you might wonder why the slice includes both the start and the stop. This is actually a requirement for CFFI. Not always problematic but a tad annoying nonetheless. Currently, however, it's unavoidable.

ABI or API?

As always, there are some caveats—unfortunately. The examples so far have partially used the ABI, which loads the binary structures from the libraries. With the standard C library, this is generally safe; with other libraries, it generally isn't. The difference between the API and the ABI is that the latter calls the functions at a binary level, directly addressing memory, directly calling memory locations, and expecting them to be functions. Effectively, it's the difference between ffi.dlopen and ffi.cdef. Here, the dlopen is not always safe but cdef is, because it passes a compiler instead of just guessing how to call a method.

CFFI or ctypes?

This really depends on what you are looking for. If you have a C library that you simply need to call and you don't need anything special, then ctypes is most likely the better choice. If you're actually writing your own C library and trying to link it, well, CFFI is probably a more convenient option. If you're not familiar with the C programming language, then I would definitely recommend ctypes. Alternatively, you'll find CFFI to be a more convenient option.

Native C/C++ extensions

The libraries that we have used so far only showed us how to access a C/C++ library within our Python code. Now we are going to look at the other side of the story—how C/C++ functions/modules within Python are actually written and how modules such as cPickle and cProfile are created.

A basic example

Before we can actually start with writing and using native C/C++ extensions, we have a few prerequisites. First of all, we need the compiler and Python headers; the instructions in the beginning of this chapter should have taken care of this for us. After that, we need to tell Python what to compile. The setuptools package mostly takes care of this, but we do need to create a setup.py file:

```
import setuptools

spam = setuptools.Extension('spam', sources=['spam.c'])

setuptools.setup(
    name='Spam',
    version='1.0',
    ext_modules=[spam],
)
```

This tells Python that we have an Extension object named Spam that will be based on spam.c.

Now, let's write a function in C that sums all perfect squares (2*2, 3*3, and so on) up to a given number. The Python code will look like this:

```
def sum_of_squares(n):
    sum = 0

    for i in range(n):
        if i * i < n:
            sum += i * i
        else:
            break

    return sum
```

The raw C version of this code would look something like this:

```
long sum_of_squares(long n){
    long sum = 0;
```

```
    /* The actual summing code */
    for(int i=0; i<n; i++){
        if((i * i) < n){
            sum += i * i;
        }else{
            break;
        }
    }

    return sum;
}
```

And the Python C version looks like this:

```
#include <Python.h>

static PyObject* spam_sum_of_squares(PyObject *self, PyObject
        *args){
    /* Declare the variables */
    int n;
    int sum = 0;

    /* Parse the arguments */
    if(!PyArg_ParseTuple(args, "i", &n)){
        return NULL;
    }

    /* The actual summing code */
    for(int i=0; i<n; i++){
        if((i * i) < n){
            sum += i * i;
        }else{
            break;
        }
    }

    /* Return the number but convert it to a Python object first
     */
    return PyLong_FromLong(sum);
}

static PyMethodDef spam_methods[] = {
    /* Register the function */
    {"sum_of_squares", spam_sum_of_squares, METH_VARARGS,
     "Sum the perfect squares below n"},
```

```
    /* Indicate the end of the list */
    {NULL, NULL, 0, NULL},
};

static struct PyModuleDef spam_module = {
    PyModuleDef_HEAD_INIT,
    "spam", /* Module name */
    NULL, /* Module documentation */
    -1, /* Module state, -1 means global. This parameter is
            for sub-interpreters */
    spam_methods,
};

/* Initialize the module */
PyMODINIT_FUNC PyInit_spam(void){
    return PyModule_Create(&spam_module);
}
```

It looks quite complicated, but it's really not that hard. There is just a lot of overhead in this case because we only have a single function. Generally, you would have several functions, in which case you only need to expand the spam_methods array and create the functions. The next paragraph will explain the code in more detail, but first let's look at how to run our first example. We need to build and install the module:

```
# python setup.py build install
running build
running build_ext
running install
running install_lib
running install_egg_info
Removing lib/python3.5/site-packages/Spam-1.0-py3.5.egg-info
Writing lib/python3.5/site-packages/Spam-1.0-py3.5.egg-info
```

Now, let's create a little test script to time the difference between the Python version and the C version:

```
import sys
import spam
import timeit


def sum_of_squares(n):
    sum = 0
```

```
    for i in range(n):
        if i * i < n:
            sum += i * i
        else:
            break

    return sum


if __name__ == '__main__':
    c = int(sys.argv[1])
    n = int(sys.argv[2])
    print('%d executions with n: %d' % (c, n))
    print('C sum of squares: %d took %.3f seconds' % (
        spam.sum_of_squares(n),
        timeit.timeit('spam.sum_of_squares(n)', number=c,
                    globals=globals()),
    ))
    print('Python sum of squares: %d took %.3f seconds' % (
        sum_of_squares(n),
        timeit.timeit('sum_of_squares(n)', number=c,
                    globals=globals()),
    ))
```

And now let's execute it:

```
# python3 test_spam.py 10000 1000000

10000 executions with n: 1000000

C sum of squares: 332833500 took 0.008 seconds

Python sum of squares: 332833500 took 1.778 seconds
```

Perfect! Exactly the same results but more than 200 times faster!

C is not Python – size matters

The Python language makes programming so easy that you might forget about the underlying data structures at times; with C, you can't afford to do that. Just take our example from the previous chapter but with different parameters:

```
# python3 test_spam.py 1000 10000000

1000 executions with n: 10000000

C sum of squares: 1953214233 took 0.002 seconds

Python sum of squares: 10543148825 took 0.558 seconds
```

It's still very fast, but what happened to the numbers? The Python and C versions give different results, `1953214233` versus `10543148825`. This is caused by integer overflows in C. Whereas Python numbers can essentially have any size, with C, a regular number has a fixed size. How much you get depends on the type you use (`int`, `long`, and so on) and your architecture (32-bit, 64-bit, and so on), but it's definitely something to be careful with. It might be hundreds of times faster in some cases, but that is meaningless if the results are incorrect.

We can increase the size a bit, of course. This makes it better:

```
static PyObject* spam_sum_of_squares(PyObject *self, PyObject *args){
    /* Declare the variables */
    unsigned long long int n;
    unsigned long long int sum = 0;

    /* Parse the arguments */
    if(!PyArg_ParseTuple(args, "K", &n)){
        return NULL;
    }

    /* The actual summing code */
    for(unsigned long long int i=0; i<n; i++){
        if((i * i) < n){
            sum += i * i;
        }else{
            break;
        }
    }

    /* Return the number but convert it to a Python object first */
    return PyLong_FromUnsignedLongLong(sum);
}
```

If we test it now, we realize that it works great:

```
# python3 test_spam.py 1000 100000001000 executions with n: 10000000
C sum of squares: 10543148825 took 0.002 seconds
Python sum of squares: 10543148825 took 0.635 seconds
```

Unless we make the number even larger:

```
# python3 test_spam.py 1 100000000000000
~/Dropbox/Mastering Python/code/h14
1 executions with n: 100000000000000
C sum of squares: 1291890006563070912 took 0.006 seconds
Python sum of squares: 333333283333335000000 took 2.081 seconds
```

So how can you fix this? The simple answer is that you can't. The complex answer is that you can if you use a different data type to store your data. The C language by itself doesn't have the "big number support" that Python has. Python supports infinitely large numbers by combining several regular numbers in the actual memory. Within C, there are no commonly available provisions for this, so there is simply no easy way to get this working. But we can check for errors instead:

```
static unsigned long long int get_number_from_object(int* overflow,
PyObject* some_very_large_number){
    return PyLong_AsLongLongAndOverflow(sum, overflow);
}
```

Note that this only works for `PyObject*`, which means it doesn't work for internal C overflows. But you can, of course, just keep the original Python long around and perform operations on that instead. So, you do have big number support in C without too much effort.

The example explained

We have seen the results from our example, but if you're not familiar with the Python C API, you might be confused as to why the function parameters look the way they do. The basic calculations within `spam_sum_of_squares` are identical to the regular C `sum_of_squares` function, but there are a few small differences. Firstly, the type definition for a function using the Python C API should look something like this:

```
static PyObject* spam_sum_of_squares(PyObject *self, PyObject
        *args)
```

static

This means that the function is `static`. A function that's static can be called only from the same translation unit within the compiler. This effectively results in a function that cannot be linked from other modules, which allows the compiler to optimize a bit further. Since functions in C are global by default, this can be very useful to prevent collisions. Just to be sure, however, we have prefixed the function name with `spam_` to indicate that this function comes from the `spam` module.

Be careful not to confuse the word `static` here with the `static` before a variable. They are completely different beasts. A `static` variable means that the variable that will exist for the entire runtime of the program instead of the runtime of just the function.

PyObject*

The `PyObject` type is the basic type for Python data types, which means that all Python objects can be cast to `PyObject*` (the `PyObject` pointer). Effectively, it only tells the compiler what kind of properties to expect, which can be used later for type identification and memory management. Instead of direct access to `PyObject*`, it is generally a better idea to use the available macros, such as `Py_TYPE(some_object)`. Internally, this expands to `(((PyObject*)(o))->ob_type)`, which is why the macro is generally a better idea. Besides being unreadable, a typo can easily happen.

The list of properties is long and depends greatly on the type of object. For those, I would like to refer to the Python documentation:

`https://docs.python.org/3/c-api/typeobj.html`

The entire Python C API could fill a book of its own, but it is luckily well documented within the Python manual. The usage, on the other hand, might be less obvious.

Parsing arguments

With regular C and Python, you specify the arguments explicitly, since variable-sized arguments are a bit tricky with C. This is because they need to be parsed separately. `PyObject* args` is the reference to objects containing the actual values. To parse these, you need to know how many and which type of variables to expect. In the example, we used the `PyArg_ParseTuple` function, which parses the arguments as positional arguments only, but it is quite easily possible to parse named arguments as well using `PyArg_ParseTupleAndKeywords` or `PyArg_VaParseTupleAndKeywords`. The difference between the last two is that the first one uses a variable number of arguments to specify the destination and the latter uses a `va_list` to set the values to. But first, let's analyze the code from the actual example:

```
if(!PyArg_ParseTuple(args, "i", &n)){
    return NULL;
}
```

We know that `args` is the object containing the reference to the actual arguments. The `"i"` is a format string, which in this case will try to parse a single integer. And `&n` tells the function to store the value at the memory address of the n variable.

The format string is the important part here. Depending on the character, you get a different data type, but there are many; i specifies a regular integer, and s converts your variable to a c-string (actually a `char*`, which is a null-terminated character array). It should be noted that this function is, luckily, smart enough to take overflows into consideration as well.

Parsing multiple arguments is quite similar; you simply need to add multiple characters to the format string and multiple destination variables:

```
PyObject* callback;
int n;

/* Parse the arguments */
if(!PyArg_ParseTuple(args, "Oi", &callback, &n)){
    return NULL;
}
```

The version with keyword arguments is similar but requires a few more code changes as the list of methods needs to be informed that the function takes keyword arguments. Otherwise, the kwargs parameter would never arrive:

```
static PyObject* function(
        PyObject *self,
        PyObject *args,
        PyObject *kwargs){
    /* Declare the variables */
    int sum = 0;

    PyObject* callback;
    int n;

    static char* keywords[] = {"callback", "n", NULL};

    /* Parse the arguments */
    if(!PyArg_ParseTupleAndKeywords(args, kwargs, "Oi", keywords,
            &callback, &n)){
        return NULL;
    }

    Py_RETURN_NONE;
}

static PyMethodDef methods[] = {
    /* Register the function with kwargs */
    {"function", function, METH_VARARGS | METH_KEYWORDS,
     "Some kwargs function"},
    /* Indicate the end of the list */
    {NULL, NULL, 0, NULL},
};
```

Note that this still supports normal arguments, but keyword arguments are also supported now.

C is not Python – errors are silent or lethal

As we saw in the previous example, integer overflows are not something you will generally notice, and unfortunately there's no good cross-platform way to catch them. However, those are actually the easier errors to handle; the worst one is generally memory management. With Python, if you get an error, you will get an exception that you can catch. But with C, you can't really handle it gracefully. Take a division by zero for example:

```
# python3 -c '1/0'
Traceback (most recent call last):
  File "<string>", line 1, in <module>
ZeroDivisionError: division by zero
```

This is simple enough to catch with `try: ... except ZeroDivisionError: ...`. With C on the other hand, if you get a bad error, it will kill your entire process. But debugging C code is what C compilers have debuggers for, and to find the cause of the error, you can use the `faulthandler` module discussed in *Chapter 11, Debugging – Solving the Bugs*. Right now, let's see how we can properly throw errors from C. Let's use the spam module from earlier, but for brevity, we will omit the rest of the C code:

```
static PyObject* spam_eggs(PyObject *self, PyObject *args){
    PyErr_SetString(PyExc_RuntimeError, "Too many eggs!");
    return NULL;
}

static PyMethodDef spam_methods[] = {
    /* Register the function */
    {"eggs", spam_eggs, METH_VARARGS,
     "Count the eggs"},
    /* Indicate the end of the list */
    {NULL, NULL, 0, NULL},
};
```

Here is the execution:

```
# python3 setup.py clean build install
...
# python3 -c 'import spam; spam.eggs()'
Traceback (most recent call last):
  File "<string>", line 1, in <module>
RuntimeError: Too many eggs!
```

The syntax is slightly different—PyErr_SetString instead of `raise`—but it's the same basic principle, luckily.

Calling Python from C – handling complex types

We have seen how to call C functions from Python, but now let's try Python from C and back. Instead of using the readily available sum function, we will build one of our own with a callback and handling of any type of iterable. While this sounds simple enough, it does actually require a bit of type meddling as you can only expect PyObject* as arguments. This is contrary to the simple types, such as integers, chars, and strings, which are immediately converted to the native Python version:

```
static PyObject* spam_sum(PyObject* self, PyObject* args){
    /* Declare all variables, note that the values for sum and
     * callback are defaults in the case these arguments are not
     * specified */
    long long int sum = 0;
    int overflow = 0;
    PyObject* iterator;
    PyObject* iterable;
    PyObject* callback = NULL;
    PyObject* value;
    PyObject* item;

    /* Now we parse a PyObject* followed by, optionally
     * (the | character), a PyObject* and a long long int */
    if(!PyArg_ParseTuple(args, "O|OL", &iterable, &callback,
                &sum)){
        return NULL;
    }

    /* See if we can create an iterator from the iterable. This is
     * effectively the same as doing iter(iterable) in Python */
    iterator = PyObject_GetIter(iterable);
    if(iterator == NULL){
        PyErr_SetString(PyExc_TypeError,
                "Argument is not iterable");
        return NULL;
    }

    /* Check if the callback exists or wasn't specified. If it was
     * specified check whether it's callable or not */
```

```
    if(callback != NULL && !PyCallable_Check(callback)){
        PyErr_SetString(PyExc_TypeError,
                "Callback is not callable");
        return NULL;
    }

    /* Loop through all items of the iterable */
    while((item = PyIter_Next(iterator))){
        /* If we have a callback available, call it. Otherwise
         * just return the item as the value */
        if(callback == NULL){
            value = item;
        }else{
            value = PyObject_CallFunction(callback, "O", item);
        }

        /* Add the value to sum and check for overflows */
        sum += PyLong_AsLongLongAndOverflow(value, &overflow);
        if(overflow > 0){
            PyErr_SetString(PyExc_RuntimeError,
                    "Integer overflow");
            return NULL;
        }else if(overflow < 0){
            PyErr_SetString(PyExc_RuntimeError,
                    "Integer underflow");
            return NULL;
        }

        /* If we were indeed using the callback, decrease the
         * reference count to the value because it is a separate
         * object now */
        if(callback != NULL){
            Py_DECREF(value);
        }
        Py_DECREF(item);
    }
    Py_DECREF(iterator);

    return PyLong_FromLongLong(sum);
}
```

Make sure you note the PyDECREF calls, which ensure that you don't leak these objects. Without them, the objects will stay in use and the Python interpreter won't be able to clear them.

This function is callable in three different ways:

```
>>> import spam
>>> x = range(10)
>>> spam.sum(x)
45
>>> spam.sum(x, lambda y: y + 5)
95
>>> spam.sum(x, lambda y: y + 5, 5)
100
```

Another important issue is that even though we catch overflow errors when converting to `long long int`, this code is still not safe. If we sum even two very large numbers (close to the `long long int` limit), we will still have an overflow:

```
>>> import spam
>>> n = (2 ** 63) - 1
>>> x = n,
>>> spam.sum(x)
9223372036854775807
>>> x = n, n
>>> spam.sum(x)
-2
```

Summary

In this chapter, you learned the most important aspects of writing code that uses `ctypes`, `CFFI`, and how to extend the Python functionality using native C. These topics can be extensive enough to fill books on their own, but you should have a grasp of the most important topics now. Even though you are able to create C/C++ extensions now, I still recommend that you avoid these as much as possible. This is because bugs are so easily made by not being careful enough. It is actually likely that at least some of the examples given in this chapter contain bugs when it comes to memory management and can crash your Python interpreter when given the wrong input. Unfortunately, this is a side effect of C. A tiny mistake can have a huge impact.

While building the examples in this chapter, you may have noticed that we used a `setup.py` file and imported from the `setuptools` library. This is what the next chapter will cover – packaging your code into an installable Python library and distributing it on the Python package index.

15
Packaging – Creating Your Own Libraries or Applications

The chapters thus far have covered how to write, test and, debug the Python code. With all of that, there is only one thing that remains, that is packaging and distributing your Python libraries /and applications. To create installable packages we will use the `setuptools` package which is bundled with Python these days. If you have created packages before, you might remember `distribute` and `distutils2`, but it is very important to remember that these have all been replaced by `setuptools` and `distutils` and you shouldn't use them anymore!

What types of program can we package with `setuptools`? We will show you several cases:

- Regular packages
- Packages with data
- Installing executables and custom `setuptools` commands
- Running tests on the package
- Packages containing C/C++ extensions

Installing packages

Before we actually get started, it is important to know how to install a package properly. There are at least four different options for installing a package. The first and most obvious is by using the plain `pip` command:

```
pip install package
```

This can also be achieved by using `setup.py` directly:

```
cd package
python setup.py install
```

This installs the package within your Python environment which would be the likely `virtualenv`/`venv` if you are using it or the global environment otherwise.

For development however, this is not recommended. To test your code, you would need to either reinstall the package for every test or modify the files within the Python's `site-packages` directory, which would mean it would be outside of your revision control system as well. That's where the development installs come in; instead of copying the package files to the Python package directory, they simply install a link within the `site-packages` directory to the path where the package is actually located. This allows you to modify the code and immediately see the results in the scripts and applications you run without the need to reinstall your code after each change.

As is the case with a regular install, both `pip` and `setup.py` versions are available:

```
pip install -e package_directory
```

And the `setup.py` version:

```
cd package_directory
python setup.py develop
```

Setup parameters

The previous chapters have actually already shown us a couple of examples, but let's reiterate and review what the most important parts actually do. The core function you will be using in this entire chapter is `setuptools.setup`.

> For the most simple packages, the `distutils` package bundled with Python will be sufficient as well, but I recommend `setuptools` regardless. The `setuptools` package has many great features that `distutils` lacks and nearly all Python environments will have `setuptools` available anyhow.

Before we continue, make sure you have the latest version of both `pip` and `setuptools`:

```
pip install -U pip setuptools
```

The `setuptools` and `distutils` packages have changed significantly over the last few years and the documentation/ examples written before 2014 are most likely out of date. Be careful not to implement deprecated examples and skip any documentation/examples using `distutils`.

Now that we have all the prerequisites, let's create an example containing the most important fields with inline documentation:

```python
import setuptools


if __name__ == '__main__':
    setuptools.setup(
        name='Name',
        version='0.1',

        # This automatically detects the packages in the specified
        # (or current directory if no directory is given).
        packages=setuptools.find_packages(),

        # The entry points are the big difference between
        # setuptools and distutils, the entry points make it
        # possible to extend setuptools and make it smarter and/or
        # add custom commands.
        entry_points={

            # The following would add: python setup.py
            # command_name
            'distutils.commands': [
                'command_name = your_package:YourClass',
            ],

            # The following would make these functions callable as
            # standalone scripts. In this case it would add the
            # spam command to run in your shell.
            'console_scripts': [
                'spam = your_package:SpamClass',
            ],
        },

        # Packages required to use this one, it is possible to
        # specify simply the application name, a specific version
        # or a version range. The syntax is the same as pip
```

```
    # accepts.
    install_requires=['docutils>=0.3'],

    # Extra requirements are another amazing feature of
    # setuptools, it allows people to install extra
    # dependencies if you are interested. In this example
    # doing a "pip install name[all]" would install the
    # python-utils package as well.
    extras_requires={
        'all': ['python-utils'],
    },

    # Packages required to install this package, not just for
    # running it but for the actual install. These will not be
    # installed but only downloaded so they can be used during
    # the install. The pytest-runner is a useful example:
    setup_requires=['pytest-runner'],

    # The requirements for the test command. Regular testing
    # is possible through: python setup.py test The Pytest
    # module installs a different command though: python
    # setup.py pytest
    tests_require=['pytest'],

    # The package_data, include_package_data and
    # exclude_package_data arguments are used to specify which
    # non-python files should be included in the package. An
    # example would be documentation files.  More about this
    # in the next paragraph
    package_data={
        # Include (restructured text) documentation files from
        # any directory
        '': ['*.rst'],
        # Include text files from the eggs package:
        'eggs': ['*.txt'],
    },

    # If a package is zip_safe the package will be installed
    # as a zip file. This can be faster but it generally
    # doesn't make too much of a difference and breaks
    # packages if they need access to either the source or the
    # data files. When this flag is omitted setuptools will
    # try to autodetect based on the existance of datafiles
    # and C extensions. If either exists it will not install
```

```
        # the package as a zip. Generally omitting this parameter
        # is the best option but if you have strange problems with
        # missing files, try disabling zip_safe.
        zip_safe=False,

        # All of the following fileds are PyPI metadata fields.
        # When registering a package at PyPI this is used as
        # information on the package page.
        author='Rick van Hattem',
        author_email='wolph@wol.ph',

        # This should be a short description (one line) for the
        # package
        description='Description for the name package',

        # For this parameter I would recommend including the
        # README.rst

        long_description='A very long description',
        # The license should be one of the standard open source
        # licenses: https://opensource.org/licenses/alphabetical
        license='BSD',

        # Homepage url for the package
        url='https://wol.ph/',
    )
```

That was quite a lot of code and comments, but it covers most of the options you will ever encounter in real-life packages. The most interesting and versatile parameters discussed here will be covered in the following sections separately.

Additional documentation can be found in the `pip` and `setuptools` documentation, as well as in the Python Packaging User Guide:

- `http://pythonhosted.org/setuptools/`
- `https://pip.pypa.io/en/stable/`
- `http://python-packaging-user-guide.readthedocs.org/en/latest/`

Packages

In our example, we simply use `packages=setuptools.find_packages()`. In most cases this will work just fine, but it's important to understand what it does. The `find_packages` function looks through all the directories within the given directory and adds it to the list if it has an `__init__.py` file inside. So instead of `find_packages()` you can generally use `['your_package']` instead. If you have several packages however, that tends to get tedious. That's where `find_packages()` is useful; simply specify some inclusion parameters (second parameter) or some exclusion parameters (third parameter) and you'll have all the relevant packages within your project. For example:

```
packages = find_packages(exclude=['tests', 'docs'])
```

Entry points

The `entry_points` parameter is arguably the most useful feature of `setuptools`. It allows you to add hooks to many things within `setuptools` but the most useful two are the possibility to add both the command line and GUI commands and to extend the `setuptools` commands. The command line and GUI commands will even be converted to executables on Windows. The example in the first section already demonstrated both the features:

```
entry_points={
    'distutils.commands': [
        'command_name = your_package:YourClass',
    ],
    'console_scripts': [
        'spam = your_package:SpamClass',
    ],
},
```

This demonstration only shows how to call the functions but it doesn't show the actual functions.

Creating global commands

The first, a simple example, is nothing special at all; just a function that gets called as a regular `main` function where you need to specify `sys.argv` yourself (or better, use `argparse`). This is the `setup.py` file:

```
import setuptools


if __name__ == '__main__':
```

```
setuptools.setup(
    name='Our little project',
    entry_points={
        'console_scripts': [
            'spam = spam.main:main',
        ],
    },
)
```

And, of course, here's the `spam/main.py` file:

```
import sys


def main():
    print('Args:', sys.argv)
```

Be sure not to forget to create a `spam/__init__.py` file. It can be empty but it needs to exist for Python to know that it's a package.

Now, let's give it a try by installing the package:

```
# pip install -e .
Installing collected packages: Our-little-project
  Running setup.py develop for Our-little-project
Successfully installed Our-little-project
# spam 123 abc
Args: ['~/envs/mastering_python/bin/spam', '123', 'abc']
```

See how easy it was to create a `spam` command that installs in your regular command line shell! On Windows it will actually give you an executable which will be added to your path but regardless of the platform it will be as a separate executable that's callable.

Custom setup.py commands

Writing custom `setup.py` commands can be very useful. One example is `sphinx-pypi-upload-2` which I use in all my packages and is my fork of the unmaintained `sphinx-pypi-upload` package. It's a package that makes it trivial to build and upload Sphinx documentation to the Python package index, which is very useful when distributing your packages. With the `sphinx-pypi-upload-2` package you can do the following (which I do when distributing any of the packages I maintain):

```
python setup.py sdist bdist_wheel upload build_sphinx upload_sphinx
```

This command builds your package and uploads it to PyPI, and builds the Sphinx documentation and uploads it to PyPI as well.

But you want to see how this works, of course. First, here's setup.py for our spam command:

```
import setuptools


if __name__ == '__main__':
    setuptools.setup(
        name='Our little project',
        entry_points={
            'distutils.commands': [
                'spam = spam.command:SpamCommand',
            ],
        },
    )
```

Second, the SpamCommand class. The basic essentials are inheriting setuptools. Command and making sure to implement all the needed methods. Note that all of these need to be implemented but can be left empty if desired. Here is the spam/command. py file:

```
import setuptools


class SpamCommand(setuptools.Command):
    description = 'Make some spam!'
# Specify the commandline arguments for this command here. This
# parameter uses the getopt module for parsing'
    user_options = [
        ('spam=', 's', 'Set the amount of spams'),
    ]


    def initialize_options(self):
# This method can be used to set default values for the
# options. These defaults can be overridden by
# command-line, configuration files and the setup script
# itself.
        self.spam = 3

    def finalize_options(self):
# This method allows you to override the values for the
# options, useful for automatically disabling
# incompatible options and for validation.
```

```
        self.spam = max(0, int(self.spam))

    def run(self):
        # The actual running of the command.
        print('spam' * self.spam)
```

Executing it is simple enough:

```
# pip install -e .
Installing collected packages: Our-little-project
  Running setup.py develop for Our-little-project
Successfully installed Our-little-project-0.0.0
# python setup.py --help-commands
[...]
Extra commands:
  [...]
  spam                Make some spam!
  test                run unit tests after in-place build
  [...]


usage: setup.py [global_opts] cmd1 [cmd1_opts] [cmd2 [cmd2_opts] ...]
   or: setup.py --help [cmd1 cmd2 ...]
   or: setup.py --help-commands
   or: setup.py cmd -help


# python setup.py --help spam
Common commands: (see '--help-commands' for more)


[...]


Options for 'SpamCommand' command:
  --spam (-s)  Set the amount of spams


usage: setup.py [global_opts] cmd1 [cmd1_opts] [cmd2 [cmd2_opts] ...]
   or: setup.py --help [cmd1 cmd2 ...]
   or: setup.py --help-commands
```

```
   or: setup.py cmd --help
```

```
# python setup.py spam
running spam
spamspamspam
# python setup.py spam -s 5
running spam
spamspamspamspamspam
```

There are very few cases where you will actually need the custom `setup.py` commands, but the example is still useful since it is currently an undocumented part of `setuptools`.

Package data

In most cases you probably won't have to include the package data, but in the cases where you do need data to go with your package, there are a few different options. First, it is important to know which files are included in your package by default:

- Python source files in the package directories recursively
- The `setup.py` and `setup.cfg` files
- Tests: `test/test*.py`
- All `*.txt` and `*.py` files in the `examples` directory
- All `*.txt` files in the root directory

So after the defaults, we have the first solution: the `package_data` argument to the setup function. The syntax for that is simple enough, a dictionary where the keys are the packages and the values are the patterns to include:

```
package_data = {
    'docs': ['*.rst'],
}
```

The second solution is using a `MANIFEST.in` file. This file contains patterns to include, exclude, and more. The `include` and `exclude` commands use patterns to match. These patterns are glob-style patterns (see the `glob` module for documentation: `https://docs.python.org/3/library/glob.html`) and have three variants for both the include and exclude commands:

- `include`/`exclude`: These commands only work for the given path and nothing else

- recursive-include/recursive-exclude: These commands are similar to the include/exclude commands but process the given paths recursively
- global-include/global-exclude: Be very careful with these, they will include or exclude these files anywhere within the source tree

Besides the include/exclude commands, there are also two others; the graft and prune commands which include or exclude directories including all the files under a given directory. This can be useful for tests and documentation since they can include non-standard files. Beyond those examples, it's almost always better to explicitly include the files you need and ignore all the others. Here's an example MANIFEST.in:

```
# Comments can be added with a hash tag
include LICENSE CHANGES AUTHORS

# Include the docs, tests and examples completely
graft docs
graft tests
graft examples

# Always exclude compiled python files
global-exclude *.py[co]

# Remove documentation builds
prune docs/_build
```

Testing packages

In *Chapter 10, Testing and Logging – Preparing for Bugs*, the testing chapter, we saw a few of the many testing systems for Python. As you might suspect, at least some of these have setup.py integration.

Unittest

Before we start, we should create a test script for our package. For actual tests, look at *Chapter 10, Testing and Logging – Preparing for Bugs*, the testing chapter. In this case, we will just use a no-op test, test.py:

```
import unittest


class Test(unittest.TestCase):

    def test(self):
        pass
```

The standard `python setup.py test` command will run the regular `unittest` command:

```
# python setup.py -v test
running test
running "unittest --verbose"
running egg_info
writing Our_little_project.egg-info/PKG-INFO
writing dependency_links to Our_little_project.egg-info/dependency_links.
txt
writing top-level names to Our_little_project.egg-info/top_level.txt
writing entry points to Our_little_project.egg-info/entry_points.txt
reading manifest file 'Our_little_project.egg-info/SOURCES.txt'
writing manifest file 'Our_little_project.egg-info/SOURCES.txt'
running build_ext
test (test.Test) ... ok


----------------------------------------------------------------

Ran 1 test in 0.000s

OK
```

It is possible to tell `setup.py` to use different tests using the `--test-module`, `--test-suite`, or `--test-runner` arguments. While these are easy enough to use, I recommend skipping the regular `test` command and trying `nose` or `py.test` instead.

py.test

The `py.test` package has several methods of integration: `pytest-runner`, your own test command, and the deprecated method of generating a `runtests.py` script to test. If one of your packages is still using `runtests.py`, I strongly recommend switching to one of the other options.

But before we discuss the other options, let's make sure we have some tests. So let's create a test in our package. We will store it in `test_pytest.py`:

```
def test_a():
    pass


def test_b():
    pass
```

Now, the other test options. Since the custom command doesn't really add much and actually makes things more complicated, we will skip that. If you want to customize how the tests are being run, use the `pytest.ini` and `setup.cfg` files instead. The best option is `pytest-runner` which makes running tests a trivial task:

```
# pip install pytest-runner
Collecting pytest-runner
  Using cached pytest_runner-2.7-py2.py3-none-any.whl
Installing collected packages: pytest-runner
Successfully installed pytest-runner-2.7
# python setup.py pytest
running pytest
running egg_info
writing top-level names to Our_little_project.egg-info/top_level.txt
writing dependency_links to Our_little_project.egg-info/dependency_links.
txt
writing entry points to Our_little_project.egg-info/entry_points.txt
writing Our_little_project.egg-info/PKG-INFO
reading manifest file 'Our_little_project.egg-info/SOURCES.txt'
writing manifest file 'Our_little_project.egg-info/SOURCES.txt'
running build_ext
======================== test session starts ========================
platform darwin -- Python 3.5.1, pytest-2.8.7, py-1.4.31, pluggy-0.3.1
rootdir: h15, inifile: pytest.ini
collected 2 items

test_pytest.py ..

====================== 2 passed in 0.01 seconds ======================
```

To properly integrate this method, we should make a few changes to the `setup.py` script. They are not strictly needed but it makes things more convenient for others using your package, others that may not be aware that you are using `py.test`, for example. First, we make sure that the standard `python setup.py test` command actually runs the `pytest` command instead by modifying `setup.cfg`:

```
[aliases]
test=pytest
```

Second, we want to make sure that the `setup.py` command installs the packages we need to run the `py.test` tests. To do that, we need to modify `setup.py` as well:

```
import setuptools


if __name__ == '__main__':
    setuptools.setup(
        name='Our little project',
        entry_points={
            'distutils.commands': [
                'spam = spam.command:SpamCommand',
            ],
        },
        setup_requires=['pytest-runner'],
        tests_require=['pytest'],
    )
```

The beauty of this approach is that the regular `python setup.py test` command works and all needed requirements are automatically installed before running the tests. Because the `pytest` requirement is only in the `tests_require` section however, they will not be installed if the test command isn't run. The only package that will always be installed is the `pytest-runner` package and that's a really light package so it will be very light to install and run.

Nosetests

The `nose` package handles the installation only and is slightly different from `py.test`. The only difference is that `py.test` has a separate `pytest-runner` package for the test runner and nose package has a built-in `nosetests` command. So without further ado, here is the nose version:

```
# pip install nose
Collecting nose
  Using cached nose-1.3.7-py3-none-any.whl
Installing collected packages: nose
Successfully installed nose-1.3.7
# python setup.py nosetests
running nosetests
running egg_info
writing top-level names to Our_little_project.egg-info/top_level.txt
writing entry points to Our_little_project.egg-info/entry_points.txt
```

```
writing Our_little_project.egg-info/PKG-INFO
writing dependency_links to Our_little_project.egg-info/dependency_lin
ks.txt
reading manifest file 'Our_little_project.egg-info/SOURCES.txt'
writing manifest file 'Our_little_project.egg-info/SOURCES.txt'
..
----------------------------------------------------------------------
Ran 2 tests in 0.006s

OK
```

C/C++ extensions

The previous chapter already covered this somewhat, as it's a requirement to compile the C/C++ files. But that chapter didn't explain what and how the setup.py was doing in this case.

For convenience, we will repeat the setup.py file:

```
import setuptools

spam = setuptools.Extension('spam', sources=['spam.c'])

setuptools.setup(
    name='Spam',
    version='1.0',
    ext_modules=[spam],
)
```

Before you start with these extensions, you should learn the following commands:

- build: This is actually not a C/C++ specific build function (try build_clib for that) but a combined build function to build everything within setup.py.

- clean: This cleans the results from the build command. This is generally not needed but sometimes the detection of files that need to be recompiled to work is incorrect. So if you encounter strange or unexpected issues, try cleaning the project first.

Regular extensions

The setuptools.Extension class tells setuptools that a module named spam uses the source file spam.c. This is just the simplest version of an extension, a name, and a list of sources, but in many cases you are going to need more than the simple case.

One example is the pillow library which detects the libraries available on the system and adds extensions based on that. But because these extensions include libraries, some extra compilation flags are required. The basic PIL module itself doesn't appear too involved but the libs are actually filled with all auto-detected libraries with the matching macro definitions:

```
exts = [(Extension("PIL._imaging", files, libraries=libs,
                    define_macros=defs))]
```

The freetype extension has something similar:

```
if feature.freetype:
    exts.append(Extension(
        "PIL._imagingft", ["_imagingft.c"],
libraries=["freetype"]))
```

Cython extensions

The setuptools library is actually a bit smarter than the regular distutils library when it comes to extensions. It actually adds a little trick to the Extension class. Remember the brief introduction to Cython in *Chapter 12, Performance – Tracking and Reducing Your Memory and CPU Usage* about performance? The setuptools library makes it a bit more convenient to compile those. The Cython manual recommends you to use something similar to the following code:

```
from distutils.core import setup
from Cython.Build import cythonize

setup(
    ext_modules = cythonize("eggs.pyx")
)
```

Here eggs.pyx contains:

```
def make_eggs(int n):
    print('Making %d eggs: %s' % (n, n * 'eggs '))
```

The problem with this approach is that setup.py will break unless you have Cython installed:

```
# python setup.py build

Traceback (most recent call last):
```

```
    File "setup.py", line 2, in <module>
        import Cython
ImportError: No module named 'Cython'
```

To prevent that issue, we are just going to let `setuptools` handle this:

```
import setuptools

eggs = setuptools.Extension('eggs', sources=['eggs.pyx'])

setuptools.setup(
    name='Eggs',
    version='1.0',
    ext_modules=[eggs],
    setup_requires=['Cython'],
)
```

Now `Cython` will be automatically installed if needed and the code will work just fine:

```
# python setup.py build
running build
running build_ext
cythoning eggs.pyx to eggs.c
building 'eggs' extension

...
# python setup.py develop
running develop
running egg_info
creating Eggs.egg-info
writing dependency_links to Eggs.egg-info/dependency_links.txt
writing top-level names to Eggs.egg-info/top_level.txt
writing Eggs.egg-info/PKG-INFO
writing manifest file 'Eggs.egg-info/SOURCES.txt'
reading manifest file 'Eggs.egg-info/SOURCES.txt'
writing manifest file 'Eggs.egg-info/SOURCES.txt'
running build_ext
skipping 'eggs.c' Cython extension (up-to-date)
copying build/... ->
Creating Eggs.egg-link (link to .)
```

```
Adding Eggs 1.0 to easy-install.pth file

Installed Eggs
Processing dependencies for Eggs==1.0
Finished processing dependencies for Eggs==1.0
# python -c 'import eggs; eggs.make_eggs(3)'
Making 3 eggs: eggs eggs eggs
```

For development purposes however, `Cython` also offers a simpler method which doesn't require manual building. First, to make sure we are actually using this method, let's install `Cython` and uninstall and clean `eggs` completely:

```
# pip uninstall eggs -y
Uninstalling Eggs-1.0:
   Successfully uninstalled Eggs-1.0
# pip uninstall eggs -y
Cannot uninstall requirement eggs, not installed
# python setup.py clean
# pip install cython
```

Now let's try and run our `eggs.pyx` module:

```
>>> import pyximport
>>> pyximport.install()
(None, <pyximport.pyximport.PyxImporter object at 0x...>)
>>> import eggs
>>> eggs.make_eggs(3)
Making 3 eggs: eggs eggs eggs
```

That's how easy it is to run the `pyx` files without explicit compiling.

Wheels – the new eggs

For pure Python packages, the `sdist` (source distribution) command has always been enough. For C/C++ packages however, it is usually not that convenient. The problem with C/C++ packages is that compilation is needed unless you use a binary package. Traditionally those were generally the `.egg` files but they never really solved the issue quite right. That is why the `wheel` format has been introduced (PEP 0427), a binary package format that contains both source and binaries and can install on both Windows and OS X without requiring a compiler. As an added bonus, it installs faster for pure Python packages as well.

Implementation is luckily simple. First, install the `wheel` package:

```
# pip install wheel
```

Now you'll be able to use the `bdist_wheel` command to build your packages. The only small gotcha is that by default the packages created by Python 3 will only work on Python 3, so Python 2 installations will fall back to the `sdist` file. To fix that, you can add the following to your `setup.cfg` file:

```
[bdist_wheel]
universal = 1
```

The only important thing to note here is that in the case of C extensions, this can go wrong. The binary C extensions for Python 3 are not compatible with those from Python 2. So if you have a pure Python package and are targeting both Python 2 and 3, enable the flag. Otherwise just leave it as the default.

Distributing to the Python Package Index

Once you have everything up and running, tested, and documented, it is time to actually push the project to the **Python Package Index** (**PyPI**). Before pushing the package to PyPI, we need to make sure everything is in order.

First, let's check the `setup.py` file for issues:

```
# python setup.py check
running check
warning: check: missing required meta-data: url

warning: check: missing meta-data: either (author and author_email) or
(maintainer and maintainer_email) must be supplied
```

It seems that we forgot to specify a `url` and the `author` or `maintainer` information. Let's fill those:

```
import setuptools

eggs = setuptools.Extension('eggs', sources=['eggs.pyx'])

setuptools.setup(
    name='Eggs',
    version='1.0',
    ext_modules=[eggs],
    setup_requires=['Cython'],
    url='https://wol.ph/',
```

```
        author='Rick van Hattem (Wolph)',
        author_email='wolph@wol.ph',
    )
```

Now let's check again:

```
# python setup.py check
running check
```

Perfect! No errors and everything looks good.

Now that our `setup.py` is in order, let's try testing. Since our little test project has virtually no tests, this will come up close to empty. But if you're starting a new project, then I recommend trying to maintain 100 percent test coverage from the beginning. Implementing all the tests later is usually more difficult, and testing while you work generally makes you think more about the design decisions of the code. Running the test is easy enough:

```
# python setup.py test
running test
running egg_info
writing dependency_links to Eggs.egg-info/dependency_links.txt
writing Eggs.egg-info/PKG-INFO
writing top-level names to Eggs.egg-info/top_level.txt
reading manifest file 'Eggs.egg-info/SOURCES.txt'
writing manifest file 'Eggs.egg-info/SOURCES.txt'
running build_ext
skipping 'eggs.c' Cython extension (up-to-date)
copying build/... ->


----------------------------------------------------------------

Ran 0 tests in 0.000s


OK
```

Now that we have all in check, the next step is building the documentation. As mentioned earlier, the `sphinx` and `sphinx-pypi-upload-2` packages can help here:

```
# python setup.py build_sphinx
running build_sphinx
Running Sphinx v1.3.5
...
```

Once we are certain that everything is correct, we can build the package and upload it to PyPI. For pure Python releases, you can use the `sdist` (source distribution) command. For a package that uses a native installer, there are a few options, such as `bdist_wininst` and `bdist_rpm`, available. I personally use the following for nearly all my packages:

```
# python setup.py build_sphinx upload_sphinx sdist bdist_wheel upload
```

This automatically builds the Sphinx documentation, uploads the documentation to PyPI, builds the package with the source, and uploads the package with the source.

This will obviously only succeed if you are the owner of that specific package and are authorized with PyPI.

 Before you can upload the packages, you need to register the package on PyPI. This can be done using the `register` command, but since that immediately registers the package at the PyPI servers, it should not be used while testing.

Summary

After reading this chapter, you should be able to create Python packages containing not only pure-Python files but also extra data, compiled C/C++ extensions, documentation, and tests. With all these tools at your disposal, you are now able to make high quality Python packages that can easily be reused in other projects and packages.

The Python infrastructure makes it really quite easy to create new packages and split your project into multiple subprojects. This allows you to create simple and reusable packages with fewer bugs because everything is easily testable. While you shouldn't go overboard with splitting up the packages, if a script or module has a purpose of its own then it's a candidate for packaging separately.

With this chapter we have come to the end of the book. I sincerely hope you enjoyed reading it and have learned about new and interesting topics. Any and all feedback is greatly appreciated, so feel free to contact me through my website at `https://wol.ph/`.

Index

Symbols

A

B

basic echo server 185-187
basic metaclass 191, 192
Benevolent Dictator For Life (BDFL) 13
bidirectional pipelines
  using 158-161
big O notation 50, 51
bisect 76-78
breakpoints
  using 335-338
bulleted list 224, 225

C

C
  code, converting to 368, 369
cache fixture 289
caching 366
call stack
  displaying, without exceptions 327, 328
C/C++
  calling, with ctypes 406
C/C++ extensions
  about 443
  build command 443
  clean command 443
  Cython extensions 444-446
  Regular extensions 444
C/C++ modules
  need for 404
C/C++ packages
  installing 8
  installing, on CentOS 9
  installing, on Debian 9
  installing, on Fedora 9
  installing, on OS X 9, 10
  installing, on Red Hat 9
  installing, on Ubuntu 9
  installing, on Windows 10
C Foreign Function Interface (CFFI)
  ABI or API, selecting between 415
  about 413
  arrays, declaring 415
  complex data structures 414
  versus ctypes 415
chain function 95, 96

ChainMap 62-66
circular imports 45-47
class attributes
  metaclasses, used for obtaining sorted
    namespace 213, 214
  storing, in definition order 212
  storing, without metaclasses 212, 213
classes
  basic metaclass 191, 192
  creating, dynamically 190, 191
  decorating 125
  metaclass attributes, accessing 193, 194
  metaclasses, arguments 193
  singletons 125, 126
  total ordering class decorator 126-130
  used, for creating decorators 115
class functions
  classmethod decorator, versus staticmethod
    decorator 116-121
  decorating 116
  property decorator 121-125
class instantiation, operations
  about 207
  class body, executing 208
  class decorators, executing 209
  class instance, creating 209
  class object, creating 209
  example 209-211
  metaclass, searching 208
  namespace, preparing 208
classmethod decorator
  versus staticmethod decorator 116-121
closures 44
code documentation
  about 249
  class, documenting with
    Google style 252, 253
  class, documenting with
    NumPy style 253, 254
  class, documenting with
    Sphinx style 250, 251
code quality
  verifying 32
  verifying, with flake8 tool 32
  verifying, with pylint 35
code style
  Pythonic code 14

G

generators
  about 141, 142
  advantages 145
  benefits 141
  context managers 151-153
  disadvantages 141-145
  example 142-144
  generating, from generators 149, 150
  pipelines 146-148
  tee 148, 149
  usage 145
  versus addition 365
  versus lists 364, 379
  versus map and list comprehensions 366
get-pip.py file
  URL 7
global commands
  creating 434, 435
global interpreter lock (GIL) 363, 385
glob module
  URL 438
Google style
  class, documenting 252, 253
  selecting 254
groupby function 100, 101

H

headers, reStructuredText syntax 221-223
heapq 75, 76
Heapy 369
Homebrew
  URL 405
hyper-threading
  versus physical CPU cores 388-390

I

identity comparison
  versus value comparison 29
if statement
  versus try/except 364
image directive
  URL 230
images, reStructuredText syntax 229-231

import collisions 47
inline markup 219, 220
interactive debugging
  about 332
  debugging services 343
  with console 332, 333
  with ipdb 341, 342
  with other debuggers 343
  with pdb 333-335
IPyparallel
  ipcluster_config.py file 399-401
  ipcontroller_config.py file 397, 398
  ipengine_config.py file 399
  ipython_config.py file 397
  ipython_kernel_config.py file 397
  used, for distributed processing 396
IPython
  URL 350
islice function 101
is operator 126
items removal
  versus collections recreation 380
itertools library
  about 95
  accumulate function 95
  chain function 95, 96
  combinations function 96, 97
  compress function 98
  count function 98, 100
  dropwhile function 98
  groupby function 100, 101
  islice function 101
  permutations function 97
  takewhile function 98

J

just-in-time (JIT) compiling 368

L

labels, reStructuredText syntax 227
lambda functions
  about 86, 87
  Y combinator 87, 89
lazy imports 367
line profiler 361, 362

U

Ubuntu
  C/C++ packages, installing 9
unittest
  and py.test output, differentiating 275-280
  used, for testing packages 439, 440
  versus py.test 280
unittest.mock
  using 302, 303
useful decorators
  contextmanager class 133-135
  conversions 135-138
  single dispatch 130-133
  type checks 135-138
  validation 135-138
  warnings, hiding 138
  with statement 133-135

V

value comparison
  versus identity comparison 29
venv
  --clear argument 5
  --copies argument 5
  --symlinks argument 5
  --system-site-packages argument 5
  --upgrade argument 5, 6
  --without-pip argument 5
  creating 3, 4

  URL 3
  used, for creating virtual Python
    environment 2, 3
  versus virtualenv 6
virtualenv tool
  URL 3
virtualenvwrapper
  URL 6

W

warnings
  hiding 138
weakref module 374
Werkzeug 343
wheel package
  about 446
  Python Package Index (PyPI) 447, 448
Windows
  C/C++ packages, installing 10
  platform-specific libraries 406
  Python interpreter 404
with statement 133-135

X

Xcode
  URL 9

Y

Y combinator 81, 87-89